HARVARD EAST ASIAN MONOGRAPHS
64

CHINA CHARTS THE WORLD
HSU CHI-YÜ AND HIS GEOGRAPHY OF 1848

CHINA CHARTS THE WORLD
HSÜ CHI-YÜ AND HIS GEOGRAPHY OF 1848

by
Fred W. Drake

Published by
East Asian Research Center
Harvard University

Distributed by
Harvard University Press
Cambridge, Massachusetts
and
London, England

1975

© Copyright, 1975, by
The President and Fellows of
Harvard College

The East Asian Research Center at Harvard University administers research projects designed to further scholarly understanding of China, Japan, Korea, Vietnam, Inner Asia, and adjacent areas. These studies have been assisted by grants from the Ford Foundation.

Library of Congress Cataloging in Publication Data

Drake, Fred W   1939–
  China charts the world.

  (Harvard East Asian monographs ; 64)
  Bibliography: p.
  Includes index.
  1. Hsu, Chi-yü, 1795–1873. 2. Voyages and travels. I. Title. II. Series.
G161.H78D72   910'.92'4[B]   75-17882
ISBN 0-674-11643-7

To my parents

ACKNOWLEDGMENTS

China is so much a part of today's world that it is easy to forget that as late as 140 years ago Chinese were scarcely aware of the lands beyond the zone dominated by the Middle Kingdom. I have chosen a remarkable individual as the central figure for this study of a pioneering attempt to widen China's horizons in the 1840's. Hsu Chi-yü, a defender of China's coast during the Opium War and subsequently governor of Fukien, had seen the evidence of British military superiority and became convinced that China could no longer afford to ignore the Western world. In the decade following the war Hsu thus became a proponent of change and relayed a new vision of the world to China's leadership. But because his liberal view of the non-Chinese world undermined notions of Chinese cultural superiority, he became a target for conservative reaction; in the early 1850's he was condemned and dismissed from office. Like some American experts on China a century later, Hsu waited many years in disgrace before the truths he revealed became apparent to a more realistic leadership in Peking.

My interest in China's nineteenth-century intellectual reorientation and the story of intercultural communication between China and the West, of which Hsu's experience is a little-known chapter, stems from many sources. I am indebted to many devoted teachers of East Asian history, languages, and literature: Professors Claude A. Buss, Ch'en Chieh-hsien, John K. Fairbank, Kao Yu-kung, James T. C. Liu, Edwin O. Reischauer, and Yang Lien-sheng. Indeed, this study would not have been completed without the guidance, aid, and encouragement of Professor Fairbank.

I am also grateful to many other friends and scholars for their help and encouragement: Dr. Fu-mei Chang Ch'en, Professors Paul Cohen, Joseph Fletcher, Peter Golas, Lewis Hanke, Roy Hofheinz, Jane Kate Leonard, Archibald R. Lewis, Kwang-ching Liu, Eric Widmer, and Mrs. Rosa Ch'ang-hsu Yang. In particular I wish to thank Meena and Ranbir Vohra and my wife. Finally, my thanks to Mrs. Olive Holmes for her painstaking editorial midwifery.

CONTENTS

FOREWORD   ix
INTRODUCTION   1
I.   A SCHOLAR-OFFICIAL FROM SHANSI   7
II.   THE "INTRACTABLE BARBARIANS"   17
III.   IN TOUCH WITH A NEW WORLD   28
IV.   A VICTIM OF CONSERVATISM   44
V.   THE *YING-HUAN CHIH-LUEH*   52
VI.   GOVERNOR HSU'S IMAGE OF THE WORLD   60
VII.   DANGER IN CHINA'S MARITIME SPHERE   69
            Japan and Liu-ch'iu
            Vietnam, Siam, and Burma
            Maritime States of the "Southern Ocean"
VIII.   THREATENED ON THE INNER ASIAN
        FRONTIER   99
            India
            The Cradle of Non-Chinese Civilizations
            China's "Western Region": Russia on the
                Horizon
IX.   THE "BARBARIAN" BASE IN EUROPE   112
            A General Picture of Europe
            The Ancient Roots of Western Civilization
            Portugal, Spain, and Holland
            Russia, France, and Britain
            Other European States
X.   DESPAIR IN AFRICA, HOPE IN AMERICA   150
            The Dark Continent and European Power
            America: New Nations against Europe
            Latin America
XI.   RETURN TO CHINA'S HEARTLAND   169
XII.   CONCLUSION   189
        APPENDICES   199
        NOTES   203

BIBLIOGRAPHY   245
GLOSSARY   257
INDEX   263

MAPS AND ILLUSTRATIONS

The Eastern Hemisphere   Front endpaper
Hsu Chi-yü as an Official   Frontispiece
Asia   70–71
Europe   110–111
United States and Lands to the West   156–157
The Western Hemisphere   Back endpaper

FOREWORD

China's defeat in the Opium War of 1839–1842 called into question the values and viability of the ancient Confucian society. After the war, Governor Hsu of Fukien province, a member of the mandarin elite, made a study of the outer world in order to get perspective on China's place in it. More than a century and many wars later, Professor Drake of the University of Massachusetts, Amherst, a member of America's sinological elite, has made a study of Governor Hsu's study. Fred Drake wants to give us a view of the Chinese view of us. After all, we have just suffered a defeat that has called into question the values and viability of our American society.

Both these men, the mandarin and the sinologist, had a good idea, but found it took a lot of work. How Governor Hsu compiled his pioneer world geography in Chinese is described in this volume. How Fred Drake did it is a different story: First he took his B.A. in History at Stanford in 1961. Then he had the foresight to take his M.A. in Chinese at Stanford in 1963 and thereafter continue Chinese in Taipei, which gave him a strong running start on his M.A. in Regional Studies–China at Harvard in 1965. Thus he prepared himself.

By 1971 he had his Ph.D. at Harvard in History and East Asian Languages and was ready to rewrite his dissertation in the present form. To some, fifteen years may seem like a long time to get one's training and achieve in one's first book a basic contribution to scholarship, but Governor Hsu would not have thought so, nor will the rest of us in the still small field of Chinese studies in America.

June 1975   John K. Fairbank

HSU CHI-YÜ AS AN OFFICIAL

INTRODUCTION

"I can neither eat nor sleep, trying to think of ways to help."
"The intractable barbarians are unfathomable (*ni-i p'o-ts'e*)."[1] So
wrote the Chinese scholar-official Hsu Chi-yü after witnessing the
fall of Amoy to the British in 1841. These obstreperous Westerners
were indeed a puzzle to Hsu, scion of Confucian culture and bureaucrat for the Ch'ing dynasty. A dedicated opponent of opium, his
outrage at the immorality of the aliens who brought the "yellow
mud" to China was matched only by his wonder at their inexplicable
power.

Hsu's bewilderment typified that of China's leadership in general. The Confucian literati who governed China were unprepared,
intellectually as well as militarily, to meet the growing challenge of
the West. They viewed their "Middle Kingdom" as the center of a
universal world order in which superior China provided moral,
cultural, and political direction for inferior tributary states. It was
self-evident that the barbarians who came to China's gates to secure
wealth and legitimacy possessed nothing of lasting value; China
held a monopoly on true culture and civilization. The rudimentary
scientific and geographical information that had been introduced
to China by the Jesuits in the preceding two centuries merely indicated the "cleverness" of Westerners; it could not be taken seriously by most Chinese scholars, nor could it be considered knowledge.

When the Opium War broke out, the officials who were ordered
by the court to control the troublesome barbarians along the coast
had little inkling of the true nature of the threat. Though a considerable literature on the maritime barbarians from the West had
grown up as a result of China's contacts with European nations,
China's literati for the most part had remained indifferent. They
had neglected the signs of the great scientific and technological
transformation that had produced powerful Western states. By the
late 1830's their parochialism and out-dated views betrayed them.
The bureaucrats of China ignored the ancient wisdom of Sun-tzu:
to know one's enemies.

Yet, the Confucian stress on learning and study, as well as on the scholar's responsibility to the polity, continued to be persuasive for many dedicated bureaucrats in the mid-nineteenth century. Tutored to believe that society's stability depended on them, these scholar-officials fervently held the Confucian notion that they should be the first to worry, the last to cease worrying, about problems of state. Motivated by the hard-headed realism that operated as the cutting edge of their idealism, some of these officials seriously began to investigate the nature of Western power once they recognized the certainty of conflict with Britain.

To end the deadly flow of opium into China, Commissioner Lin Tse-hsu arrived in Canton on March 10, 1839. He immediately sought reliable intelligence on the barbarians who brought the drug. Lin employed a group of local Chinese, who were reputed experts in Western languages and knowledge, to translate Western books and provide border-watching officials with a more complete and accurate view of these aliens.[2] Lin failed to perceive, however, that the Western threat to his world order was of a quality and proportion previously unknown in Chinese history. Since he regarded non-Chinese as culturally inferior, the intelligence collected was intended only to help control and pacify them. In June Lin invited the first American missionary to China to witness the destruction of opium. Elijah C. Bridgman repeatedly warned him that the powerful British would not allow the matter to be so concluded and that war might result. But Lin responded with the summary words, *"Ta-chang, pu p'a! Ta-chang, pu p'a! "* (We are not afraid of war, we are not afraid of war!)[3] The imperial commissioner's self-confidence reflected China's faith in her ability to chastise the barbarians.

The fate of Amoy, Tinghai, Ningpo, and Chinkiang as they became targets for British military power, however, made it abundantly clear to many coastal officials (including Lin) that Western ships, guns, and organization were indeed superior to China's. The British were not to be scorned. These officials now began to see the alien invaders in a new light. Perplexed and considerably humbled, with the specter of defeat before them they began to seek more precise information regarding foreigners. A few scholar-officials, who were sensitive to the relationship between knowledge and power, now began to expand their geographical awareness and to delve into the politico-cultural background of the Westerners.

Such pioneering explorations into the sources of Western wealth and power provide a key to our understanding of the beginnings of Chinese modernization. Publications that resulted from this research in world geography not only belied the myth of China's supremacy in the world, they also introduced ideas that ultimately helped to undermine the Confucian order.

Though the early efforts of Lin Tse-hsu and later of his friend, Wei Yuan, produced the first important world geography of post-Opium War China, their book left much to be desired as a balanced and objective scholarly treatment. Lin and Wei advocated the adoption of Western-style armament in the *Hai-kuo t'u-chih* (An illustrated gazetteer of the countries overseas) published in 1844. But they remained committed to a limited vision of the outside world and attempted to demonstrate the continuing validity of traditional Chinese foreign policy: how, for example, barbarians could be used to control barbarians in the expanded global setting.[4]

In his 1848 treatise entitled *Ying-huan chih-lueh* (A short account of the maritime circuit) Hsu Chi-yü (1795-1873) provided a more accurate and open-minded outlook on the world. When he recognized the superiority of Western power during the Opium War, he too was shocked and disoriented. (Imagine for a moment the trauma that today's world leaders would feel were they suddenly to sight a technologically superior civilization bearing down on earth from outer space.) Yet, secure in the mastery of his own culture and feeling a deep sense of duty to it, Hsu began a dramatic quest for knowledge of the non-Chinese world. While he resided in the coastal marches of Fukien in the years after the war, he persistently sought geographical facts from Westerners and studied available geographical literature in an attempt to assess the sources and quality of Western power. As a member of the *ching-shih* (statecraft) school and as a proponent of Wang Yang-ming's view that knowledge and action were inseparable, Hsu was driven by his desire to comprehend the culture which now practically covered the globe with a network of control. His fellow literati had to be alerted.

By the end of the 1840's Hsu had become one of China's foremost experts on foreign lands. Because of his administrative abilities and his expertise on the world outside China, he climbed high in Ch'ing officialdom. As governor of Fukien province he published the *Ying-huan chih-lueh*. In this scholarly work he presented to his Chinese audience both a basic picture of the earth's geography and a view of a pluralistic world of competing states—a situation on a global scale not unlike the Warring States period (403–221 B.C.) of ancient China. Hsu acknowledged that the most successful states in this world-wide struggle of recent times were those of the West. Using effective institutions that had been patterned after ancient prototypes, these states had produced a powerful order which now challenged China's position in the world.

Based on the results of scientific geography, Hsu's work was a significant step toward a modern view of the world which contributed to the deterioration of Confucian cosmography. But because this image conflicted with the Confucian world view, Hsu Chi-yü's bold endeavor to reconnoiter the world outside China at first failed to evoke a favorable response from the literati in general. Ultraconservatives felt that Chinese culture would be contaminated if contact with Westerners was not strictly contained. To them Hsu's dealings with Westerners and his realistic and frank presentation of the non-Chinese world only proved that he had been seduced by barbarians and their knowledge. This sentiment no doubt was strengthened by the outbreak of the Taiping Rebellion, which in the eyes of the literati had acquired its contemptible Christian elements through the nefarious activities of Western missionaries. Consequently, in his attempt to strengthen China by modifying the literati's view of the world, Hsu proved himself to be a man ahead of his time. In the 1850's he and his book became victims of China's inability to face up to a changing world order. By offering the facts of Western military, economic, and institutional power to post-Opium War China, he and his treatise became targets of the conservative literati's attack. They damned him and finally drove him from office. Disheartened, Hsu retired for more than a decade to teach Confucian literature and to work in the suppression of rebels in his native province of Shansi.

After the second war with European powers a decade later, however, such opposition to change could no longer prevail. Hsu's message of China's need to deal with the new world situation finally struck a responsive chord with reforming statesmen of the 1860's. As a new corps of Ch'ing officials emerged to deal more realistically with the West, Hsu won prominent positions in Peking. His book at last gained wide acceptance and respectability as an effective and concise synthesis of the information and concerns that "statecraft" scholarship had produced in the 1840's.

The *Ying-huan chih-lueh* thus became a convenient manual which now provided China's leadership with an enlightened view of the world as well as a potent statement of themes for modernization: self-strengthening; official-merchant cooperation; a more realistic diplomacy; and, with admiring reference to the program of Peter the Great, the introduction of useful knowledge. In addition to basic geographical information, Hsu's book offered facts on Western forms of organization. He suggested that representative institutions which effectively related people to their governments operated as the ultimate sources of European and American power. In George Washington's victory over imperialist Britain, Hsu recognized—as did Mao Tse-tung nearly a century later—that people's militias, properly led and inspired by patriotic fervor, could serve to ward off European aggression.

In 1866 Hsu's book was reprinted and assigned as a text in the T'ung-wen kuan, the school established by Peking in 1862 to train Chinese in Western languages and affairs. More than a decade later it was used as the primary source of information on the West by Kuo Sung-tao when he journeyed to Europe as China's first resident diplomat.[5] Even at the end of the Ch'ing dynasty Hsu's account, then a classic, continued to serve the Chinese as a popular though dated source on the world outside. It helped promote the nationalism and reformism of more radical thinkers and statesmen such as K'ang Yu-wei and Liang

Ch'i-ch'ao, as well as that of Yen Hsi-shan, warlord and "model governor" of Shansi.

Remarkably, as part of the anti-Confucius, anti-Lin Piao campaign begun in the People's Republic of China in 1974, Hsu and his work have once more gained attention. The *Ying-huan chih-lueh* is now cited as the work of a Legalist scholar who overcame Confucian orthodoxy to present a realistic picture of the new international world.[6]

But Hsu the "Legalist" was quintessentially Confucian in his motivation. An eclectic scholar who was sensitive to a wide variety of concerns within the complex Confucian heritage, Hsu indeed was able to transcend the cultural myopia of the majority of his peers. He could acknowledge that the civilized world extended far beyond the Chinese world order without concluding that the Confucian system was bankrupt; moreover, he could admit that the new strengths of European civilization were in juxtaposition to weaknesses in the Chinese polity. But he remained devoted nevertheless to rational humanism and to the higher ideals of his Confucian tradition. He sponsored change in order to strengthen his state and protect his cultural heritage. Hsu was a Confucian realist.

This portrayal of Hsu Chi-yü's life and writings will, I hope, lend some insight into the adaptability of the Confucian mind and personality in a time of prodigious change.[7]

Chapter I

A SCHOLAR-OFFICIAL FROM SHANSI

Hsu Chi-yü was born to a gentry family in Shansi in 1795.[1]
Until he entered the Hanlin Academy in 1826, Hsu spent much of
his life in his native province. He felt great pride in the region of
his ancestral home and looked upon it not only as a cradle of early
civilization but as an area where, even in the turmoil of the nineteenth century, Chinese culture could be fostered and protected.
A cultural crossroads in Chinese history, Shansi indeed contributed
to the intellectual resilience that enabled Hsu to inquire into other
cultures of the world. The commercial life of Shansi, for example,
with its highly developed banking and trade connections, made him
cognizant of the benefits of international trade in spite of the
area's pronounced conservatism.

Shansi's people had developed strong centripetal ties early in
Chinese history. The province was justly revered not only as a primary part of the ancient heartland of China, but also as one of the
fundamental units of all the great empires.[2] Fortress-like, the rugged
province enclosed a spectacular variety of land: high plateaus, jag-
ged and deforested mountains, broad and fertile valleys, and pre-
cipitous gorges. Its mountains and rivers formed a natural defense
network.

Hsu's Shansi was a harsh land. Because of limited rainfall it
was semi-arid and subject to drought. In winter the freezing winds
off Inner Asia spread a loess veneer (the "winter dust" of North
China) over much of the province. Located on a primary fault, the
province shook with disastrous earthquakes. These tremors, threatening to the mud-walled houses that dotted the inhabited areas
above ground, spelled calamity for the cave dwellings so popular in
this loess region.

Though much of Shansi's rugged 60,000 square miles was
sparsely inhabited, the river valleys supported a dense population.
The concentration of people in the upper Fen Valley by T'ai-yuan,
for example, was not unlike that of the lower Yellow River delta.

Population figures for the province exceeded fifteen million by 1850. People had come from early times to Shansi's valleys to grow agricultural products, including wheat, millet, and kaoliang as well as some rice. Locally produced fruits such as sour crab apples, apricots, pears, cherries, sour haws, jujubes, persimmons, and grapes added color and a variety of flavors to what otherwise might have been an unusually bland diet. Indeed, Shansi was famous for its purple grapes, rare in China and perhaps a vestige of contacts with the West via the Silk Route.[3]

People had also been attracted to the province's rich natural resources. The salt brine lakes in the south had made Shansi one of the ten major salt-production zones during the Ch'ing dynasty. The province boasted a wealth of minerals: high grade bituminous and anthracite coals, iron, cinnabar, copper, marble, lapis lazuli, and jasper.[4]

This economic base was partially responsible for the development of Shansi's vibrant trading community. Situated below Inner Mongolia and wedged into the abrupt right-angle bend of the Yellow River, Shansi's location in North China also made the province a transfer zone from water transport to camel caravans along the north-south and east-west routes of trade. Consequently, the merchants of Shansi had become famous by the nineteenth century not only for their role in domestic trade and banking, but also for their trade to the north with the Mongols and Russians. These shrewd merchants, some of whom learned pidgin Russian, brought a cosmopolitan veneer to provincial Shansi, as did the officials of the emperor.[5]

As a youth Hsu Chi-yü witnessed the bustling trade centers along the Fen River. Here Chinese exports were prepared and transshipped to the north: teas from Fukien in chests—the "flower teas" and "family teas," and brick tea; silks; nankeen cloth; preserves; lacquer ware. And in exchange came the woolen cloths of Moscow and its environs—the Mezeritsky, Masloff, Karnovoy; velveteens; Dutch camlets; linens; leather, skins of lamb; and the furs of squirrel, otter, lynx, and muskrat.[6] In these cities along the Fen River arose institutions which functioned on a national scale. In P'ing-yao, T'ai-ku, and Ch'i-hsien were located the home offices of famed Shansi banks as well as letter hongs, commercial mail firms that grew up around them.

Hsu's ancestral home was located at an elevation of 3,600 feet in a crescent-shaped basin above the Hu-t'o River valley, nestled in the southern foothills of the Wu-t'ai Mountains in northeastern Shansi. It was near Wu-t'ai, city of "five terraces," the three-mile-square walled administrative center of Wu-t'ai district. In Hsu's time the city of Wu-t'ai served both as the economic center for the agricultural products of surrounding villages and as the political headquarters for a hilly district which covered an area of about 1,085 square miles. This administrative unit had been known by the name Wu-t'ai since the Sui dynasty, more than a thousand years before. In the nineteenth century it fit into the Ch'ing order under the jurisdiction of the independent department of Tai to the northwest and of the seemingly unwieldy Yen-P'ing-Ta-So-Ning-Hsin-Tai-Pao circuit.[7]

Roughly forty miles to the northeast rose the Five Terraces, the city's namesake, five sacred peaks named for each of the Five Directions. Here in the nineteenth century over 150 Buddhist monasteries still remained of the 360 or more of the T'ang dynasty, when the center reached its zenith. Visited four times by the K'ang-hsi Emperor, this site with its living Buddha still resident in Hsu's time continued to attract thousands of Mongol votaries each year.[8] Such proximity to a Buddhist mecca, however, did not dampen Hsu's strong Confucian antipathy for the Indian religion.

In this Shansi home Hsu Chi-yü inherited the ideas and ambitions of a gentry family. Over the generations a concrete family tradition formed which was passed on to him. In China's clan-oriented society this tradition was a potent influence in the construction of his own attitudes, ideals, and image of himself and family within society at large.

Hsu's paternal family had lived in the district of Wu-t'ai for the eight preceding generations that can be traced in the available sources.[9] The surviving records of the late-Ming and early-Ch'ing ancestors of Chi-yü indicate that the Hsu family at Wu-t'ai had

established itself sufficiently by the end of the Ming period to edu-
cate at least some of its members. Scholarship had become a tool,
if not in all cases an ideal. Yet the highest academic degrees and
high-ranking offices eluded the family in the late Ming era. Only
with the Manchu invasion did one of Hsu's ancestors, following a
military path, secure the rewards of rank and position for the
family. This was a fact not forgotten by later generations of Hsu
scholar-officials who were proud of their family's early support of
the Manchu conquerors.

During the century and a half of Manchu control over China
before Chi-yü's birth, his ancestors had declared their loyalty to
the new rulers and pursued scholarship as the ladder to prestige.
The Hsu family of Wu-t'ai was totally committed to honest and
able service, a daring tradition in an era when honesty was not always the best policy. Chi-yü's forebears had been identified with
middle-ranking offices connected with grain transport and storage
as well as with local administration and bandit suppression. Though
they were comfortably established and undoubtedly had opportunities to enrich themselves, every evidence would suggest that
the family never became exceptionally wealthy.

Chi-yü's grandfather, Ching-ju, scored the first major success
in "plowing fields with the brush." Chi-yü's father, Hsu Jun-ti, also
was encouraged in his studies and showed great promise as a scholar
from early childhood. Jun-ti secured the *chin-shih* degree (the third
and highest) in 1795, the final year of the Ch'ien-lung reign. After
serving in a variety of minor posts, both in Peking and in the provinces, Jun-ti retired to his native place in 1820. He spent the rest of
his life teaching at Chin-yang (T'ai-yuan), K'uo-hsien, and Chieh-
hsiu in Shansi, using these years to master his favorite work, the
Book of Changes (Chou i). He reckoned that the eight-legged essay,
for which he found origins in the Han dynasty, served as the most
effective method to organize thought and to analyze contents; this
was a view at least to an extent accepted by his son. During the
last years of his life, though bedridden much of the time and under
the continuous care of the family doctor "who practiced the love
of Mo-tzu" and was greatly respected by Chi-yü, Jun-ti became a

famous teacher in the province and was known by his students as
Kuang-hsuan hsien-sheng (vast and lofty teacher). After his death
at Chieh-hsiu in 1827 Chi-yü, his only son, collected Jun-ti's
miscellaneous essays from his students, which he published post-
humously around 1831 in seventeen chüan under the title *Tun-ken-
chai i-shu* (Remaining writings from the Tun-ken Study).[10]

Chi-yü spent his childhood in Wu-t'ai district, in Peking, and
probably also in Hupei, where his father was assigned. His younger
brother, Chi-wan, died as a boy. There was also at least one sister.
But little appears in the available materials about Chi-yü's childhood
days. The *Hsu pei-chuan chi* biography of Hsu, for example, simply
repeats the account of his epitaph that Chi-yü was a precocious
child.[11] Chi-yü was his father's only hope of placing a son in the
high ranks of the Chinese bureaucracy. Consequently much of his
early life was spent studying the Confucian Classics, and his scholarly father introduced Chi-yü to his own interpretations. For several years he studied under his father's supervision along with a few
other boys.[12]

A glimpse into Chi-yü's childhood days is found in his 1853
reminiscence of Hsu K'o-chia (1751-1827), his mother's cousin.
Each time Chi-yü visited the home of his maternal grandparents
as a child, K'o-chia would talk with him for a long time, asking
about his studies and encouraging him. Chi-yü sometimes went
into K'o-chia's study to read some of the books which were stacked
up to the ceiling. They would discuss matters far into the night, and
Chi-yü became very familiar with his relative's interpretations and
arguments.

The eclecticism that characterized Hsu's later intellectual life
undoubtedly had its roots in such early encounters with interpretations that differed from his father's. On every occasion he became fascinated by things he had never heard before. K'o-chia, a
student of Neo-Confucianism, loved the philosophy of the two
Fangs of the T'ung-ch'eng School in Anhwei, who attacked Han
Learning and stressed instead the relevance and application of
Confucian morality to the world of action. K'o-chia also condemned the eight-legged essay style as useless. Having failed his

examinations in spite of his "profound learning," K'o-chia traveled widely in the realm, purchasing books wherever he went. Surrounded by these books, he isolated himself in his study; he wrote poems, loved to study ancient times, and delved into the history of each dynasty. The children of his clan all looked up to him, and he was particularly talented in settling arguments. Chi-yü finally noted that his mother's cousin especially admired talent and often gave money to promising scholars. Such were Chi-yü's recollections of a man he obviously admired as a child.[13]

Hsu also reminisced about his days as a student in Peking. When he was fighting rebels in Shansi in 1853, he wrote the following sketch about an old friend. Wang Ch'iu-pao, childhood classmate of several years, was subdirector of schools at P'ing-yang, Shansi, in that year. His young son had been killed when rebels broke through the walls of the city in early autumn. "I think back on the years 1807 and 1808," said Hsu, "when Ch'iu-pao and I studied together in the capital. We read the *Historical Records (Shih chi), History of the* [Earlier] *Han (Han shu)*, and the various scholars of ancient writing. We took up our brushes to practice eight-legged essays. When our fathers had free time, they both taught us. His father (Wang Yueh-t'an) corrected the essays, and my father lectured on the Classics. On many cold nights we kept the lamp burning late as we chanted in unison into the middle of the night. My father would lie down and listen, extremely happy. When I now recall these times, it seems just as if it happened only yesterday."[14] Soon after this, in 1810, Chi-yü married at the age of sixteen *sui*. He became devoted to this wife who shared his life for the next thirty-six years, refusing to take a concubine till after her death even though she failed to bear him children.

Little information is available concerning Chi-yü's later education. In his youth, before he was twenty *sui*, a certain Chou Chih-kuei instructed him. Years later Hsu Chi-yü, then associated with the Hanlin Academy, visited Chou in Ch'ang-an to continue his studies. In an essay written to honor the ninetieth birthday of his teacher's mother, Hsu noted that Chou, when sent as an official to Kwangsi (to which Hsu too would later be assigned) where the "frontier tribes were wild and the people were voicing complaints," was both strict with the local officials and liberal with the people; therefore the area soon was pacified and harmony regained.[15]

Hsu's early childhood and education in preparation for the government examinations were obviously of fundamental importance in forming the young man's attitudes, ideas, and intellectual curiosity, as were also the personal relationships formed both in Shansi and Peking. Instructed so many years by his father, a disciple of the Lu-Wang School, he favored this branch of Neo-Confucianism.[16]

Despite the decadence of his school in a later era, Wang Yang-ming's (1472-1529) rejection of abstract speculation and his dedication to the search for solutions to fundamental moral and social problems on a practical level, strongly influenced a group of Confucian reformists in the early nineteenth century. Wang's stress on sincere purpose as well as concrete action for problems of state appealed to a concerned minority; some of these men were the best and brightest minds of the day. They opposed the sterile Neo-Confucian "investigation of things," which they criticized for its failure to relate to realities and for its inadequate attention to results. Such people agreed with Wang that the search for facts was indispensable, but before information could have meaning it had to be internalized and placed in harmony with one's intuition. Only then would information become knowledge and result in effective action. This notion of Wang Yang-ming, a pragmatic Confucian official and military leader for the troubled Ming dynasty, that knowing was inextricably tied to action, indelibly colored Hsu's own approach to the problems of dynastic breakdown when he served as an official for Peking.

As we have seen, Hsu also encountered the teachings of Mo-tzu and the ideas of the T'ung-ch'eng School. But precisely what other influences the young Chi-yü absorbed from the atmosphere of intellectual ferment that characterized latter-day Confucianism —that of Ku Yen-wu and the School of Empirical Research, for example—remains a mystery only partially revealed by the loyalties and scholarly productions of his later years. Whatever the specific sources, however, Hsu's intellectual life featured a significant degree of eclecticism, one which was able to place together without apparent contradiction diverse elements of traditional and Confucian thought as well as information from beyond China's cultural boundaries.

Hsu earned his *chü-jen* degree (the second highest) when he was nineteen, in the eighteenth year of the Chia-ch'ing reign. But he waited another thirteen years before he won the *chin-shih* in 1826, early in the reign of Tao-kuang and just a year before his father's death. Little is found about his life during these years, but he must have been studying hard as he prepared for the highest level of examinations. Perhaps these were also years of frustration, though despite the long wait for his *chin-shih* degree there is no mention of his having failed the examination.

When he took the final court examination after earning the highest degree of the land at age thirty-one, Hsu placed high on the roster. After an imperial audience, he won the honor of joining the Hanlin Academy as a bachelor to continue his studies. When his father died in 1827, however, he was obliged to return to Shansi for a lengthy period of mourning.[17]

Upon his return to the academy he was promoted, after further examination, to be compiler of the second class, rank 7A.[18] During his years in the capital with the Hanlin Academy, Hsu maintained close ties with his cousin, Liang Wen-ch'ing, a son of his mother's sister. He and Liang had been childhood friends and classmates. But while Hsu had become a scholar, his cousin entered his family's trade of brickmaking; nevertheless, he too was a student of Hsu's father and "accepted the thought of Wang Yang-ming." Liang supervised the family brick kiln on the outskirts of Peking and specialized in the production of fine bricks and tiles for the imperial palace and tombs. When Hsu entered the academy in 1826, Liang invited him to his spacious home as tutor for his two sons. Later, when Hsu had to travel from Peking to Ch'ang-an in 1833, since he had no transportation of his own, Liang provided a Peking cart and helped him with expenses for the long journey. Hsu was not to forget such kindness and wrote years later that of all the high officials he had known, only one or two could be compared to Liang—a very high compliment indeed for a merchant.[19]

Hsu's association with the Hanlin Academy was crucial for his later career along China's coast. In addition to enhancing his chances for advancement in the bureaucracy, it brought him under the influence of the powerful Manchu minister, Mu-chang-a, then chancellor of the academy and close friend of the emperor since childhood. In 1834 Chi-yü wrote, in an essay honoring the eightieth birthday of Mu-chang-a's mother, that he had visited the residence of Mu-chang-a on returning to the capital after traveling to various places for the past half-year. He further noted that upon his admission to the academy in 1826, Mu-chang-a "did not regard me as being without talent."[20] This relationship would prove decisive for Hsu's role in the Ch'ing system which depended so heavily on personal ties.

Hsu left the Hanlin Academy a decade after he entered it when he received an appointment as provincial censor of Shensi in 1836, rank 5B. Although he was in this position for less than a year, he greatly impressed the Tao-kuang Emperor with several memorials calling for the simplification of the central government's administrative procedures and recommending a closer relationship between the emperor and his officials. His recommendations sought to eliminate useless red tape, to take power away from bureaucratic clerks, and to relieve the emperor from duties that were clearly superfluous; both the emperor and his officials then would be able to concentrate more on the crucial matters that involved the state's structure and order.[21] Hsu advocated reforms in the salt administration for the sake of the common people, citing the adverse situation in Shansi and noting the desirability of new methods for distribution. He also impeached several local officials in Shansi and Shantung, accusing them of taxing the people too heavily. Struck by Hsu's ideas and actions, Tao-kuang summoned him. During the audience the emperor inquired about the general state of affairs in the empire and the condition of the people. Hsu's answers "moved him to tears."[22] Clearly against the irresponsible attitude of much of China's nineteenth-century bureaucracy, Hsu was facing up to the obvious dysfunctions of the Ch'ing apparatus. And Tao-kuang rewarded him.

The next day the emperor cut short his term as censor, ordinarily supposed to last three years, and appointed Hsu (in 1836) prefect of Hsun-chou, Kwangsi, rank 4B. Now wearing the official dress appropriate to his rank—embroidered wild geese on breast and back, a necklace, and the azure-colored button on his cap—the young bureaucrat was on his way up Manchu China's ladder of success.[23]

Chapter II

THE "INTRACTABLE BARBARIANS"

Hsu Chi-yü's life during the years after 1836 was hardly prosaic. Transferred to the difficult coastal region on the eve of the Opium War, this talented Ch'ing bureaucrat, who was committed to a strong defense of the coast and the exclusion of foreigners, encountered pressures that converted him to a position of moderation and made him an expert in barbarian matters.

His appointment in 1836 as prefect of Hsun-chou, Kwangsi, brought him deep into the southern part of China, just north of the Luichow Peninsula. The prefectural yamen that he occupied was located 200 miles west of Canton in the district city of Kuei-p'ing on the Hsun River, the West River of Kwangtung, nearly on the Tropic of Cancer. This was a territory to a large degree inhabited by minority groups, most notably the Chuang and Hakka. Here in this Hakka country, just fifteen miles to the north of Kuei-p'ing, lay Chin-t'ien-ts'un, in 1837 an ordinary village under Hsu's jurisdiction, but shortly thereafter famous as the first center of the massive Taiping Rebellion.

Hsu went into this office in early 1837 at age forty-two to rule over a considerable area of southeastern Kwangsi, where his northern ear must have been distressed by the seemingly infinite, cacophonous tonal variety of the local dialects. His job was to coordinate the affairs of the five districts under him. He headed a staff of assistant prefects who were assigned specific duties in the locality, such as the control of aborigines or military preparations.[1] In addition to these men Hsu enjoyed the services of a large assortment of lower assistants who were charged with the multiplicity of tasks that in good times kept the machinery of local government running.

During the few months Hsu occupied this position, however, he obviously could not have had time to understand the local problems adequately; nor could he solve them. Yet, had he not been transferred prematurely to the coast, one wonders what a man with

Hsu's dedication and effectiveness might have done to improve local conditions for the potential followers of Hung Hsiu-ch'üan, leader of the Taiping Rebellion, then an unrecognized young scholar of twenty-two. This question must have haunted Hsu nearly two decades later when he led the local militia against the Taipings in his own home province.

Hsu's next promotion, less than six months after taking his post in Kwangsi, was crucial, for it brought him to the southeastern coast. Hsu had already gained a reputation as a troubleshooter. Now he was assigned as taotai, rank 4A, over the Yen-Chien-Shao circuit of Fukien. The circuit was one of four in the province; it encompassed the upper reaches of the Min River, including the rich Bohea tea-producing district. It was an area long troubled by secret societies and bandits. In this chief subdivision of the province Hsu as taotai was now considered part of the high governing authority of Fukien. He functioned as the intermediary between the governor-general and governor above and the prefects and magistrates below.[2]

When he arrived in Fukien in the second month (February 24–March 25) of 1838, Hsu promptly set about to control the gangs who hid in the circuit's mountains and were involved in opium smuggling and other nefarious activities. He issued a public proclamation to the seventeen districts under his jurisdiction in which he cited some of the more spectacular cases of banditry and noted how easy it was for brigands to hide in the "10,000 mountains" of Yen-Chien-Shao.[3] But for those who had been forced into banditry from lack of work he held out the carrot of government employment as laborers; the rest would ultimately, he assured his readers, be suppressed by the *pao-chia* stick—a traditional collective-guaranty system.

At the same time Hsu made contacts with the province's higher officials, among whom was Wu Wen-yung, governor of Fukien from May 1839 to January 1841. Hsu and Wu became devoted friends, a relationship which lasted until Wu's death in battle against rebels when he was governor-general of Hunan-Hupei in 1854. Hsu also became acquainted with Teng T'ing-chen, governor-general of

Fukien-Chekiang from January 1839 to September 1840, who thought highly of him.[4] Meanwhile, he kept busy with the numerous functions of his office. For example, in the eighth month (September 8–October 6) of 1839 Hsu reported that he had supervised the local examinations; apparently he was still not fully aware of the storm that was gathering along China's coast.

Because of the threat to the coast of Fukien during the Opium War, on the recommendation of Governor Wu Wen-yung, Hsu again was transferred in the seventh month (July 29–August 26) of 1840 to be acting taotai of the T'ing-Chang-Lung circuit in southern Fukien.[5] It was here, with his headquarters at Chang-chou, a city opposite Amoy, that he first encountered the direct influence of Western power.

When he took office in this coastal area, not only did he move into a semi-tropical land of destructive typhoons, of oppressive heat, and humidity; Hsu moved into a new magnetic field. A northern landlubber had come to sea-conscious Fukien, with its rugged coastline of good harbors facing on the Taiwan Strait; hundreds of small islands, many of which were perfect lairs for Chinese buccaneers; junks for fishing and trade; and vibrant communities of Chinese merchants. He was now in a region with a long history of maritime relations. Control of the offshore islands, Taiwan and P'eng-hu, was maintained from this provincial base, and regular missions from Liu-ch'iu and Sulu entered the Ch'ing tributary system at the two main ports of Foochow and Amoy. The province also had had considerable experience in times past with barbarians from faraway places. Zayton (Ch'üan-chou), between Foochow and Amoy, was the site of a large Arab trading community as early as the T'ang dynasty. Fukien had been exposed to the curse of the infamous Japanese pirates during the sixteenth century. The first Portuguese carracks to enter the junk trade routes of the East also came here to trade before finally locating their base at Macao. In the seventeenth century Fukien had become the target for "pirates" of a different cloth; European Dominicans and Franciscans came to preach in the streets to steal the hearts and minds of the people.

Fukien in Hsu's time, as it had been in the past, was a Chinese

Phoenicia. Her merchant junks traversed the seas to Southeast Asia to bring back the exotic products of the Moluccas, Java, Borneo, Malaya. The people of Fukien, a tough breed, carried their distinctive and complicated Min dialect, composed of some 108 sub-dialects, to Taiwan and to the Overseas Chinese settlements of Southeast Asia: the Philippines, Batavia, Malacca, Siam.[6] Such Overseas Chinese maintained close contact with their home bases in Fukien via the fleets of junks which followed the trade winds from Foochow and Amoy to Southeast Asia and back each year. These Fukienese Overseas Chinese and their relatives in China had long been in contact with the bizarre Western peoples from across the seas who had gradually infiltrated their routes of trade.

From the point of view of the court and its officials, the people of Fukien thus could not be completely trusted. The Manchu court, remembering Ming resistance movements in Fukien, constantly worried about collusion between local Chinese and the foreigners who frequented the coastal waters. Here lay in hiding large, vigorously anti-Manchu secret societies such as the troublesome Triads. From Peking's perspective it appeared that Fukien's coastal people, isolated from the inland areas by rugged terrain, were possibly more tolerant of non-Chinese from the maritime outside world than they were of the continental non-Chinese rulers who occupied the Middle Kingdom.[7]

To Northerners like Hsu the people of Fukien appeared in sharp contrast to people of the North: they seemed smaller on the average, more delicate of frame; they were rice-eaters instead of wheat-eaters; they could seem to a man from the North, who pictured himself to be frank and straightforward, as cunning, scheming, and yet often strangely compliant. A man from Shansi in particular might stereotype people from his home province as honest, perhaps even simple, business-minded, and resolute, keen on sour food and liberal with vinegar, while these Fukienese seemed to be clannish, petty-minded, willing to take risks, and crazy about sweets.[8]

Hsu's transfer to the coastal area in the South in the summer of 1840 coincided with the arrival of the British expeditionary force, led by the *Alligator* and followed by the *Rattlesnake* and others, which moved north to the coast off Tientsin, blockading Amoy and bombarding Tinghai enroute. When Admiral George Elliot arrived soon after for negotiations off Tientsin on August 9, Tao-kuang, in what was to many officials a bewildering display of imperial tergiversation, reversed his adamantine position against the British.[9]

The following month witnessed the replacement of Lin Tse-hsu by Ch'i-shan as imperial commissioner to Canton, and the governor-general of Fukien-Chekiang, Teng T'ing-chen, was removed the same day. As Hsu noted later, the emperor had decided "to take [the foreigners] to his bosom in order to win their hearts (*huai-jou*)." A new policy of appeasement emerged in the court of Peking, with Tao-kuang's favorite from childhood and Hsu's former teacher in the Hanlin Academy, Mu-chang-a, calling the tune.[10]

Hsu recorded later that he was ordered to the new position near Amoy after an alert was posted regarding "barbarian pirates" (*i-k'ou*). At this time the taotai of Hsing-Ch'üan-Yung, Liu Yao-ch'un, who became Hsu's friend and was praised by him as being "an incorrupt official from Kiangsu," was posted at Amoy. Since this was just across the bay from Hsu, who was stationed at Chang-chou, the two exchanged messages to coordinate their preparations for defense "three or four times every ten days, so that the messenger was [soon] exhausted." In the third month (March 23–April 20) of 1841 the two met for the first time when Hsu visited Amoy. Liu was ten years Hsu's senior and treated him as a younger brother. Hsu lodged at Liu's residence in the most pleasant surroundings, and very special Kiangsu dishes appeared on the table, much to Hsu's delight. The two loved to discuss current problems of state, especially border policies. The heated arguments usually continued into the early hours of the morning, so the annoyed servants were sent on to bed. Hsu, along with Liu and another officer, Ma Chih-chai, often would meet far into the night too with Governor Wu Wen-yung to discuss and argue about state policies, "even to the point of forgetting propriety." But Hsu noted that Wu appreciated his candor.[11] And Wu, while very critical of most of the officials he found in charge of coastal defense, paid high compliments to Hsu, Liu, and Ma.

Regardless of the court's new but uncertain policy of appeasement, Hsu and his fellow officers in Fukien still faced the difficult assignment of defending Chinese soil. In a letter to "a certain governor," Hsu complained of the situation he found along the coast. He was most concerned about the problems of defending Hai-ch'eng, just across the bay from Amoy. The city was protected by only a thousand-odd soldiers, of whom hundreds were sick. Many of those called soldiers were really merchants. If the "intractable barbarians" landed and attacked, these forces would surely run away or be defeated. Why was the situation so bad? According to Hsu his men lacked the essentials of all good soldiers from ancient times: good clothing and sufficient food. Therefore, Hai-ch'eng was "in the tiger's mouth."[12]

Hsu's task in southern Fukien proved to be most demanding, but here he found other dedicated, competent men as colleagues who had also assumed a responsibility for coastal defense. For example, in 1841 Hsu worked closely with the governor-general of Fukien, Yen Po-t'ao, a native of Kwangtung. In the spring of 1841 Yen had come to direct preparations in the Amoy region and Hsu met with him in that city for the first time in the third month (March 23–April 20). For six months the two worked together feverishly before the fiasco of August 26, when Amoy was taken.[13] Yen and Hsu at this time extensively used a treatise on border defense written by the Mongol, Pi-ch'ang, one-time Tartar General of Foochow and a man whom Hsu regarded as a patriot. This work, entitled *Shou-pien chi-yao* (A summary [of items] to protect the border), was typical of the kind of literature then available to barbarian-suppressing officials located on the maritime frontiers of China. It focused in great detail, in a proto-scientific manner, on the construction of walls, including several illustrations that listed detailed specifications for thickness and size.[14]

After Yen's dismissal and return to Kwangtung in early 1842 as a result of Amoy's fall, Hsu wrote a lengthy defense of Yen's work in Fukien. He recorded that altogether over four hundred cannon had been positioned in and around Amoy, with the largest weighing ten thousand catties. There Yen had posted six or seven thousand soldiers. This testimony jibed with that of John Francis Davis, for when Davis visited Amoy in October 1844 he found a two-hundred-gun battery facing Kulangsu. Most of these guns, then spiked, had been cast in 1806, but nearby he discovered a foundry where cannon were being cast when the city fell. "The largest bore the inscription that it was cast in the summer of 1841 by Yen the viceroy . . . and that it weighed 10,000 catties, or nearly six tons." Davis concluded after seeing the preparations for defense at Amoy that "had the Chinese known only half as well how to annoy us as to protect themselves, the result might have been very different."[15]

As Hsu noted later, "One could not say there were no preparations."

> But suddenly in the first ten days of the seventh month [August 17-26, 1841], thirty-odd rebel ships sailed into Amoy and opened fire. Our forces also fired. But our iron cannon were not as good as their brass cannon, which were light and easy to manage. Our cannon on land were not as close together as theirs were aboard the ships. Thus in half a day our gun emplacements were destroyed, the entire army defeated, and we lost about a thousand men [including several officials].[16]

To add to Hsu's troubles, the people and the officials of Chang-chou under him were "frightened nearly to death" by the British attack on Amoy. He related that the "officials sent their families from the city, and people were thinking of running away." He tried to calm them and promised to defend Hai-ch'eng, at the mouth of the Lung River which led to Chang-chou, in a battle to the death. Gradually the people then settled down and continued to work on military preparations. Luckily, when a "rebel barbarian fire-wheel ship" attempted to come to Hai-ch'eng it was unable to enter the area because the water was too shallow.[17]

Hsu had learned a hard lesson in this coastal region: that the Chinese had underestimated British power and that these Western maritime barbarians possessed a technology in advance of China's.

Before the war he was aware of European penetration into Asia, "gobbling up harbors like silkworms eating leaves." But at the time he advocated policies as unrealistic as those of his fellow officials. He reflected, after analyzing the history of opium traffic in China, that since it was impossible for China to cut off the supply coming in on "barbarian ships," the market would have to be closed on the Chinese side by punishing "Chinese traitors" (*Han-chien*) as well as any offending officials and soldiers. A gradual policy should be adopted to eliminate the poison, root and branch. Addicts should be allowed to break the habit, but each year every district should execute ten or more addicts as examples. After ten years, he reasoned, those who were able to break the habit would have done so; the others would have been eliminated.[18]

Hsu blasted the British barbarians for importing the bulk of China's opium supply, which came from places they had stolen: Bengal and Bombay. They were akin to dogs and sheep, and they sought profit. The British did not comprehend sincerity and right conduct, but they were successful in gaining wealth and power (*fu-ch'iang*) for their state. Hsu cited what they and other Europeans had already done to the states of Southeast Asia as a warning to China.[19]

After learning of the ransom of Canton in May 1841, Hsu wrote that "everyone knew it was like using kindling to put out a fire." He considered Ch'i-shan, because of the Chuenpi Convention, to have been duped by the "intractable barbarians."[20] Yü-ch'ien on the other hand, Mongol governor of Chekiang, who had tortured to death several British captives, had opposed the conciliatory policies of Ch'i-shan and I-li-pu, and finally had committed suicide after the fall of Ningpo in October 1841, was a great patriot and hero in Hsu's eyes.[21]

In early 1842, however, after experiencing the Amoy debacle, Hsu wrote a long letter to two scholar friends in Shansi which evidenced a new sense of appreciation of the quality of the Western threat. Here he analyzed the causes of the war, the character of British power, and the reasons for China's failures. He called the British the strongest tribe of the Red Hairs. They lived in a place

70,000-odd li from China, and they had invaded and occupied several tens of sites along the coasts of the Large Western Ocean (Atlantic), the Small Western Ocean (Indian), and the Southern and Southeastern Oceans (Southeast Asia). Their ships were the very strongest and largest sort, their cannon the fiercest. The English had traded at Canton since the beginning of the dynasty, but had only gradually seized on opium to fill their coffers. Chinese confiscation and destruction of 20,000 cases of opium in 1839 had been taken as a pretext for their attack in 1840 on Tinghai.

Hsu continued that these "intractable barbarians" were creating serious trouble for the dynasty which had "brought prosperity to China for two hundred years"; they had already caused numerous civil and military officials, one after another, to give up their lives fighting. But this Chinese defense, supported at great expense, had not hindered the British one iota. Though he considered himself a bookish person, Hsu asked how he could simply sit by and witness this. The authorities had placed their trust in him and assigned him to a crucial border area, so for a full year he had worked on defenses, with but too few hours in the day. Yet his attempt had been fruitless.

That China was still intact was due to "luck from Heaven." Despite all expectations to the contrary, the British were defeating a China caught unprepared. Hsu belittled the Chinese small arms which would not shoot farther than forty paces. "But in addition to these there are but short swords, and that is it." China's cannon did not equal British cannon, and the army itself was inferior because it lacked military discipline. British seapower was great, while "Naval warfare is not one of our strong points." Consequently, Hsu explained to his bewildered friends in Shansi, he was unwilling to attack the British who were left behind to occupy Kulangsu, a small island opposite Amoy. He noted with approval the recent appointment of I-liang as imperial commissioner (and governor-general of Min-Che, in January 1842) to implement a "defense first, offense second" policy.[22] For Hsu and many others, the rashness of Lin Tse-hsu's actions against Western power had been proved unrealistic and foolish. As observed later by John

Francis Davis, "it became clear . . . to all discerning persons that Amoy, with its vast defensive operations, having thus fallen, the English might with equal ease capture other places."[23]

Furthermore, Hsu lamented, the British possessed the great advantage of information. The wily Westerners had employed Chinese traitors, so that "of our strengths and weaknesses, none is not known to them." Hsu concluded his letter with a remarkable if plaintive passage, which hinted strongly that China's ignorance of Britain was in large part responsible for the debacle:

> The intractable barbarians depend on trade for their liveli-hood and regard profit as their sole goal. They did not want to attack [our] cities, steal land, and occupy territory. All they wanted [originally] was to secure some famous Chinese harbors in order to facilitate the trade of their goods.[24] [But] now they see our officials and soldiers have been regularly defeated in these years, and they know China is weak and incapable [of defense]. As [Britain's] desires increase, the more cunning are her plans. If we do not defeat their van-guard decisively there will be no end to it. Now suddenly without means to win, if we wish to negotiate terms of peace they will demand 15-20,000,000 ounces of silver as well as every important port along the coast. How could we consent to that?[25]

Indeed, Hsu was fast becoming conscious of some of the in-controvertible realities which now forced their way into China from the vague world beyond. Like Lin Tse-hsu when he arrived in Canton and began to assemble materials about the West, Hsu finally was beginning to recognize the necessity of bringing informa-tion about the British and other Westerners to China in order to learn their strengths and weaknesses.

Early in 1842 (in the first month, February 10-March 11), Hsu assumed concurrent duties with the grain intendancy at Ch'üan-chou, the harbor just north of Amoy.[26] Since his good friend, Liu Yao-ch'un, was also there, "there was no day we did not meet." During these weeks the two continued to discuss affairs

of the empire (*t'ien-hsia shih*) and to "compare the present with
the past." Although they did not always agree initially, they
usually reached a common view after much discussion. Hsu noted
that while Liu was high-strung and had a severe temper, he himself
in contrast was rather lethargic, slow to respond, and had a lenient
personality. Balanced by an inquiring mind, these traits were to
prove invaluable in his work with the Westerners on China's coast
whom he would soon be forced to accommodate.

   Hsu's recognition of his nation's weakness in the face of
Western ships and guns caused him, a patriotic official, to search
for ways to buy time for China. War with Britain without proper
preparation had been foolhardy. Now rational and effective policies,
premised on the facts of European military superiority on China's
coast, had to be devised. Long before the final shots of the Opium
War, Hsu thus saw that the people of the West were aliens that
China could no longer disregard.

Chapter III

IN TOUCH WITH A NEW WORLD

Hsu's work in the T'ing-Chang-Lung circuit was amply rewarded by recognition from his local superiors. Governor Liu
Hung-ao, who replaced Wu Wen-yung in January 1841, praised him
highly, as did Governor General Yen. Liu stated that Hsu was
"pure, incorrupt, and clearly understands everything."[1]

The numerous promotions that followed indicate that Hsu
had also found favor with Peking. In the last days of the war, on
May 26, 1842, he was promoted to the post of salt controller of
Kwangtung, rank 3B. The order arrived so late that before he was
even aware of this assignment he was informed, on the morning of
July 2, 1842, of a new appointment as provincial judge of Kwangtung, rank 3A. On July 5 he sent his letter of departure and thanks
to Governor Liu Hung-ao, who some years later wrote one of the
laudatory prefaces for Hsu's world geography.[3]

Hsu did not arrive at Canton until late September, after the
Mid-Autumn Festival. As a realist who had reconciled his view of
China's fundamental weakness with a pragmatic position about
what should be done next, Hsu had joined potent allies within the
Ch'ing order. From this time on his heart and career lay with the
advocates of conciliation, and he was thereafter known as a practi-
tioner of the flexible *chi-mi* ("loose-rein") policy of managing
barbarians—a term which suggested that Chinese, if wise and
knowledgeable, could sit in the driver's seat and guide non-Chinese
at will.[4]

On the way to Canton Hsu left his family at Nanchang,
Kiangsi, until "barbarian affairs were peacefully settled."[5] Negotiations had been completed already by this time at Nanking and a
treaty signed on board the *Cornwallis*. Among other points, this
treaty ceded Hong Kong, opened five ports, and paid Britain a
twenty-one million dollar indemnity—all of which Hsu had found
unacceptable just a few months before.

In his new position as judicial commissioner of Kwangtung, Hsu resided in Canton as one of the three or four top officials of the province. He was the supreme judge of the province and now had the right to memorialize the throne directly. Above him, as governor general, was Ch'i Kung, Ch'i-shan's replacement, a barbarian-tamer of some repute in the Chinese records and like Hsu Chi-yü, a native of Shansi. Ch'i had employed Liang T'ing-nan, the prolific author of, among other things, material concerning foreign countries. While in Canton Hsu was the guest of his friend, Huang En-t'ung, lieutenant of Ch'i-ying and *chin-shih*, like Hsu, of 1826.[6] Huang had played an important role in the negotiations for the Treaty of Nanking and was known as one of the leading figures in the so-called appeasement party. He now served as Ch'i-ying's assistant in the discussions being continued with the British while Hsu resided in Canton.[7]

Precisely what influence this short assignment to Canton may have had on Hsu's later career is a matter of speculation. Was he involved in the experimentation with Western-style ships in Canton to rebuild a Chinese navy along modern lines? Did he have personal contact with Westerners? Or with the so-called barbarian experts, who were supposedly capable of eliciting confidence from the foreigners?[8] Unfortunately almost nothing concerning this period is found in Hsu's records. After only three months in Canton he was again promoted, this time to the office of financial commissioner of Fukien, which he occupied from 1843 for over three years. He had been gone from Canton for months before the European community was apprised in the *Chinese Repository* for the first time of his presence, noting that he "has given satisfaction during the short period he has been in office here." Before he assumed office once again in Fukien the emperor summoned Hsu to the court of Peking.[9]

At age forty-eight Hsu, in the office of financial commissioner (or lieutenant governor), had become the third highest official in the province (since the governor general of Min-Che also resided in Foochow). He held the same rank, 2B, as the governor and supervised the affairs of provincial finance and taxation as a deputy of his superior. His appointment to Foochow came directly from the emperor and he was affiliated in the capital with the Board of Revenue. Like that of the governor, his official hat now sported a red coral button and embroidered golden pheasants decorated his official dress on back and breast. As a top provincial bureaucrat, he headed a large staff of assistants and secretaries to enable him to keep on top of the enormous correspondence of his office.[10]

Less than a decade after his departure from Peking and the Hanlin Academy, Hsu Chi-yü thus became one of the most powerful officials of the realm. He had bounded up the ranks, sometimes advancing a grade in just a few days or months, into the heady atmosphere of high officialdom denied both his grandfather and father. While in the provinces he had been catapulted six classes in rank, from 5B to 2B. Obviously Hsu was a talented administrator, a concerned and able coastal official; but it is also clear that he was being watched closely and supported by people powerful in Peking.

The ancient walled city of Foochow, where Hsu took up residence, held over 600,000 people, including a large boat population. The city had occupied this site from at least the Chou dynasty and was known as Fuju in Marco Polo's tale. It nestled by the scenic Min River, a stream flanked by cliffs and terraced rice paddies as its narrow valley penetrated rugged inland mountains to provide an avenue of commerce from the sea to Fukien's hinterland. On its way to the coast the river flowed through heavily forested mountains, the lair of tigers, and passed picturesque temples; in its verdant valley were groves of orange, pear, plum, peach, lichee, loquat, and longan.[11] Flowing down to the sea past Foochow, the river passed beneath the famous shop-covered bridge outside the city, past Nantai Island, where foreign residences soon were to be located, and past Pagoda Anchorage nine miles below Foochow where Yankee clippers fashioned by Donald McKay were destined to arrive for trade.

Foochow's people produced fine lacquerware, famous inside China and out. Local artisans also specialized in making high quality paper. Timber, brought from the inland forests, was plentiful in Foochow's yards, and camphor from this wood became another major item of trade. Bamboo, abundant in supply, was fashioned by ingenious craftsmen into scores of shapes and sizes to make a cornucopia of utensils and other useful gadgets. Practically everything made or sold by Chinese could be found here. There were "image-makers, lamp-makers, tailors, gold and silver leaf beaters, umbrella-makers, cotton-beaters, grocers, druggists, jade-stone cutters, seal-engravers, and decorators." After the Opium War one could even find "picture shops hung with the tawdry performances of native artists and caricatures of English admirals, colonels, ladies and steamboats."[12]

Had he not been so heavily burdened with the problems of office during an inauspicious period of Foochow's history, Hsu may well have delighted in the variety of the city. Life in such a place offered many fascinations for an official from the North: cormorant fishing on the Min River; fine "flower boats" tied up along the river banks; *fan-t'an*, the city's popular form of gambling, all surrounded by a sea of quiet countryside, away from the noise and bustle of the city and from the ever-present firecrackers of celebrations. The landscape resembled scenes of nature famous in Chinese paintings of the South. Buffalo wallowed in summer mud holes to escape the heat of the day; and even high officials interrupted busy schedules to ride out of the city, drawn to the cool air of retreats in the nearby hills such as the Ku-shan monastery northeast of the city where monks displayed a tooth of Buddha.[13]

Composed of Min and Hou-kuan districts, the prefecture of Foochow had achieved particular academic and official success under the Ch'ing even though the city had long served as a center of anti-Manchu sentiment. Foochow had been the capital of the refugee Ming court after it fled from Nanking. The Triad Society, whose slogan was "overthrow the Ch'ing, restore the Ming," claimed to have been founded in a Buddhist temple near Foochow in 1674. And Cheng Ch'eng-kung (Koxinga), pirate supporter of the Ming, was still a local hero. Nevertheless, Foochow produced a total of 723 *chin-shih* degrees during the dynasty's 267 years—an enviable record of which the local literati were justly proud; one surpassed only by Hangchow and Soochow.[14] The dynasty relied on these literati, who retained clear loyalties to the Confucian center in spite of the Manchu presence, to control the local populace and keep order.

While Hsu occupied this new post he was nominated by Ch'i-ying as an officer "who has usually been trusted by the barbarians," and consequently given an imperial appointment on November 7 to supervise trade in Fukien after the opening of Amoy on November 2, 1843. This meant the necessity of frequent visits to his old haunts in and around Amoy, where Hsu now entered into personal contacts with a variety of Westerners.[15]

Communication between the provincial capital and Amoy was by sea, for the mountains of Fukien made transportation by land along the coast too difficult. While Hsu supervised China's trade with the outsiders in Fukien after the Opium War, he therefore traveled several times by boat along this rugged coast, whose shoreline equaled ten times the distance of the 140 miles that separated Amoy from Foochow. Amoy was the chief naval station on the Fukien coast, and the province's squadron, assigned to guard the coast from outsiders as well as to suppress pirates, was reputed to be better than that of any other in China.

Amoy bay, one of the finest along China's coast, had long been known to Westerners. Indeed, Amoy had received some of these early traders from the West before they were forbidden to trade anywhere but Canton. The small island of Kulangsu in Amoy harbor, with its distinctively enormous granite boulders, sheltered English gravestones dating from 1698.[16] The large outer harbor, guarded by Quemoy Island, was considered to be good holding ground, and easy and unobstructed passage was afforded to the inner harbor, which was further protected from swells by Amoy Island itself. Just west of Amoy, a city with perhaps over 200,000 inhabitants in the 1840's including a large boat population, lay the island of Kulangsu. Not quite one mile square, this island once again served as the location of a Western settlement.[17] Many other islands, scattered over the harbor, lent added protection to the inner harbor and provided scenic variety. Numerous small villages and green fields dotted the surrounding coastal plains. The hills nearby were stunning in their barrenness, with some terracing where the land and the availability of water would permit. The city of Amoy sat at the western end of Amoy island; its people covered the valleys and hills of a large portion of the island. Beyond the city's suburbs thousands of horseshoe-pattern graves testified to the city's long habitation.

Amoy functioned as a link connecting China's domestic commerce with international trade. Exports to the international trade included tiles, granite, bricks, china, mats, paper, preserves, silk, shoes, sugar, tea, tobacco, vermilion, iron ware, rice, vermicelli, woods, mushrooms, oils, combs, joss-sticks, paints, and salt. Numbered among legitimate imports came a curious mixture of ordinary as well as exotic items from beyond China: betel nut, sea slugs, birds' nests, camphor, cotton, shirtings, cloths, cotton yarn, elephants' tusks, flint, glass, tin, rod iron, lead, various peppers, rattans, sharks' fins, skins, grains, various woods, dried meats, medicines, and wool.[18]

By 1843 Amoy already had attracted foreign vessels on a regular basis, ships bearing exotic foreigners as well as strange sounding names: *Inca, Panama; Cohota, Montauk; Clarendon, John Q. Adams, Paul Jones; Eliza Ann, Mary Ellen, Ann Maria.*[19] On such ships came Western consuls, medical doctors, and missionaries. These Westerners came to the coast of Fukien to promote change for China: to open China fully to trade and diplomacy with the outside world; to spread Western medicine and eliminate infanticide; to bring the message of Christianity and of Western knowledge in general. This foreign influence, for an official from the North like Hsu, provided an additional layer of variety to an environment already in striking contrast to that he had known in Shansi or Hopei. Hsu's genius in this location was his attraction and openness to information from beyond China. It was here that he began to display a remarkable readiness to borrow knowledge from non-Chinese sources to help him gain a more realistic perspective for Chinese. The Westerners with whom he came in contact discovered in Hsu qualities most unusual in their eyes for a high-ranking Chinese official. Not only was he open and fair, he was respectful and friendly.

For Hsu these were difficult times; on one hand he had to learn the techniques and problems of dealing with Western traders and their diplomatic representatives, while on the other he needed to satisfy the demanding requirements of his office as financial commissioner. In a letter to relatives in Shansi, written after his appointment to manage "barbarian affairs" in Amoy, he noted that this was both an important and a difficult assignment. He was "not afraid," but was nevertheless extremely worried about the unsettling effects of the foreign presence in places where the local people were in such a bad state. Hsu hinted that he might not succeed in his new job. He inquired about buying land in Wu-t'ai, saying he disliked living in cities and could hardly wait to return to the country. He had heard that a certain Feng-en was offering land for sale at less than a thousand taels; he wanted very much to buy it to build a house but was concerned over the expense. He concluded that if forced to resign soon he would not be able to afford the land. Such were the worries of an apparently incorrupt official.[20]

In spite of his official obligations, somehow Hsu had already found time to begin work in 1843 on his world history-geography. During visits to Amoy in January, February, and May of 1844 Hsu on several occasions met an American missionary who introduced him to Western maps of the world. Britain's first consul at Amoy, Captain Henry Gribble, who had spent time in a Canton prison during 1839–1840, had called on David Abeel to be his interpreter when he met Hsu.[21]

One of the first two American missionaries to China, Abeel had arrived at the island of Kulangsu in late February 1842 with William J. Boone, another missionary. The two took up residence in an unoccupied house on the island, now occupied by the British, and began their work. Both spoke Fukienese. By June they had been joined by a medical doctor, William Henry Cumming. Abeel had already begun preaching, first at Kulangsu in March, and later in January 1844 at Amoy. He and his fellow missionaries even distributed religious tracts and Western books translated into Chinese to the officials of Amoy. Abeel could scarcely believe the changed attitude of the officials he encountered there. On several occasions

Chinese officers had returned his calls and at all times showed the best of manners. "If I had never lived in China before the new order of things," he noted, "I should probably not be so much struck with the astonishing change in the conduct of the officers. Their present condescension and suavity are quite equalled by the disdainful pride they formerly assumed." On April 26, 1843 Abeel reported that he had helped the British at Kulangsu entertain four of the highest officials of Amoy who had arrived two hours before dinner. In this time before the feast they were shown "books and anatomical plates; in the latter of which they took a laudable interest."[22]

Abeel reported on January 27, 1844, that Hsu Chi-yü, erroneously labeled "imperial commissioner," had already been in Amoy for some time to locate a suitable place for the future residence of the foreigners who were to be removed from Kulangsu and to determine the limits for foreign activities in and around Amoy. It was on the occasion of Hsu's talks with Gribble in January that he met Abeel for the first time. Abeel jumped at the opportunity to peddle Christian influence.[23] His objective in Fukien after arriving at Kulangsu under British protection had been to present ideas to the Chinese by word and books which might "through the guidance of the Holy Spirit, lead some of them into the narrow way of life."[24] On some Chinese, however, his influence did not have that precise effect. For Hsu the contact with Abeel and his books opened up new vistas; his provincial view of the world expanded to take notice of all the known lands and seas of the planet. Hsu, a sophisticated representative of the Confucian humanistic heritage, found it useful to collaborate with the eager American because he lacked a knowledge of the outside world.

Abeel was delighted to provide Hsu with statistics and facts related to history and geography; he also introduced him to Western maps and helped him to prepare copies with place names written in Chinese. "We saw his excellency several times. He is next in office to the lieut.-governor [sic], and bids fair to be the governor-general of this and the neighboring province. He is the most inquisitive Chinese of a high rank I have yet met. After asking many

questions about foreign countries, we proposed bringing an atlas
and showing him the position and extent of the places which were
most interesting to him. To this he gladly assented, and we have
given him as much general information as we could compress into
part of an afternoon. We promised to send him Christian books,
and yesterday I made up a package for him containing the New
Testament and other books."[25]

Hsu did not resolve the residence question on this visit, for
Abeel noted soon after that he had been sent again to Amoy.
Abeel visited Hsu again on February 19, 1844, and described the
visit as follows: "Knowing that his excellency had returned, we
called upon him, and had a peculiarly gratifying visit. He said he
had been reading the Christian books, and begged to make a number of inquiries, which related principally to the characters and
places he had met with. He had evidently read the New Testament
with attention, and gave me an opportunity of explaining many
most important truths, which I pray God may be impressed upon
his heart."[26] Abeel could not but show some disappointment, however, that Hsu was "far more anxious to learn the state of kingdoms
of this world, than the truths of the kingdom of heaven."[27]

The next day the "sub-prefect" of Amoy, probably Hsu's
aide, Huo Ming-kao, informed Abeel that Hsu was busy reading
the literature he had received from the missionaries. Abeel was
delighted. Already interested in learning more about the non-
Chinese world, Hsu was happy to find a man from the West who
could provide accurate information. In late March Abeel received
a visitor, a young official he had first met in Hsu's party, who discussed with him matters of religion and of the various countries.[28]
Hsu was already employing subordinates to gather information
from a wide variety of sources, including Western publications in
Chinese.

Hsu readily admitted Abeel's contribution in the preface to
his *Ying-huan chih-lueh*:

In the *kuei-mao* year of Tao-kuang [January 30, 1843–
February 17, 1844] when I was temporarily staying in Amoy

in official capacity, I met an American named Abeel. [He was]
a scholar who was able to speak Fukienese and who was very
well-informed regarding Western countries. He had a book of
maps which were finely drawn and carved [i.e., engraved].
Unfortunately, however, I did not understand the characters.
But I traced ten-odd maps and asked Abeel to transliterate
them so as to get a rough idea [of the pronunciation] of each
country. But I was in a great hurry and was not able to examine
them with care [at that time] . . . The following year [i.e.,
after February 17, 1844] I again went to Amoy [and saw]
two [books of] maps purchased by the first class sub-prefect,
Huo Ming-kao. One was over two feet in size while the other
was a little over one foot; and these were even more detailed
than Abeel's volumes. [Huo] had also found several kinds of
miscellaneous books written by Westerners in Chinese.[29]

Hsu mentioned Abeel by name in at least six other places in
his book.[30] While Hsu and Abeel cooperated on their maps, Hsu
also became acquainted with Abeel's American medical colleague
in Amoy, Dr. Cumming, known to Hsu as *Kan-ming*. After he
arrived at Kulangsu with Abeel, Cummings had opened a hospital at
Amoy by early 1844, where he remained until his retirement in
1847. Cumming is also mentioned by name in the *Ying-huan chih-
lueh* as being very knowledgeable concerning Switzerland.[31] Another doctor, James C. Hepburn of the American Presbyterian
Board and later famous for standardizing a romanization system
for Japanese, was connected with the Amoy hospital at the time.[32]
Although Hsu did not refer specifically to Hepburn, it is most likely
they were in touch because of Hepburn's connections with Abeel
and Cumming.

Hsu's duties continued to press him. He had rushed again to
Amoy in early May, where he hoped to dissuade "an American
(*Mi-li-chien*) barbarian ship" (Caleb Cushing and party) from going
to Tientsin. He waited in Amoy twenty days with no news till at
last learning that, contrary to expectations, the Americans had
negotiated in Kwangtung; he was able to return to Foochow by
June 4, 1844. This left him with only two months to prepare a

detailed memorial concerning taxes. He lamented that if he did not
raise at least 874,001 taels by then, he would be punished.[33]

Foochow was opened to Western trade in the summer of 1844,
and on July 3 Hsu helped the port's first British consul locate a
place to lodge outside the city wall at Nantai Island. He found that
George Tradescant Lay, married to Mary Nelson, a distant relative
of the naval hero, could speak Chinese and that he was most respectful. Lay, who founded a line of British officers in China, had first
come to China as a naturalist in 1825. He had returned in 1836 as
a missionary before entering government service under Sir Henry
Pottinger and had served as the first British consul at Canton before
his transfer to Foochow. During his years in China Lay had learned
much of the etiquette expected by Chinese officials and had developed a sincere appreciation for things Chinese.[34]

Even though Lay appeared in Chinese documents of the time
under the pejorative title "barbarian chief," he made a favorable
impression on Hsu Chi-yü. Hsu admitted that he often consulted
with Lay while he was in Fukien and learned much about the Middle
East from him; Lay was mentioned by name at least three times in
the *Ying-huan chih-lueh*, always as "the English official (*Ying-kuan*)
Lay." Lay for his part wrote in early 1843 in preface to his remarks
on the "Chinese character and customs" that "the kindness I have
at any time exercised towards them, they have returned, and that
too with usury."[35]

Lay's admiration of China's ways and traditions apparently
convinced Hsu that Lay hardly fit the stereotype of a Western barbarian. That Lay had learned Chinese was evidence of his attraction
to Chinese civilization. But Lay even in this sense was not the typical continental frontier barbarian who was able to appreciate the
material benefits of Chinese civilization. He was a gentleman and
a scholar, universal qualities recognizable to a liberal Chinese. Even
though Hsu and Lay were subsequently caught between their governments on the sticky residence question, Hsu continued to find
him respectful and conciliatory.

Later in the year, on October 12, 1844, Hsu received orders
from his superior, Governor General Liu Yun-k'o, to meet Governor

John Francis Davis. Davis had arrived outside Foochow the previous evening on board a "fire-wheel ship" while on an inspection tour of the ports. Liu passed on Hsu's report to the throne that Davis had "observed the rules of propriety and was very respectful."[36] Davis, however, was unhappy about Lay's residence outside the city and reported this meeting somewhat differently, noting that "the provincial treasurer [Hsu], accompanied by the praefect of the city, came on board the *Proserpine*, with abundance of apologies from Lew Tajin [Liu Yun-k'o], for which I was fully prepared."[37] Davis departed the next morning for Amoy, so Liu was able to report to Peking that all was peaceful at Foochow and Amoy. No reference was made at this point to Davis's demands to remove the consular office to a more comfortable place, preferably inside the walls of Foochow. But after Consul Lay had resorted to "persevering firmness and determined remonstrances," the consulate at Foochow was allowed inside the city wall on the grounds of a temple at Black Rock Hill.

Hsu and his fellow officers were ready to make every reasonable effort to pacify the British. Having learned from missionaries that Westerners did not work on Sunday for religious reasons, the Chinese officials, "of their own accord, introduced into their agreement with the building contractor, viz. that none of the masons or carpenters should ever perform any work on the Sabbath day, or in any wise interfere with religious observances of the English." Moreover, "the mandarins, before paying the consul a visit, frequently sent to enquire whether it was the Sabbath day or not." Proclamations were repeatedly issued in Foochow commanding all citizens to show respect to the new foreign strangers, and punishment was promised to all offenders.[38] Conciliators on both sides—moderate Chinese officials, more fearful of Western ships and guns than personal contacts and ideas, and Westerners, insistent on their war-won role in China but sympathetic with Chinese who treated them with civility—were able to communicate during this period in a manner previously impossible.

In the fall of 1844, even while working to establish a system of treaty ports to accommodate Westerners outside the tributary system, Hsu, in addition to his other tasks, managed the affairs of the Liu-ch'iu tribute mission which was waiting in Foochow to begin its journey north to the capital.[39]

After Liu Hung-ao's retirement on March 30, 1845 Hsu served concurrently as acting governor of Fukien. During this time he reported regularly to Peking on financial matters: currency problems; the loss of silver from Fukien, historically and currently; taxation; yields of rice harvests; defense costs, including expenditures for the construction of war junks in Taiwan, Foochow, Changchou, and Ch'üan-chou.[40] Since the emperor had required notification on all costs of shipbuilding above 500 taels, Hsu diligently recorded such details in lengthy memorials. He also notified Peking of the arrival of marooned fishermen from Liu-ch'iu; but little mention is found regarding his regular contacts with Westerners. When reports on them did go in, they usually stressed that everything was under control. For example, as acting governor, Hsu reported in a joint memorial with Governor General Liu Yun-k'o that Consul Lay, transferred to Amoy in the summer of 1845, was extremely pleased with the accommodations that had been prepared for him there.[41] Meanwhile, Hsu continued to learn everything he could about the outside world from translated materials and from the Westerners who now resided in the treaty ports under his supervision.

In his account of a visit to Foochow from December 1845 to January 1846, George Smith of the Church Missionary Society noted that Hsu was "a man of liberal views, and remarkably well versed in the geography and politics of the west." Smith apparently repeated information about Hsu gained from Lay's successor, Rutherford Alcock, who assumed duties at Foochow in March 1845, his medical career cut short by the loss of the use of his thumbs as a result of rheumatic fever.[42]

> Of all these officers of the local government the acting governor of the province far exceeds the rest in the varied extent of his information and liberality of his view . . . he is far in advance of the generality of his countrymen. In his intercourse

with the British consul, he has alluded to the more prominent
events of modern European history, and shown his general
acquaintance with the whole cycle of European politics; as for
instance, the difficulty of governing Ireland on account of
popery, the revolt of Belgium from Holland, the separation
from Britain and Spain of their colonies in North and South
America, the ambitious career of Napoleon, and the closing
victory of Waterloo. He also seems to have heard of the excite-
ment in England consequent on the discussion of the Maynooth
grant. For hours together he will converse on geography, and
has pasted the Chinese names over an expensive American
Atlas presented to him by one of his subordinate officers
from Canton.[43]

Indeed, Consul Alcock and his wife provided additional geographical and historical information for Hsu, whose book about
the non-Chinese world was now well under way. Alcock promised
to provide him with a globe of the world, and at Hsu's request, Mrs.
Alcock drew him a map of the world, in which she indicated with
different colors the global territories controlled by Britain, France,
and Russia. "Shortly after receipt of it, he sent a note inquiring the
reason why Afghanistan had been omitted, and whether it had become amalgamated with Persia or was no longer an independent
kingdom."[44]

But the peace and quiet cited by Hsu and Liu Yun-k'o in their
reports to Peking was soon shattered in Foochow with the admix-
ture of foreigners and their Cantonese linguists in the local populace. In late March and early April of 1846 this unfortunate com-
bination caused a riot. On April 8 Hsu met with Rutherford Alcock
and his interpreter, Harry Parkes, to discuss the problems born of
the recent commercial and cultural contacts. Hsu "ordered" Alcock
to thereafter control the "barbarian mob," while the Chinese officials for their part would control the local people in order to restore
peace. "Alcock was happy and sincerely submissive," Hsu reported.
However, shortly afterwards local "bandits," upset by the foreign
presence, stole money and goods from the English at Nantai, and
Hsu again was summoned to settle the matter.[45]

That July, however, a personal tragedy wrenched Hsu away from the increasing worries of his office. He wrote to his relatives in Shansi to report his wife's death on July 3. After thirty-six years of marriage Hsu was still childless. He deeply loved his wife and during these years had not taken a concubine. In his letter Hsu lamented that after suffering all the ordinary hardships of an official's wife in the provinces, when he brought her south she was unable to adjust to the uncomfortable climate. "She was bothered by the extremes of cold or heat and the wind, and she was often ill." After their arrival at Foochow in 1843 she wished to return to Shansi, but Hsu did not want her to go alone and had persuaded her to remain until arrangements could be made to resign his post. During the spring of 1846, however, the weather had been particularly unsavory. It had rained continuously for eighty days and was so cold that padded clothing was still worn in late May. But suddenly it became intensely hot at the end of June, and his wife's heart was affected. After dinner on July 2 she felt ill and cold. During the night she perspired "like rain" and suffered chills. He gave her several bowls of rice gruel during the night to quench her thirst, and finally she slept. Worried, Hsu summoned a doctor after dawn. She said she was only weak now and that the sickness had passed. The doctor, after taking her pulse, agreed and wrote out a prescription. But after taking the medicine and another drink, she began to vomit. "Her breathing stopped and there was not the slightest pulse. She failed to respond to the needle. Alas!"[46] The oppressive climate of southeastern China's coastal cities, fatal to so many missionary families in the nineteenth century, was hardly less so for the families of Chinese officials from the North.

The funeral was a big affair in Foochow, attended by over two hundred civil and military officials, from the governor general down to low-ranking officers. On the "third seven" (the twenty-first day of the traditional forty-nine days of mourning), Hsu planned to move the coffin to the K'ai-hua Temple just outside the city. There it would await return to Wu-t'ai district for burial later in the fall when Hsu planned to take sick leave.

The death of his wife awakened Hsu's concern for the con-

tinuation of his family line. He desperately wanted a son. He was
extremely shaken by his wife's death, since he "held her in such
high regard;" but he was not willing to remarry and give her place
to another. Instead he would have to purchase a concubine. He
commented, however, that to find a pretty woman was easy, while
to discover one with a good disposition was indeed difficult. He
thought that purchasing a woman in the South would not be the
best solution, since on his return to Shansi she would find life hard.
"Hopei women are reputed to be good for bearing children," but
he feared they were rather boorish. The best solution after all
would be to find a girl from Wu-t'ai who would know the customs
there. He therefore requested his relatives to keep this in mind and
to try to find him a girl from a poor family. "But who would be
willing to give a girl to an old fellow over fifty? How could people
not laugh at such a groom—with bald head and missing teeth?"[47]

Hsu's duties left little time, however, to mourn his loss. When
Alcock received a group of foreigners (Robert B. Jackson and M.
C. Morrison, a woman and girl, plus servants) on September 8, 1846,
at his consular residence inside the wall at Chi-ts'ui Temple on Black
Rock Hill, Governor General Liu ordered them to visit Hsu at his
yamen on September 10.[48]

Though it is impossible to trace the full extent of Hsu's contacts across the cultural barrier with foreigners during his difficult
assignment in Fukien as financial commissioner and acting governor
—with missionaries, doctors, consuls, and even perhaps with traders
and seamen—nevertheless the above examples indicate the nature
of the connections Hsu plugged into on China's maritime frontier
after the Opium War. His personal contacts with some exceptional
Westerners, men such as Abeel and Lay, who had taken the trouble
to learn Chinese, revealed them to be men of culture and knowledge.[49]
They served as catalysts which aided Hsu's reaction to literature
about the world outside China, and they were fundamental to his
formation of a new world perspective.

Hsu's demonstrated ability to deal with these Westerners raised
him even higher in Ch'ing officialdom.

Chapter IV

A VICTIM OF CONSERVATISM

On December 2, 1846, Hsu was appointed governor of Kwangsi. On receipt of this order he requested, and was granted, an audience with the Tao-kuang Emperor. During the audience Hsu appears to have stressed the pivotal role he was playing in foreign affairs and argued that he be allowed to remain in Fukien. Soon after, he received notice of his appointment as governor of Fukien; by March 17, 1847, he had reached Yenp'ing, a city on the Min upriver from Foochow, and five days later he assumed his duties in the governor's yamen at the provincial capital.[1]

For the second time in his career Hsu was removed from a substantive role in Kwangsi, this time on the very eve of the Taiping Rebellion. According to the account of the *Wu-t'ai hsin-chih* (New gazetteer of Wu-t'ai [Shansi]), the switch in assignments had been negotiated by Fukien's Governor Cheng Tsu-ch'in. Cheng had been assigned as governor to Fukien on September 13, 1845, but since this was such a difficult post with little opportunity for private gain he had convinced the court that Hsu, with his experience as a barbarian expert, was the man for Fukien. Cheng was then assigned instead as governor of Kwangsi where he remained until his dismissal in late November 1850 after the rise of rebellion in his province. Because Cheng was a devout Buddhist, he had refused to execute criminals; thus, according to the gazetteer's authors, the bandits of Kwangsi were treated so leniently that rebellion was inevitable.[2]

Whatever the reason for his transfer, the Ch'i-ying—Mu-chang-a clique finally had its man Hsu in Fukien as governor. In this office for over four years, he became one of the fifteen governors of the empire, in charge of a large, troublesome, but extremely important region. He was laden with concurrent offices: vice-minister of war; junior associate censor general; and others, such as supervisor of waterways. To his normal duties as governor—investigating and reporting on the work of all officers below him, supervising provincial examinations, and a multiplicity of others—Hsu still carried the additional responsibility of managing the affairs of foreign trade in his province. Since his yamen was located in the same city as that of the governor general, he further was required in almost all cases to memorialize and make announcements under a joint signature with the governor general. Hsu was fortunate during his years as governor to have as his superior Liu Yun-k'o, who also had become a convert to the policy of conciliation while governor of Chekiang during the war.[3]

In his report to Peking on arrival in Foochow, Hsu noted that he had already worked in Fukien for seven years and consequently had had opportunities to become familiar with the maritime foreigners. In spite of the problems that resulted from the presence of barbarians, however, Hsu assured the court that he would continue to work diligently to apply the techniques of *chi-mi* (loose-rein) to control them. The emperor, in his vermilion endorsement, opined that Hsu had exerted himself with complete conscientiousness to manage barbarian affairs satisfactorily.[4]

During the following years Governor Hsu continued to deal with the everyday concerns of his office. Reports flowed from his yamen to Peking on financial and administrative matters: transfer of officials; taxation of foreign trade; problems with local bandits and pirates; the expenses of building war junks, and appeals for more support to strengthen China's defenses against Western naval encroachment. Hsu argued that the time should be used to prepare ships and cannon while the barbarians were still "very docile and obedient."[5]

Governor Hsu also completed the work on his geography of the non-Chinese world during this period. Despite the moderate tone of his book, Hsu's reports to Peking revealed that he was tough-minded regarding the foreign threat. In a joint memorial submitted in late 1848 or early 1849 Hsu and Liu Yun-k'o complained about the complicity of "Chinese traitors" with barbarians; they reiterated the cliché that "the barbarian nature is like that of dogs and sheep."[6] Clearly Hsu separated his role in officialdom from his commitment to objective scholarship. He was not above using the jargon of the day in order to work effectively within the bureaucracy.

By 1850, however, after the death in February of the Tao-
kuang Emperor, twilight was already upon the party of officials
who had taken a soft position toward the non-Chinese in the
coastal region. Ch'i-ying's foreign policy of conciliation failed at
the court, now headed by the young Hsien-feng Emperor. Palmerston's attempts in the spring of 1850 to communicate with the
capital and to bypass Hsu Kuang-chin at Canton spelled the end of
the Ch'i-ying—Mu-chang-a clique of officials, Hsu Chi-yü included.[7]

In a memorial to Peking in the summer of 1850 Hsu reported
the situation at Foochow, finally peaceful after numerous problems
due to the friction between foreigners and local Chinese. He observed that large foreign ships could not come to Foochow because
the water was too shallow. Nevertheless, he and Liu Yun-k'o had
just inspected the batteries in Foochow harbor in case of trouble.
In the ritualistic documentary style of the period, Hsu consistently
referred to the British as *ying-i* (British barbarians), a term written
with the mouth radical attached to the characters to connote the
meanness and barbarity of such people.[8]

Despite his precautions, however, Hsu soon encountered a
series of events that served as a pretext for his removal from officialdom. Though he had finally allowed Lay and subsequent British
consuls to reside at the Chi-ts'ui Temple inside the walls of Foochow, a strong position had been maintained forbidding residence
inside the walls to all other foreigners. However in 1850 Hsu and
Liu both became trapped in a case which proved particularly difficult. This was the so-called Shen-kuang Temple affair.[9]

The case centered on the rental of rooms in an old temple
on Black Rock Hill by two Englishmen, one a missionary, the
other a medical doctor. Xenophobic local literati, reflecting the
sentiments of their Canton counterparts, called the situation to
the attention of the authorities and the emperor, who in turn
demanded that Hsu and Liu expel the foreigners. After several
months the Westerners were finally moved to another temple,
but the impassioned literati of Foochow thought action had been
too slow. Critics repeatedly called for Hsu's removal. That Hsu's
new book about the outside world had just appeared further

complicated his life, for this too was used as a pretext by his critics.[10]

The first gentry protest of foreign residence in the Shen-kuang Temple occurred sometime soon after June 26, 1850. And the attack against Hsu and Liu in Peking was initiated on August 25 when Sun Ming-en, a member of the Hanlin Academy, memorialized Hsien-feng and stated the Foochow scholars' position. In response the emperor issued an edict the same day notifying the Grand Council of the report that foreigners were trying to live in that city.[11] The emperor instructed Hsu and Liu to do the impossible: to keep peace between the people and the barbarians.

A few days later a joint memorial from Hsu and Liu reached the court reporting the history of the British consuls' residence inside the wall on Black Rock Hill, but noting that all other foreigners had been kept outside. "We have been playing it by ear for the last six or seven years." But now two English barbarians "who teach the classics" (i.e., missionaries) had rented two rooms in the Shen-kuang Temple. Details of the case having been roughly sketched, the memorial reported more serious matters: the recent intelligence that an English fire-wheel ship had stopped outside of Keelung in Taiwan on May 7 hoping to buy coal.[12] Hsu and Liu were still banking on the foreign threat to keep themselves in office as barbarian-tamers.

The emperor's reply of September 1, 1850, urged Hsu and Liu to resolve the case. But foreigners should not be allowed inside the city in any case. The emperor was also concerned about the report of the English spying on Taiwan's coal resources, however, and he issued an edict the next day ordering preparations for the island's defense.[13]

But on September 4 and 6, censors who represented the case of the ruffled Foochow literati sent two additional memorials to Peking. In the first, Lin Yang-tsu cited a public letter written to Hsu by Lin Tse-hsu (then on sick leave in his native city, Foochow) and others which strongly opposed his handling of the case.[14] The memorialist noted, however, that the gentry had been motivated by the example of Canton's exclusion of foreigners and reported that

Hsu had responded to this letter of the gentry point by point. The second memorial, sent by Ho Kuan-ying, was a clearer attack on Hsu. The emperor, noticeably disturbed by this report, ordered Liu Yun-k'o to memorialize regarding Hsu's actions there.[15]

Meanwhile another joint memorial arrived from Hsu and Liu on September 8. This was ostensibly a report on the movement of barbarian ships, stating that "the barbarian nature changes and is not dependable," but it finally raised the topic of the Shen-kuang Temple. The memorial depicted the unfortunate Hsu in the difficult position of a conciliator between the barbarians and the gentry. Hsu and Liu assured the emperor that all was being done and that the able barbarian expert, Lu Tse-ch'ang, had been spying on the two foreigners in the temple.[16]

In another memorial sent to Peking shortly afterward and received on October 30, Hsu and Liu briefly reviewed the history of China's relations with Britain. The *Ying-chi-li* (all with mouth radicals) "are island barbarians from the Western Sea." "The intractable barbarians having attained their wish [for trade], have become arrogant and their acquisitive desire has not been suppressed." But with their memorial thus carefully spiced with anti-barbarian epithets, Hsu and Liu pointed out again China's coastal exposure, from Manchuria to southern Kwangtung, to the maritime power of Britain. They noted that trade should be used to control the British. "Cutting them off from trade is like taking [a mother's] breast away from an infant."[17]

On the same day the emperor received the memorial he had requested from Liu concerning Hsu's management of the Shen-kuang Temple affair. Though the memorial exonerated Hsu, the emperor angrily ordered Hsu to "act decisively."[18] Hsu received the edict with this message on December 9 and finally moved to transfer the missionaries to the Taoist Tao-shan Temple on the hill by the British consulate. Liu Yun-k'o, no doubt having guessed the obvious outcome of these events, had already resigned due to "ill health."

But Hsu held on stubbornly. On November 21, 1850, the emperor received another memorial from Ho Kuan-ying further accusing Hsu. So now the court ordered the conservatives' darling, Hsu Kuang-chin, to investigate the charges. At the same time the emperor again urged Hsu to get on with the case's settlement and not to delay the least bit.[19]

A few days later on November 30, 1850, the emperor denounced Ch'i-ying and Mu-chang-a. Apparently undaunted, Hsu continued business as usual. In a memorial written shortly after November 18 he dealt with the affairs of Liu-ch'iu and the British threat against that island tributary.[20] But this did not stop imperial edicts concerning the residence problem. On January 12, 1851, the emperor upbraided Hsu for being so tardy in reporting the details of the case. "Have the foreigners been removed?" "Are the gentry and people at peace?"[21] With the inadequate lines of communication between Peking and the coastal provinces of the South, this edict on its hurried flight to Fukien passed Hsu's memorial announcing the foreigners' transfer to the Tao-shan Temple.[22]

Soon thereafter, Hsu submitted a final report, stating that the foreigners had been removed from the Shen-kuang Temple— one on December 2 and the other on December 23. Now fully aware of his plight, he briefly reviewed the case and apologized for his mistakes. Following proper procedures to show his loyalty to the court and the Chinese order, he noted in even this memorial, however, that the nine American barbarian missionaries and the one Swiss (with mouth radical) missionary residing on Nantai Island were all "good and peaceful."[23]

The court, upset by the cascade of criticism from the gentry of Foochow, instructed the new governor general of Min-Che, Yü-t'ai, to continue the investigation into Hsu's and Liu's management of affairs. Though Yü-t'ai's report cleared both officials of all charges in a memorial received on April 23, 1851, the Hsien-feng Emperor that day summoned Hsu to the capital, and abruptly removed him from involvement in foreign affairs. He was not to return to officialdom until thirteen years later. The emperor replaced him as governor of Fukien on June 22, 1851.[24]

Westerners were quick to identify Hsu's dismissal as a sign of Chinese retrogression in foreign affairs. The editors of the *Chinese*

Repository observed that his removal had been "on the ground that he allowed his attention to be distracted from the duties of his of-fice—which may be interpreted that he published books not flatter-ing to Chinese prejudices, and moreover valued the companionship of intelligent foreigners." [25] When informed of Hsu's replacement, Rutherford Alcock, long one of Hsu's admirers, wrote of the gov-ernor's "great progress" in Fukien and viewed his removal as a step backward for China. [26]

During his imperial audience, however, Hsu impressed Hsien-feng with his patriotic sentiment; the emperor turned to those in court and said that he was "trustworthy and not deceitful." Con-sequently he assigned Hsu to a post in the capital as a sub-director of the Court of the Imperial Stud, in charge of the imperial herds and grazing lands of southeastern Mongolia. Though demoted, Hsu was instructed by the emperor to speak out when he wished to sub-mit any recommendations to the court. [27] In 1852 Hsu indeed sent a memorial that favorably impressed the emperor, who then ap-pointed Hsu to serve as chief examiner for the provincial examina-tions that year in Szechwan. [28]

The spectacular sights of the mountains particularly pleased Hsu as he traveled into Szechwan. He concluded that it was little wonder that such an inspiring place had produced scholars like the famed Ssu-ma Hsiang-ju and Han Yü. But the pleasant change of scenery did not alter the realities of his shaky position in Ch'ing officialdom. Soon censors reopened his case and presented a request for settlement to the Board of Civil Appointments. In the sixth month of 1852 (July 17–August 14) while he was still in Szechwan, Hsu received notification of his impending dismissal. Whereupon he resigned and returned to his native place in Wu-t'ai to "mourn the death of his mother," who had probably passed on many years before. [29] Thus came to an abrupt end the promising official career of Hsu Chi-yü, obliged now to spend the following thirteen years in the Shansi of his past as a suppressor of rebels and as a teacher of Confucian truths. Because of his Western connection, Hsu learned early what China specialists in the United States were to discover a century later: that an individual who attempted to explain to his countrymen the events and dynamics of the civilization that lay beyond the culture gap separating China and the West risked identification as a subversive agent.

But though Hsu was forced to return to his native province in the heartland of traditional China, he left behind a compelling treatise that would draw the attention of other concerned Chinese to the implications of what he had heard and seen along China's coast.

Chapter V

THE *YING-HUAN CHIH-LUEH*

Like Westerners of an earlier age, such as Marco Polo who came to China to discover a remarkable people with a highly advanced civilization, in Kwangtung and Fukien Hsu had encountered another world civilization and the information that accompanied it. Along China's coast he had learned that his limited view of the non-Chinese world, especially of the Western world, was not based on current realities. He realized that Chinese literati required a new field of view, a more accurate vision that would encompass the globe. Therefore Hsu set off as a vicarious explorer in geographical materials to provide answers about the new international world. Unlike Western explorers, however, for Hsu there were no promises of loot, no El Dorado, no seven cities of gold. A Confucian realist on China's frontier, Hsu was motivated by geopolitical concerns as he searched out the facts that would help Chinese understand the non-Chinese world.

Even though Chinese scholarship after the early Ming dynasty had become too restricted, specialized, and inward-looking, China could not be hermetically sealed from outside influences, either on its inland frontiers or along the coast. Indeed, the maritime commercial activities of the coastal communities provided a milieu that fostered a literature on the maritime states which engaged in trade with China; coastal scholar-officials thus had produced a corpus of material. Some was of use to Hsu.[1]

The level of knowledge about the Western world in most of this literature, however, was inadequate. It was obsolete and limited by stereotypes. Such materials often contained fantastic tales, myths, and always Chinese preconceptions. At its worst this literature portrayed Westerners as less than human, as oddities, as hobgoblins and bugaboos. Such creatures appeared vile, cruel, insidious, cunning, uncanny, grotesque. At its best the more objective and straightforward examples simply described places, people, and scenes of the outside world with a superficial content that was comparable to that of the peep shows which became popular in China of a later day: peoples dressed in weird costumes; engineering marvels, such as large bridges and ships of war; black men from Africa; odd buildings; peculiar customs. Western penetration of China's zone, though worrisome, was hardly a unique threat from such a vantage point. Were not the Japanese "pirates" of the sixteenth century even more threatening?

While the Western world continued to be haunted by its ignorance of China in the early decades of the nineteenth century, China thus seemed oblivious to the need for a thorough reappraisal of her position vis-à-vis the outside world in general and the West in particular. Clearly, China required a more timely, realistic, dependable, and detailed literature concerning the developments beyond her ken. This the Protestant missionaries— William Milne, Walter H. Medhurst, Karl Friedrich August Gützlaff, and Elijah Coleman Bridgman—who appeared along China's coast, attempted to provide.[2] When these missionaries came to China, beginning with Robert Morrison in 1807, they followed the example of the earlier Jesuits by printing not only religious materials but also accounts of foreign lands.[3] This literature, added to information by Chinese authors and to his Western-style maps, provided a crucial ingredient for Governor Hsu's geographical potpourri.

Hsu surveyed the information concerning the non-Chinese world that was available to him in Fukien—materials old and new, Chinese and Western. From both books and personal contacts he meticulously assembled facts that he recognized as reliable. The "proto-scientific" manner by which Hsu proceeded to gather and organize his information reflected his identity with the school of empirical research (*k'ao-cheng-hsueh*), as well as his attraction to the early Ch'ing scholar, Ku Yen-wu (1613-1682).[4] Ku's condemnation of Ming Neo-Confucian scholarship for restricting Chinese thought—thereby reducing Chinese awareness of political realities and opening China to the Manchu invaders—held an irresistible appeal for Hsu who now faced foreign invasion by an even more potent foe. Hsu's heavy reliance on Ku Yen-wu's research to depict the Asian tributaries of China further suggests the influence of this early Ch'ing intellectual.

Hsu did not attempt to conceal the use of Western information for his book. In the author's preface of the *Ying-huan chih-lueh* he related the methodology of his research, as well as the nature of his materials. The author's objective approach to the materials of Westerners stressed the factual accuracy of Protestant publications rather than the style of the earlier Jesuit accounts.

> I continuously sought and collected a considerable variety [of Western works]. If they were unpolished and lacking in elegance so that a cultured and refined person could not look at them, I condensed them and recorded them on slips of paper so that they too would not be discarded. Each time I met a Westerner I would at once open a volume for his corrections [regarding] the appearance of the land and the present conditions of all the countries beyond our borders. [In this way] I gradually derived an outline of the boundaries [of the various states]. Then with maps as a basis I selected what was credible in all the books and expanded this to make sections which after a long time grew into a book. Whenever I received a book or there was some new information, I immediately revised [the draft] or added to it, so that it was changed altogether many tens of times. [I have done this] from 1843 [or early 1844] to the present, for five years, in addition to my official duties, with only this as a hobby and without stopping a day.[5]

Westerners like Ricci, Aleni, and Verbiest all lived in the capital for a long time and became well-versed in the Chinese language. Consequently the style of their books is quite clear and agreeable, but there is not a little boastfulness and craftiness in their accounts. Today's Westerners are not profound in [their use of the Chinese language] and their books are mostly vulgar and inelegant. But the facts related by them of the rise and fall of states are indisputably reliable. So I realize the elegance of the former cannot replace the sincerity of the latter.[6]

The author continued that despite their rustic and vulgar flavor he had nevertheless found most of the materials of recent Westerners—including printed books, manuscripts, periodicals, and newspapers—many dozens in all, to be factually reliable concerning the boundaries, conditions, historical development, products, and events of the various Western countries. Where dissimilarities in the accounts were found he followed that of the latest. When he met Westerners he sought additional information by word of mouth to add to his written account. Consequently because this material from the West was so miscellaneous in nature, Hsu explained that he did not add notations to specifically identify Western sources.[7]

Hsu also used a variety of Chinese materials, citing at least twenty-six such works or sections in compendia (see Appendix A). The author relied heavily on various dynastic histories, primarily to cite contacts between China and non-Chinese areas as recorded in Chinese documents, and to equate modern place names with their equivalents in the histories; on a variety of works specializing in particular areas, such as *An-nan chi-ch'eng* (Record of a journey to Annam) and *Lü-sung chi-lüeh* (A brief description of Luzon); and on works which surveyed Chinese past and present tributary states, such as *Hai-kuo wen-chien lu* (A record of things heard and seen among the maritime states) and Ku Yen-wu's *T'ien-hsia chün-kuo li-ping shu* (A critical account of the world's divisions and states).

Hsu finished the *Ying-huan chih-lüeh* in late August or September 1848, but the work probably did not appear in published form until late summer of 1849.[8] Despite S. Wells Williams's observation that the opinion of Hsu's "friends and fellow officers to whom he showed [his work], is not too high," the prefaces written by high officials in the Ch'ing government uniformly praised the *Ying-huan chih-lüeh* as the best book then available to Chinese readers who wished to understand the foreign situation.[9] Indeed, Hsu's own preface assigned a significant role to his fellow officers: "Financial Commissioner Ch'en [Ch'ing-hsieh] and Taotai Lu [Tse-ch'ang] saw this [work] and thought it should be preserved; [so] for this reason [they] corrected its errors and it was divided into ten chapters. Other colleagues also asked to see it and many urged me to have it printed. Thereupon it was named *Ying-huan chih-lueh*."[10]

P'eng Yun-chang, for example, found earlier Chinese geographies inadequate to portray the world as it really was; only with knowledge of the world could China understand the threat to her borders. This was indeed a book that would bring peace to the world.[11] Liu Yun-k'o also lauded the work, saying that of all the accounts concerning the outside world, only Hsu's "cleared away incredible statements."[12] Liu Hung-ao noted that Chinese records and ideas about the nature of the world were false.[13] He criticized Wei Yuan's *Hai-kuo t'u-chih* (An illustrated gazetteer of the countries overseas), published in 1844 as an elaboration of Lin Tse-hsu's earlier compilation project at Canton. Liu estimated that over half of the information in Wei's book could not be relied upon. He praised Hsu's maps and dependable information which the author had obtained from English and Americans. It was only when he read Hsu's book that he learned there was a "northern frozen sea." "The book can be used as a guide to the world for a hundred generations!" To Ch'en Ch'ing-hsieh the book was "like a candle in a dark room." Lu Tse-ch'ang too paid high compliments to Hsu and his work; he wrote that the author had empirically evaluated (*k'ao-cheng*) even the most obscure materials to compile the book and concluded that the results of his work would enable the dynasty to be better prepared to deal with foreigners.[14]

Tung Hsun's preface to the 1866 edition also complimented Hsu's work. He stated that he was so happy when he received it that he read the book even while riding in his sedan chair. Only when he read this book did he finally understand all "that was covered by heaven and carried by earth." Of all the available Chinese geographical works on foreign areas, Tung thought, only the book of Hsu was to be trusted. The absurdities of other books had been eliminated and ridiculous explanations ignored. The book was detailed and carefully compiled, so Tung, one of China's great Restoration leaders, hoped it would be read by many.[15]

Indeed, Tung's favorable opinion of the book led to its reprinting in 1866.

The above indicates that the *Ying-huan chih-lueh* was not the freak product of one individual. Even in the decade of the 1840's many high-ranking officers in the Ch'ing government appeared willing to attach their blessings, names, and careers to this book about the non-Chinese world. Hsu later wrote from retirement to the son of his former mentor in Fukien, Wu Wen-yung, that just after the book was printed there arose slanderous criticism from all sides. Yet, even then Wu praised and approved the work and advised Hsu to improve its style before presentation to the throne.[16]

But, as Western contemporaries pointed out at the time, Hsu's book was not without blemishes. Since he was not a translator and knew no foreign language, Hsu did not evidence concern for the problems that beset translators of information from one cultural context to another. He acted instead as a synthesizer of materials already written in Chinese. But Hsu too inevitably encountered the hoary problem of fitting foreign ideas and information into materials written with characters in classical Chinese.[17] Although he ultimately accepted translations of both Chinese and Western origin, Hsu had to decide which terms best conveyed what he thought to be the intended meaning. Hsu's own message was therefore usually clear, but the original ideas and information became subtly distorted as they were modified by the medium of Chinese characters and syntax, as well as by Chinese patterns of thought and assumptions. As vehicles for alien ideas the Chinese language and its written form, indeed Chinese culture in general, maintained a high index of refraction—the original image was altered by the lens of language and its context.[18]

As an interpretive work on the outside world Hsu's pioneering book thus fell prey to the tyranny of a language that could not accurately convey new meaning without considerable explanation of new terminology. Hsu himself probably did not realize the extent or significance of this problem, for he judged all translated material on the basis of whether it "made sense" within his own cultural context. His sleep was not disturbed by the nightmares of

later generations of translators in China which finally gave rise to
the National Institute of Compilation and Translation, with its
thirty-seven committees, to standardize neologisms imported via
translations.[19]

Hsu's intent was simply to transmit information about foreign
places to prepare Chinese to deal with a challenging new world.[20]
But inevitably foreign ideas were also imported via translated terms.
While these were usually rudimentary in content, nevertheless some
inkling of the idea of democracy could be found in the work; of
world religions; of Western governments; of social and economic
developments in Europe and America. Yet much of this information
was understandable to the reader only in terms of what was known
already in China. Relatively few literati had been to the shores of
China to see that Western ships did not really look like junks;
"wild cow" did not accurately describe to the Chinese the bovine
beasts which roamed America's plains. On a more abstract level,
the practice of "democracy" harmonized with certain Confucian
values and seemed similar to gentry control of local politics in
China. And so on.

Therefore the work's effectiveness as a tool to import accurate
new information and ideas depended on the author's ability to reveal the context of his new terminology. For a synthesizer like Hsu
who had never left China, the quality of his sources was thus as
important as his critical method of selection and evaluation. Given
such problems, Hsu's book was reasonably successful. But throughout, even in the description of the United States which closely
followed a Western translation, its information was characterized
by a quaint ring. Indeed, Hsu viewed the outside world of the
1840's through a Chinese glass darkly. But it is, at least to a degree,
this very imperfection which makes Hsu's book so appealing as an
early document on the eve of China's reassessment of her place in
the world.

Yet, Hsu's primary message was valid. He had realized that
the Confucian image of China as a supreme power in the center
of a moral order was no longer accurate. China now competed for
survival in a world of states which looked not to morality or virtue

for legitimacy, but rather to industrial and military power. Though it was presented as a "geography," Hsu's exposition was basically concerned with the relation of China and her order to a militant European order. What the European penetration of Asia already meant for India and the tributary states of Southeast Asia indicated to him that China's fate clearly depended on her ability to dance to the tune of new demands.

But could the spirit of the old China—the preservation of the internal system, if not the letter in foreign affairs—be maintained in this new world by quickly learning how to deal with it on its own terms? This was the conundrum Hsu raised for himself, his dynasty, his nation, and his culture.

What then did Hsu Chi-yü have to report to his Chinese audience after his contact with Westerners, after his lengthy research about the mysterious world beyond the seas and the steppes?

Chapter VI

GOVERNOR HSU'S IMAGE OF THE WORLD

When Hsu met David Abeel in Amoy early in 1844 Abeel introduced him to Western maps, which with their fine details impressed him from the first. The additional maps provided by Huo Ming-kao, his aide, apparently further convinced Hsu of the scientific accuracy and dependability of Western cartography and they became one of the organizing features of his book, as Hsu explained to his readers:[1]

> A geography without maps is not clear, but maps not [based on actual] observation are not [accurate] in detail. The world has a form and its protuberances and indentations cannot be conceived [by merely thinking about them]. Westerners are accomplished in traveling to distant places. Their sails and masts encircle the Four Seas. Wherever they go they immediately take out brushes to draw maps. For this reason only their maps can be relied upon . . . This book uses maps as its guiding principle; these maps have been copied in outline from original maps in the books of Westerners. [In these maps] the veins and arteries of rivers are as fine as hair. Mountain ranges and cities, large and small, are all in place. But since it is impossible to translate all of the names and because the strokes of Chinese characters are so numerous that there is little room to write them on the maps, only the most important rivers and mountain ranges have been included [on the book's maps]. Also I have only given notice to cities which are capitals of states (*kuo-tu*). The remainder has all been summarized.[2]

The maps Hsu included in his work totaled forty-two (see Appendix B for titles and location). Of these, all but one, that depicting Japan and Liu-ch'iu, were based on Western sources. For the one exception Hsu reasoned that because Western traders rarely traveled to Japan their maps of these islands were not reliable. Consequently Hsu's work was marred by the inclusion of an absurdly inaccurate map based on an eighteenth-century Chinese source.[3] The other maps, however, show a reasonable degree of accuracy as simple maps which reveal the basic outlines of continents, oceans, positions of states, and political divisions. None could argue that Hsu's maps reproduced the quality of the original atlases he used, but they were sufficiently accurate and detailed to present to the Chinese reader a practical view of the physical world's shape and its political units. In any case, with Hsu's reintroduction of Western cartography to China after its failure to gain acceptance in the early Ch'ing, his maps were better than any then available on the non-Chinese world in Chinese geographical sources. They would impress some of Hsu's readers as much as he himself had been by the original maps in Western atlases.[4]

Before Hsu traced the world in terms of political divisions, he introduced the planet's physical features, its continents, and its seas. To illustrate these for his readers, Hsu presented two maps of the hemispheres, which he then explained in his text.*

The earth is like a ball, and it is divided [on maps] into warp and woof [longitude and latitude] based on the period of one revolution, with perpendicular and horizontal lines drawn across it. Each revolution [of the globe] equals 360 degrees (*tu*), while each degree equals 250 Chinese li. The sea covers over six-tenths of the globe, while land is less than four-tenths. (Westerners are very accurate in their reckonings, but I need not repeat this now.) . . .
If we cut the globe from east to west [to make hemispheres], *the northern extreme* [North Pole] *is on the top and the southern extreme* [South Pole] *is on the bottom. A crimson line* [equator] *encircles the globe horizontally in the center and this is the path followed by the sun.* Twenty-three degrees, twenty-eight minutes (*fen*) south and north of the equator are the yellow lines [Tropics of Capricorn and Cancer] and

*Since Hsu stressed passages that he considered particularly important by placing a series of circles beside the characters, all such material has been italicized in the following translations to preserve the author's emphasis.

this is where temperatures gradually become mild. Forty-three degrees, four minutes farther north and south are the black lines [Arctic and Antarctic Circles] and as one goes gradually farther away from the path of the sun, it becomes dark and frozen. This is the location of the Southern and Northern Frozen Seas [Antarctic and Arctic Oceans] . . .

If we view the globe from the top or bottom, the North and South Poles are in the center . . . Everyone knows of the Arctic Ocean, *but I had previously never heard of the Antarctic.* When I first saw a map of the globe drawn by Westerners [written in Chinese] and saw they had labeled the southern extremity as Southern Frozen Sea, I thought they perhaps did not know Chinese well and had mistakenly called it this by copying "frozen sea" from the northern sea. [Hsu apparently thought the Westerners did not understand the character for "ice"]. I therefore asked the American, Abeel, about this; he said it was accurate and one should not doubt it . . .

The equator is the path followed directly by the rays of the sun and it encircles the earth exactly in the center. China is north of the equator, but the most southerly coastal reaches of Fukien and Kwangtung are just inside and outside the Tropic of Cancer . . . I had imagined that the farther south one went the hotter it would become until one reached the South Pole; there it would be hot enough to melt stones and fuse metals, *for I actually did not know that the sun followed a path around the center of the globe.*

If you cross the sea from Fukien or Kwangtung to a distance of about five or six thousand li, you will reach Borneo, which lies just below the equator. Here winter is like early summer in the interior of China. But if you continue on south beyond the Tropic of Capricorn the weather gradually becomes mild. Going farther toward the southwest you will eventually reach the Cape of Good Hope in Africa where frost and snow can be seen. Continuing toward the southwest you will reach Cape Horn in South America, quite close to the Antarctic Circle, where ice never melts and it is cold. Thus how can one doubt the explanation that the South Pole is a sea of ice? . . .

The continents of the earth encircle the Arctic Ocean *and*

they hang down in a disorderly fashion, like luxuriant leaves, with hollows and projections which are not at all uniform. Westerners divide the earth into four continents known as Asia, Europe, Africa (connected together and located in the eastern half of the globe), and another separate continent called America (which is situated in the western half of the globe). (The names of the continents are those coined by Westerners. Originally these were not dependable, but now I am discarding the old [Chinese names] and am following the statements of Western maritime maps. Recently the name of Australia, an archipelago in the Southern Ocean, has been added as the fifth continent in the world, but this is really stretching a point.) . . .

Asia extends north to the Arctic Ocean, east to the Great Ocean-Sea [Pacific], and south to the Indian Sea; it includes all of the Moslem areas in the west and extends to the Black Sea in the southwest. *Of the four continents Asia is the largest.* China is located in the southeastern portion [of Asia].[5]

Hsu removed the Middle Kingdom from the center of the world, but he was quick to describe China with the most complimentary phrases. He observed, for example, that all things originated in China and all peoples were envious of her. He continued in this vein.

The extensiveness of the land controlled by our dynasty has never been matched in ages past. The northeastern corner of the three eastern provinces [Manchuria] connects with Russia. Due north, all of the tribes of Inner and Outer Mongolia have been enrolled in the Eight Banners as servants and slaves. Kokonor and Tibet in the southwest are peaceful under our direct military control. Sinkiang and Turkestan in the northwest are composed of many of the states cited in Han records of the Western Region; the various tribes of Kirghiz and Burut from beyond the frontier annually contribute cattle to pay their tribute. Korea and Liu-ch'iu of the Eastern Sea and the various states bordering on the south, such as Cochin China,

Siam, Burma, Laos, and Nepal, have regularly sent tribute.
From this continent of Asia the only ones who have not submitted to our authority are Japan in the Eastern Sea, the
northern border tribes of Russia, the various weak and small
Moslem tribes of the extreme west, and the various states of
India in the southern region. So that the part of Asia held
by China is not quite half . . .

Europe is at the extreme northwest corner of Asia. The
land and the sea mutually gnaw and swallow one another [the
sea coast is very uneven]. It is not even one-fourth the size of
Asia. There are many tribes (*pu-lo*), but if one speaks only of
the large ones there are ten-odd states (*kuo*). The people have
dispositions which make them very careful and exact; they
produce machines and are accomplished in sailing ships, so
there is nowhere they have not reached within the Four Seas.
They cover 70,000 li in order to reach China. Those who are
called "Great Western Ocean people" in China are all from
this continent . . .

Africa is southwest of Asia and lies to the southwest [of
China]. It is surrounded by oceans to the east, west, and south;
it borders on two inland seas to the north (the Red Sea and
the Middle-of-Land Sea). It is connected to Asia only by a
thread. Its land is extensive and is approximately one-half of
Asia's. In the north there are Moslem tribes while the remainder of the continent is inhabited by black barbarians.
*The weather is hot and oppressive; the soil is coarse and good
for nothing. The people are chaotic. It is the worst of the four
continents* . . .

America is in the western half of the globe; it is not connected to the other three continents. The land is divided into
two portions, one in the north and one in the south, and these
are connected in the middle by a narrow waist. North America's northern boundary reaches the Arctic Ocean. Its northwestern corner is close to the northeastern corner of Asia and
the two are separated only several tens of li by sea. The east
side faces the states of Europe and looks out over the sea of
the Great Western Ocean [Atlantic]. The Pacific Ocean in
the West reaches to the eastern part of Asia. South America

and North America are connected by a thread and South America's most southerly point is close to the Antarctic Ocean . . . From the beginning of the world this land had no relations with other continents until Europeans discovered it in the middle years of the Ming dynasty . . .

The four continents all hang down in a disordered way from the North Pole. South of the Tropic of Capricorn there are only islands; further south there is only open sea reaching to the South Pole without even a slice of land [in between]. *That land is above and water is below is a principle of the earth's nature.* Abeel states that two years ago the four states of France, England, the United States, and Spain sent four ships to the south to explore the area. In the region of the Antarctic Ocean there is land belonging to these states, but it is impossible to know its size precisely.

Aside from the four great continents there are very many islands. The largest is Australia. Beside this there are the various islands in the area of Southeast Asia and the archipelago of the American gulf. These are all places frequented by numerous merchant ships.

Beside land there is only the sea. And if one tries to determine its boundaries according to the various continents, it will be incorrect [because there are no clear lines of demarcation] ; *consequently the waters are arbitrarily divided into five oceans known as the Pacific, Atlantic, Indian, Arctic, and Antarctic.* The Pacific Ocean reaches from the east of Asia to the west of South and North America; *this is the same ocean known to China as "Great Sea of the Eastern Ocean."* Because of its vast surface, *it encircles half the globe* and covers more of the earth than any other ocean. Americans say they can reduce the distance to Kwangtung to buy tea by 30,000 li if they follow this route. But because they must pass hazardous regions of extreme danger [Cape Horn] and because on the open sea for several thousand li there is no place to take on water and food, it is rare that anyone travels by this route.

The Atlantic Ocean reaches from the west of Europe and Africa to the east of South and North America; its greatest breadth is over 10,000 li while its narrowest part is less than

10,000 li. The Indian Ocean reaches north to Asia, east to Australia, and west to Africa. *Westerners call it by this name because they looked out at it from the centrally-located land of India. It is the same as China's "Southern Ocean" and that which is recorded as the "Lesser Western Ocean."* The Arctic Ocean encircles the northern boundaries of the three continents of Asia, Europe, and North America; somewhat over 1,000 li from the shore frost and snow have congealed. There is solid ice which never melts. The sea holds great fish [whales] which are able to swallow ships. Chuang-tzu probably referred to these when he said that in the northern vastness there was a fish known as *k'un* [leviathan]. The Antarctic Ocean is at the South Pole and the climate there is similar to that of the Arctic.[6]

In his introductory presentation of the world the author's concerns were thus purely geocentric. He did not place his globe in the context of a universe or even a solar system; he failed to make it clear to his readers that the sun did not revolve around the earth, though he was fascinated with the scientific exactitude of Western measurements; he did not show how the angle of the earth's axis accounted for the change of seasons. Such things were not part of his interests. His attention was riveted to the geographical nature of the terrestrial orb and the history of its peoples. Yet invariably the book presented a fascinating juxtaposition of Western-derived scientific facts and Chinese misconceptions: "land is above and water is below," an example of Hsu's misapprehension, was not an uncomfortable concept for Hsu in order to explain the relative positioning of continents and seas which he observed in Western atlases.

Hsu remained sensitive to his Chinese identity. In his discussion of the continents, he attempted to compensate for China's occupation of only a corner, and control of less than a half, of Asia by observing that Asia was the largest of the world's continents. He also felt compelled to deliver an opening statement on China's magnificence.

The author followed a uniform pattern in his approach to the world. General descriptions of the continents preceded a discussion of the particular political units therein. Thus, in the first chapter, following a general description of the globe, Hsu introduced Asia. He then began a broad clockwise sweep of the areas and states surrounding China: from Japan and Liu-ch'iu in the east to the states of China's "Southern Ocean," the various countries of Southeast Asia and the islands of the South Pacific; then to India and the border states between India and Tibet, sweeping up finally to complete an Asian arc around Chinese-controlled lands with a treatment of the Moslem states in Western and Central Asia.

Following a general description of Europe, Hsu completed China's ring with a treatment of Russia. The account then shifted to a counterclockwise sweep, from China's perspective, of Scandinavia, Central Europe, and Southeast Europe. The outer rings of Hsu's circle of European countries concluded with the Western maritime nations of Holland, Belgium, France, Spain, Portugal, and Britain. Africa and the isolated lands of North and South America were presented last.

Hsu thus revealed his new world edifice to Chinese literati in an account that totaled over 145,000 characters. Contained within his geographical framework were the basic political configurations of the mid-nineteenth century as well as a treasure chest of miscellaneous information about the states of the world. Into this mixture Hsu injected material that outlined the emergence of Western power, its penetration of Asia and the rest of the world, and its effects on the tributary arrangement of states which seemed so important to China as buffer zones, as sources for trade, and as inferior members of an order premised on the superiority of the Chinese system.

For its time, Hsu's book on world geography was a great achievement. Most of the harsh language and ridiculous lore about non-Chinese peoples were eliminated, and the author sincerely attempted to construct a realistic perspective. In addition to bringing China a more accurate picture of the location of the world's states, Hsu's account presented a rudimentary historical view that stressed the ancient heritages on which Western civilization was based.

But before scanning the outside world in detail, Hsu presented a map of the realm controlled by the Ch'ing dynasty. Here he again paid his compliments to China, explaining why he would not treat the Middle Kingdom in his geography of the world. As noted by S. Wells Williams, Hsu thus escaped comparing China in an obvious fashion to the powerful Western nations that occupied such a prominent position in his story about the new world.[7] Hsu said:

> China is the lord of Asia and everyone knows its borders, its mountains and rivers, so it is not necessary to bother with these complicated details. Our dynasty (*kuo-chia*) established imperial rule over Liaoyang and Shenyang [i.e., Manchuria] by firmly controlling and settling the area . . . The province of Heilungkiang straddles the Lesser Khingan Mountains and encompasses 10,000-odd li, all of which is land that had never been [a part of China] even from ancient times. [The empire] reaches to the northern area where people live scattered over the region wearing felts and furs and living in felt tents (the various tribes of Inner and Outer Mongolia). The Himalayas and Tienshan Mountains encircle the Western Region (Sinkiang and Turkestan). The fief that now takes the place of Hsiang-p'ing and Chi-tzu [ancient place names in Korea] and the old areas of Wu-szu and Turfan (Ch'ing-hai and the two Tibets) formerly did not have relations with China. *Recently they have again come under our control as dependencies, and communications with China are frequent; China and these border lands are not clearly demarcated.* The information in available accounts of China is very detailed, and records by various scholars are especially numerous. *China cannot be definitively treated with all-embracing expressions; also it cannot be treated in a history of foreign places.* Thus I have respectfully copied out the map of the Imperial Ch'ing to place it at the head of this work, but I will not repeat [what is already available elsewhere].[8]

Having thus safely tucked China outside his scope, Hsu was now ready to lead his readers into the details of lands beyond.

Chapter VII

DANGER IN CHINA'S MARITIME SPHERE

Though Hsu relied primarily on Western materials for information on other areas of the world, for Japan, Liu-ch'iu, and the states of Southeast Asia he based his study chiefly on Chinese documentation. The detailed evaluation of the states presented in this portion of his book reflects the traditional concern of Chinese bureaucrats for the maintenance of China's tributary network. Yet, the history and present situation of these cultures, and even old Chinese lore relating to the area, served as a cloak under which disturbing realities of new power politics could be revealed.

The treatment in Hsu's world geography of these states on China's circuit followed a general description of the Asian continent. This account introduced the details of Hsu's map at the head of the section, a map quite accurate in outline except for the position of the islands of Japan.[1]

Asia was originally the ancient place name for "Turkey Minor" (*T'u-erh-ch'i mai-no*; . . .[2] *Westerners know the area east of this land by the general name of Asia.* The land is so extensive that it is the largest of the four continents . . . In the sea [east of China] are the three islands called Japan as well as small islands called Liu-ch'iu. To the south and connecting with China's provinces of Yunnan, Kwangsi, and Kwangtung are Annam, Siam, Burma, and Laos. Those scattered in the midst of the Southern Sea are called the Archipelago of the Southern Ocean. Lying northwest and connecting with Sinkiang and Turkestan are the various Moslem tribes of the Western Region. Southwest and connecting with the two Tibets are Nepal and the Five Indias. Farther west are the various Moslem tribes of Afghanistan, Baluchistan, and Persia. Farther southwest are the Moslem tribes of Arabia, and farther to the northwest is the eastern part of Turkey (which is the same as the land [formerly] held by the various tribes of Judah).

ASIA

大洋海即東
洋大海又名
太平海

斯羅我
克薩哈

斯羅我
海島梁

斯羅我
上湖
車臣
國

斯羅我

黑龍江

庫瓦島

多布科

普布 疆新
疆回

大戈壁
後藏
前藏
密薩阿
陶

圖克薩札
顏語三
海潮
愛新古函

蕎拉阿
山西
陝西
河南

甘肅

青海
四川
雲南

湖北
江西
湖南
安徽
江蘇
浙江

直隸
山東

京畿

朝鮮

內蒙古
東四盟
盟西

吉林

日本三島

琉球

臺灣

呂宋

貴州
廣西
廣東
福建

越南

羅暹

緬甸

孟加拉

南洋

州瓊

婆羅洲

蘇祿
呂宋薰島

西晉

歷鹿加

亞布巴

巴羅鳴

閩池

Farther west is the central portion of Turkey, "Minor," the so-called "Lesser Asia."

The north reaches to the Arctic Sea, the east to the Pacific, the south to the Indian Ocean (same as the Southern Sea and the Lesser Western Ocean). The western part reaches to the Red, Mediterranean, and Black Seas. This then is the complete map of Asia.[3]

Japan and Liu-ch'iu

Having omitted Korea from his work because it was "like China," Hsu presented Japan and Liu-ch'iu in a section entitled "The Two States of the Eastern Ocean." The author's portrayal of Japan relied on the various dynastic histories and a few other miscellaneous sources, but primarily on Ku Yen-wu's monumental *T'ien-hsia chün-kuo li-ping shu* (A critical account of the world's divisions and states) and Ch'en Lun-ch'iung's *Hai-kuo wen-chien lu* (A record of things heard and seen among the maritime states).[4] However, the author followed Ch'en's account (author's preface, 1730) more than Ku's, which was published sixty years earlier. He noted that Ch'en, a native of Ch'üan-chou (Fukien) had often traveled to Japan as a child aboard merchant junks and was therefore thoroughly familiar with Japan's situation.[5] Betrayed by the outdated and grossly inaccurate information of Ch'en's work, Hsu extracted his general introduction to Japan. But he first explained his unwillingness to use Western materials for either Japan or Liu-ch'iu.

The Eastern Ocean is vast and its waters reach to the western boundary of America; across several thousands of li there is no land of any size. Near China there are only the two states of Japan and Liu-ch'iu, *and these cover China's left wing.* (The maritime maps of Westerners place the three islands of Japan to the north of Korea and are thus in error. [Westerner's] ocean-going merchant ships seldom reach [this part of] the Eastern Ocean, so the information they transmit is based on impressions only. I will now [avoid such mistakes] by reference to the *Hai-kuo wen-chien lu*.)

Japan was known in ancient times as Wo-nu ["dwarf-slaves," a pejorative term dating from at least as early as the *Hou Han shu*]. The state is located in the Eastern Sea on three islands. The northern island is called Tui-ma-tao [Tsushima], which is across from the southern edge of Korea. It can be reached [from Korea] in one night . . . The center island is called Ch'ang-ch'i [Nagasaki]. The land area is comparatively large and is opposite [the island of] P'u-t'o-shan off the coast of Chekiang. *China's merchant ships trade at this place.* The southern island is called Sa-szu-ma [Satsuma] and is opposite Wen-[chou] and T'ai-[chou] in Chekiang. Its people are strong and healthy and their swords are the sharpest; horses are also raised. In the Chia-ching period [1522-1567] of the Ming dynasty the *Japanese pirates who raided the coasts of Fukien and Chekiang were from Satsuma.* In addition to these three islands there are numerous small ones. The king resides to the northeast of Nagasaki in a place called mi-yeh [?]-ku, meaning "capital" in Japanese [Japanese: *miyako*]. The officials all receive hereditary emoluments and still follow Han regulations by allocating provincial governors two thousand piculs of rice. The written characters are the same as China's, but they are read according to Japanese pronunciation. The authority over state affairs resides with a generalissimo [shogun]. The king does not attend to such affairs, but only serves in a ceremonial capacity. The shogun infrequently has an audience with him and that is all. *Throughout the ages people have not fought to become king, but rather to become shogun.* Therefore the residence of the shogun at times is taken over by a new master, but the king's surname does not change. The reign title K'uan-yung [Kan-ei, 1624-1629] is used. Throughout the ages this [system] has not been changed. Laws are strictly enforced and the people seldom fight. Those who have broken the law go at once to a ravine and commit suicide. To summon a servant-boy one has only to clap and he will respond; a whole day may pass without hearing a person's voice. [The Japanese] love Buddha and revere their ancestors. If they obtain fragrant flowers or good fruit, they must offer this to Buddha or present it to their ancestors' graves. It is the custom to esteem cleanliness;

the streets are always swept. Men and women both [wear garments] with large collars and broad sleeves. The women's [clothes] are made longer so as to trail on the ground. They draw and paint flowers [on them]; on the inside of their loose trousers is a silken border. They wear short stockings and let their silk [clothing] trail on the ground as they walk. The men shave their heads and beards, leaving hair a bit wider than an inch along the temples to the back of the head. This hair is then bound up. When it grows out it is cut. The women all fix up their hair and wash it daily; for fragrance they wash it with cedar. From front and back it is done up in a knot with a tortoise shell hairpin stuck in. *Both the men and women have handsome features and look similar to Chinese. Truly the elegance of the East is gathered here.*[6]

This favorable if dated and often inaccurate introduction to Japan was followed by a record of the distances between Japan and various ports in China, such as from Amoy, Keelung, and P'u-t'o-shan. The author then mentioned the influence of Westerners in Japan:

In the middle years of the Ming dynasty, because the Portuguese from the Great Western Ocean desired to occupy [Japan's] ports, and also because the Catholics were enticing the local people, Japan fought them. Holland sent war ships to aid Japan; the Portuguese withdrew. Consequently Japan trades only with China and Holland. The products are such things as copper, sulphur, and agar-agar.[7]

A lengthy section from Ku Yen-wu's work was next quoted by Hsu.[8] This account traced the historical development of Japan, listed ancient political divisions, outlined the history of the royal line, and dealt with the relations between China and Japan from the Han dynasty on. Hsu interrupted Ku's account occasionally with "footnotes;" in one such note he remarked that originally Japanese customs were not different from those of the various aboriginal islanders of Southeast Asia; it was only during the Han period that Japan finally learned the arts of civilization. Ku cited the *Yuan History* for information about the Mongol campaigns against Japan in the thirteenth century, and he noted the typhoon that destroyed the attacking naval force. From the *Ming History* Ku took reports of tribute missions to China, of Japanese raids on the coast of China, of Chinese "traitors" who collaborated with the Japanese, of conflict between China and Japan in Korea. Hsu added his own conclusions to Ku's information; he cited the Mongols' invasion of Japan with Chinese naval power as an example of reckless stupidity in the history of Chinese foreign relations, an adventure that had caused the Japanese to lose respect for China— strong words indeed in an era when the Ch'ing rulers were notoriously sensitive to Chinese criticism of non-Chinese from the inner frontiers who could be in any way associated, as could the Mongols, with the Manchus.

I have called Japan a state; to the east of the Great Sea it alone *has regulations and a written language similar to those of China.* [The Japanese] *are not customarily people who rob and steal. From the time of their earliest contacts with China, although they held on to Liu-ch'iu and did not* [send tribute] *according to the established times, nevertheless they had never caused a loss to* [China] *that was not paid for beyond the regulations. So how did they threaten China's authority?* Yuan Shih-tsu [Khubilai Khan] had great ambitions and bragged recklessly. He suddenly sought to force [the Japanese] to be his slaves and concubines. He commanded them, but they did not respond. So he tried to intimidate them with military force. He finally raised 100,000 troops to attack, but on the open sea they encountered a typhoon. Having learned his lesson [Khubilai] did not again *scheme to gather another force. The Japanese since that time have held China in low regard.* The robbing and pillaging during the Ming dynasty which gradually reached to the southeastern side [of China], the oppressive behavior there from which there was no real shelter, as well as Korea having several times suffered the gnawing of silkworms [i.e., invasion] *all stem from the misfortune caused* [to Japan] *by the Mongols.* [When] our dynasty established its imperial rule over Liaoyang and Shen-yang, *its fame and spirit first reached out to Japan as the sun into a valley, and she was fearful. For a long time now the eastern border has been quietly maintained, and* [the Japan-ese] *have not dared to encroach on China. Moreover tribute ships have not been permitted. Our trading vessels have gone there, but their merchant ships have not come here. In two hundred years there has been peace in having no dealings with her. Only this method can be relied upon as a good policy in planning frontier defense.*[9]

The ineffective actions of the Mongols which had caused Japan to hold China "in low regard" rankled a patriot like Hsu, who was bent on maintaining Chinese prestige in foreign relations. But little evidence is found in Hsu's summary of a clear understand-ing of Japan's potential threat to China, something that would be-come of primary concern to Chinese leaders a few decades later. No positive recommendation for future Chinese policy toward Japan is to be found, except for the impracticable call for a con-tinuation of Japan's isolation from China.

The *Ying-huan chih-lueh's* coverage of Japan concluded with a short quotation from the *Fan-hai hsiao-lu* (A short record of sail-ing on the sea) which listed distances and sailing directions to ports in Japan as well as some descriptive material on the Japanese. Hsu also cited the *History of the Later Han Dynasty* and the *Shih-chou chih* (A record of the ten continents), a work about foreign geog-raphy of the Han period.[10]

Shifting his attention to the Liu-ch'iu, the author noted that this small tributary, although long caught between the magnetic poles of China and Japan, was a state that had succeeded tolerably well in serving two masters.[11]

Distances from the ports of Fukien were included in the account, as were the details of Liu-ch'iu's administrative divisions. Hsu quoted only one source by title for this section of his work, a book entitled *Chung-shan chih* (An account of Chung-shan) and written by one Chou Hai-shan, "a board president who had often been sent as an ambassador to Liu-ch'iu."[12] From this source Hsu sketched the island-state's historical relations with China beginning with the Sui dynasty; it became a tributary state in the early Ming. It was noted, however, that during the Ming period Japanese had attacked the state and captured the king, so that relations with China had been temporarily interrupted. Hsu concluded his short treatment of Liu-ch'iu with a frank recognition, one not generally acknowledged by Peking, of Japan's influence in the islands:

> The small islands of Liu-ch'iu in the Eastern Ocean have become the servants (*i*) of Japan. Being poor and weak [the state] cannot survive on its own, but must rely on its tribute vessels to trade [with China]. Of the goods [taken in this trade], eighty to ninety percent is transported to Japan; for the people of the country are extremely poor and are unable to buy anything . . . *They earnestly send tribute according to the established precedents and have received* [the Chinese calendar's] *New Year's Day. Consequently* [Liu-ch'iu] *is a vassal in the Eastern Sea comparable to the states of Korea and Cochin China. How can we believe that it does not value its independence (tzu-li)* [from Japan] ?[13]

Ahead of his time, Hsu in the 1840's had already pinpointed a major trouble-spot on China's periphery, one which suggested that China's maintenance of her tributary system and world order was being undermined by even a weak and poor off-shore Asian island state, namely Japan.

Vietnam, Siam, and Burma

Continuing his account of peripheral and tributary states, Hsu presented "the various states bordering on the seas of the Southern Ocean": Vietnam, Siam, and Burma. These areas, tied to China by politics and trade, were crucial for China's traditional system of foreign relations. How did Hsu view this part of the globe which was increasingly exposed to Western maritime pressures? In his directions to the reader the author had already pointed out that after the Han and before the Ming dynasties the various places in

Southeast Asia had been inhabited by weak and small barbarian tribes (*fan-pu*) who paid tribute to the court of China: "Now however they have changed to become marts for all of the European states." "This is one of the great transformations of all times, so I shall be somewhat more detailed in describing this area."[14]

The author looked first to Vietnam, noting that this was also the land known as Annam and Champa in ancient times. The country's history was sketched in relation to China's dynastic periods beginning with the Ch'in, when China controlled Vietnam. The text identified various place names, and the state's position in relation to China and the surrounding states was established before Hsu introduced general comments on the people, customs, and products of the area.

Again Hsu relied heavily on Ku's *T'ien-hsia chün-kuo li-ping shu* for ancient place names and a fairly detailed historical summary of China's relations with the area from the Ch'in dynasty on. Ku recorded that Chinese during the Han period taught the people to farm, gave them a system of administration, introduced marriage, and founded schools. Ku's chronicle covered the vicissitudes of the royal line, noting even that there was at one time a "woman king" and stressing the tributary relationship of Vietnam with China.[15] The *Hai-kuo wen-chien lu* also provided information in Hsu's account regarding the situation of Vietnam in the eighteenth century with the names of cities, distances, and points of reference in coastal navigation between Amoy and Vietnam.

Further influence of Ch'en's account on the *Ying-huan chih-lueh* may be seen in the author's discussion of Vietnamese techniques to repel Westerners, although Hsu appears to have maintained a healthy skepticism as well as an appreciation of the value of practical experimentation:

> It is commonly said that the "Red Hair" (*hung-mao*) [Western] ships fear Annam most of all and do not dare penetrate its boundaries. The [Annamese] are skilled in swimming. If they encounter a Western *chia-pan* [ship, lit. "layered-board"], several hundred people are sent carrying bamboo pipes [to

breathe through while under water].[16] They [then] take fine silk lines under the water and nail them to the bottom of the vessel. [With this] they get in small crafts and pull [the Western ship]. As soon as it has become stranded in the shallows, they burn it and take the goods. It is also said that the people of Annam build small vessels called "battering ships." These attack the hulls of Western vessels, so the Westerners fear them. *Lately I have inquired about these stories and they do not appear to be very reliable.*

The sea north of Cochin China is shaped like a half moon; the seas rush with great force toward the gulf. If ocean-going ships sail into the gulf, they cannot come out without a westerly wind. *Western ships have come in and run aground. This has already destroyed numerous vessels. Up to the present, therefore, Europeans who sail the seas regard seeing the mountains of Kuang-nan to be strictly forbidden.*

When a [Western] merchant ship enters a harbor in Annam the natives all tow it in with ropes from small vessels and try to make it run aground on the rocks. Now with this as a guide, the pilot boats of each harbor in China *can copy the principle for destroying enemy ships. But just how to go about getting under water to fasten the line onto the ship is vague.* As to the construction of battering ships, some already have been built according to drawings. But when tried on the open sea they were no different than ordinary ships. *The talk which is consumed by the ear should be verified by facts. One frequently chisels the handle* [to make it fit]; *this applies not to this one matter only.*[17]

Hsu concluded his section on Vietnam by citing the *An-nan chi-ch'eng* (Record of a journey to Annam) by Ts'ai T'ing-lan, a *chin-shih* degree-holder from the Pescadores Islands who had been caught in a typhoon while at sea and driven to Annam. The king had sent him back to China via a land route. Ts'ai's book recorded his adventures in that country while enroute to China. Wherever he went Ts'ai found both Cantonese and Fukienese; most of the Fukienese were from T'ung-an and Chin-chiang, and Ts'ai estimated altogether there could not have been less than 100,000 Overseas Chinese in Annam.

The *Ying-huan chih-lueh* presented Siam in much the same organizational pattern. In the author's introductory piece he located the state, quickly sketched its history and named the important rivers, ports, capital, and other important cities. Various "tribal areas" (*fan-pu*) such as Sungora, Patani, and Trengganu were listed as "vassal states" (*shu-kuo*) of Siam, which was in turn a loyal tributary of China.[18]

Again Hsu utilized the accounts of Ku and Ch'en: Ku for Siam's historical development, and Ch'en for maritime routes and distances from China. The author concluded his treatment of Siam with a short sketch.

> Both Fukienese and Cantonese live in Siam, but the majority [of the Chinese there] is Cantonese. They amount to about one-sixth of the population. There are those who came by the maritime route and those who came [by land] across Vietnam from Wang-kuang and Shih-wan-shan by Ch'in-chou [in Kwangtung]. The land of Siam is open and the people are few; the fields are fertile and it is easy to cultivate and reap. Consequently there are many people who rush to get there. But the state has many evil spirits, and the people believe in incantation. The customs and government are vaguely similar to those of Annam. *But while Annam is now perhaps gradually being made to fit* [within the tribute system], *Siam has submitted from the earliest times. Now that dangerous times have come, it is fitting that* [Annam and Siam] *are dissimilar* [i.e., that Siam has not faced the difficulties of Annam with Westerners].[19]

A third tributary state attached to China's underbelly was Burma, a "large state of the southern barbarian area." Wild barbarians (*yeh-i*) inhabited its northern borders. Hsu described the state's location and listed the names of mountains, rivers, and cities:

> [Burma] sends tribute by way of Yunnan. Some time ago the British occupied several sections of India and approached Burma's frontier. In 1824 the king of Burma led a large force

and attacked them. The British forces were completely defeated, but then they brought warships into the inner harbor.
(That is, at the mouth of the Irrawaddy River.) The Burmese
jumped them and fought with vigor, but were dispersed by
the exploding fire from cannon. The [British] forces pressed
on for the capital. The king had no alternative but to negotiate
peace; they ceded the uninhabited coastal area for British
ports . . . [20] The Burmese today still cherish the ambition
for revenge, but as yet have not made any moves . . . *Now
because* [Burma] *is between* [China] *and India, it is the screen*
[buffer zone] *of the Southern Sea; our relations with her are
not insignificant.* [21]

An excerpt from Ku's work again was used to outline the history
of relations between China and Burma, to list the names by which
Burma had been known in the Chinese records, and to treat the
administrative system of the state.

Hsu concluded his discussion of the three Southeast Asian
states with general comments concerning the Western threat to the
entire area. Here appeared Hsu's theme of the current superficiality
of European power in Southeastern Asia, which he viewed as a weak
network susceptible to the pressures of effective local organization;
such opposition would bring diminishing economic returns to the
European states. For Hsu Western power in China's zone was a
paper tiger that would ultimately fall prey to patriotic resistance
movements if only these could be launched; and they certainly
would be, according to Hsu, in the states that possessed traditional
methods of organization and an appreciation, gained from their
contacts with China, for international order. A people motivated
by the spirit of revenge could do wonders even against superior
weaponry.

In the various barbarian areas of the southern wilds (*nan-
huang*) the conditions of the states of Annam, Siam, and
Burma are similar. [People from] the various states of Europe
from the middle years of the Ming have sailed eastward and
have established ports everywhere in the barbarian islands of

the Southern Ocean. Since the three states [of Annam, Siam, and Burma] all border on the sea, *how can there not be many places* [in these states] *that will elicit* [European] *covetousness? . . . If we are able to go there, how is it that* [the Europeans] *are not also able? . . .* Why have [the Europeans] not yet deeply penetrated and occupied these [states]? *It is a mistake to say this is because of the* [local] *poverty or a disregard for business . . . It is* [also] *unrealistic to say that Westerners (hsi-jen) are generally following* [a policy of] *abandonment.* [It is] because Westerners rely on commerce for their livelihood; they establish ports along the seas for the sole purpose of gaining profit. But if they [must] assign soldiers everywhere to guard and protect [their holdings], there is no way for them to be repaid for this expense.

The various islands of the Southern Ocean are dissimilar . . . [The area] is inhabited by tribes of aboriginal Malays. They are stupid and weak; they do not understand military [systems]. *The land is so situated that it can be encircled and completely inspected; using clever techniques it can be known on the first attempt. With the firing of cannon* [the people] *are in fear like the birds and beasts. They flee and hide, and do not dare move again. Consequently the Westerners occupy* [these areas] *with confidence.*

But as for the three states of Annam, [Siam, and Burma], even though they border on the sea, their land frontiers touch China . . . *Their populations are abundant. If invaded, they are able to fight; if* [the enemy] *withdraws, they are able to guard. Their conditions are very dissimilar to those of the various islands isolated in the sea.* Moreover, they have been established states for several thousands and hundreds of years. *In battling for land or cities, there is mutual rivalry in using the powers of cunning in warfare. Formerly Westerners were unable to fathom the extent of their strategems.* The [recent] forceful occupation of their ports was a lucky temporary victory. Can [Westerners] guard against the various states' desire for revenge? *If they assign heavy military forces, it will be too expensive; but without soldiers they will fear that the various states will take advantage of their lack of prepara-*

tion and assemble troops, so that they would be wiped out.
It is almost to the point that even though [Western] *merchant*
ships go [to these places] *they do not establish* [new] *ports.*[22]

In Hsu's eyes, continental Southeast Asia therefore remained
at least temporarily in an uneasy balance, with real or potential
local resistance the primary factor in deciding the extent of Western penetration. The question that surely concerned Hsu was what
China could do to push the balance against the West. It was obvious
to Hsu that China should use trade links more effectively with these
states to exert political influence and counteract Western penetration of the region. Also, with his consistent and detailed treatment
of the Overseas Chinese communities in Southeast Asia, Hsu was
perhaps hinting that they offered a potential base for Chinese-
directed resistance.

Maritime States of the "Southern Ocean"

Hsu's treatment of the Southeast Asian islands was encyclo-
pedic. The major themes were European occupation of the area and
Chinese immigration, but there was also a concern for local customs;
the position of the area in relation to the surrounding states; descriptions of the people; religions; products—gold, diamonds, foods,
woods; contacts with China—the exploits of the great Ming eunuch
naval commander, Cheng Ho, as he "summoned" these states to the
Chinese political order; tributary relations with China; and Overseas Chinese activities in the various states.

Throughout this section Hsu continued to refer especially to
the writings of Ku Yen-wu and Ch'en Lun-ch'iung, but additional
books were cited. For example, he found Wang Ta-hai's *Hai-tao*
i-chih (An informal record of the islands in the sea) the best record
of Java, for Wang had lived there for over ten years.[23] Hsieh Ch'ing-
kao's *Hai-lu* (A maritime record) was, according to Hsu, the most
accurate account of Siam's dependencies, Borneo, and Sumatra. The
author even consulted "old helmsmen" in Amoy who had frequently traveled to the ports of Southeast Asia, and he also

inquired with Westerners about these places. Though the maps drawn of the region by Westerners were the most detailed and accurate, Hsu found Western descriptions too abbreviated and their transliterations too confusing. Ch'en's *Hai-kuo wen-chien lu* also had to be used with care, according to Hsu. While generally reliable, it contained many errors concerning borders, distances, and directions relating to these island states. Chinese governmental publications were also not very dependable. Therefore Hsu admitted that though he had carefully pieced information together from numerous sources, he could not guarantee the accuracy of his findings.[24]

Hsu began his discussion of Luzon by locating it in reference to Taiwan; he noted its distance from Amoy, its shape, size, ports, mountains, jungles, volcanoes, earthquakes, and "wild aborigines (like those of Taiwan)." He recorded the coming of Europeans to Luzon, Spanish deception—with the well-known cowhide tale of the *Ming shih*, and the fate of the indigenous state.

> The land was originally a Malay barbarian state. In the Lung-ch'ing reign of the Ming [1567-1573], the European state of Spain sent an officer, Magellan, to come east in a great warship. When he reached Luzon he saw the land was both extensive and fertile, so he plotted to take it. In the Wan-li reign [1573-1620], [the Spaniards] used several large warships to carry soldiers, and these vessels were disguised to look like merchant ships. They presented the aboriginal king with gold and asked for land the size of a cowhide on which to display their wares. The king assented. *But they cut the cowhide* [into thin strips] *to form a square, and they then claimed this as the land* [promised them]. They collected monthly taxes [on this land]. The aboriginal king permitted this without bothering them again. Thereafter [the Spanish] built walls and established a fort. Without warning they attacked Luzon with cannon, killed the aboriginal king, and destroyed his state. The Spanish use a headman (*ta-ch'iu*) to direct affairs, and they gradually sent people from their state to consolidate their holdings.[25]

People call [this island] *Lesser Luzon, while Spain is Greater Luzon* . . . Ships collect at Manila, and goods are exchanged. *The flourishing of this harbor makes it one of the primary ports of the various oceans. The land is fertile and wet, so it is suitable for producing rice.* Other products are sugar, cotton, hemp, tobacco, coffee, cocoa (coffee is like a flat bean, and is greenish-black in color; it is first roasted and then boiled; it has a bitter flavor, but is fragrant like tea; Westerners use this as a substitute for tea; sugar is added before it is drunk; cocoa is also the name of a seed, and is a sort of medicinal astringent nut; Westerners also use this instead of tea), gold and pearl hair pins, Baroos camphor, swallows' nests, sea slugs, ebony, and eucalyptus.[26]

Hsu listed both Fukienese and Western transliterations for other islands of the Philippine archipelago, which were said to be like Luzon in climate as well as products. All had attracted Chinese merchant junks for trade, and most were controlled by the Spanish. The author cited the account of Shao Hsing-yen, the *Po-hai fan-yü lu* (A record of the maritime barbarian regions) for information concerning Luzon's presentation of tribute to China in the early Ming period and the beginning of Chinese trade with the area. According to this account, by 1602 there were tens of thousands of Overseas Chinese in Luzon, most of whom were natives of Fukien. Hsu corrected Shao's use of *Fo-lang-hsi* as the name for the Spanish.[27] He repeated the account of the massacre "in 1602" [1603?] of over twenty thousand Overseas Chinese by the Spanish due to a misunderstanding when a Chinese official was sent to search for a mountain which allegedly produced nuggets of gold.[28] But gradually thereafter, he found, Chinese returned to the place to live. Also quoted by Hsu was spellbinding material concerning the Spaniards' religion taken from Chen's *Hai-kuo wen-chien lu.*

Luzon originally belonged to the local aborigines, but it is now controlled by the Spanish. Those Chinese who marry local aborigines must join the religion [of the Spanish]. They

worship in a hall of God (*t'ien-chu*), and use oil-water to draw
the cross [lit. "to draw the character ten"] between their eye-
brows; this is called "cleansing with water." They burn the
ancestral tablets of their parents. When someone dies of old
age, he is taken to the hall of God and the local relatives
gather to bury him in a deep pit. The wealthy pay a bit more
and bury their dead in the foundations of the hall. The poor
bury their dead outside the walls. Every three years there is a
cleansing, and the skeletons are cast into a deep river.[29]

Hsu also quoted the book of Huang I-hsien entitled *Lü-sung
chi-lueh* (A brief description of Luzon). This work used older terms
for European countries and provided Hsu with more exotic information.

The appearance of the Spanish is similar to that of the Chinese.
Their hats are tall and pointed, and their clothes have tight
sleeves. The utensils used for eating and drinking are approximately the same as those of the Dutch. The silver wafers
[dollars] used in Fukien and Kwangtung are cast with the like-
ness of their king.[30]
In the Ming period [the Spanish] occupied the state [of
Luzon] and established a padre (*pa-li*) hall.[31] (This religion is
the same as Catholicism.) They practice the religion by wor-
shipping [a god]. The padres are foreign priests. (This is the
same as a teacher of the Catholic religion.) They follow the
command to be covered with water. They do not sacrifice to
their ancestors. The only god (*shen*) they worship is Jesus
(Liu-shih [with the mouth radical]; this is the same as Yeh-su).
Those who have been covered with water take the body of
the pope [lit. "king of the padres"] (the same as the king of the
Roman religion) and render it into lard. When they worship
they are ordered to swear that their bodies have come from
Jesus. The padres take oil-water and drip it on the heads [of
the people]. Consequently this is called "immersion." Taking
a wife is called "connecting hands." On the day [the couple]
meets in person, the father of the religion (the same as a
teacher of the religion) places a chain around the necks of the

man and woman. Every seven days [they] go to the hall to
entreat the padre to do away with their crimes. Daily they
attend mass (*mi-sa*). There is a hall for nuns, and they special-
ize in superintending the wealth [of the church] in order to
help with the state's expenditures. Their hall is securely barri-
caded, and men are forbidden to enter.[32]

Even though the author included such absurdities in his book,
he did so with some hesitation. Hsu suggested, for example, that
the books of Ch'en and Huang were of little real use for an accurate
description of Luzon since they both stressed the practices of
Catholicism. He further noted that the Spanish themselves did not
now follow such customs as described, but only the natives at an
earlier time.

Hsu estimated that the number of Overseas Chinese in Luzon
from Chang-chou and Ch'üan-chou, Fukien, alone amounted to
not less than several tens of thousands. These people were allowed
to reside there if they paid five or six ounces of silver per year as
head tax. The rice of Luzon had long been imported by Fukienese
merchants, especially before Taiwan began to produce a surplus,
and it was still considered important by the merchants of Amoy.
He noted that "all the barbarians (*fan*) who have come to Canton
have also been gathering in Manila: chieftains (*ch'iu*) of America
and France, for example."[33] Because of such trade, in Hsu's view,
Luzon had become the most prosperous of all the islands of the
Southern Ocean. He concluded his notice of Luzon and the other
islands of the Philippines by referring again to Huang's *Lü-sung
chi-lueh*. Huang had mentioned the arrival and sudden departure
from Luzon of an English force in the eighteenth century. From
this Hsu drew some thought-provoking conclusions, albeit in terms
of Chinese psychology, about English behavior.

Again Huang I-hsien's *Lü-sung chi-lueh* records that during
the Ch'ien-lung reign [1735-1796] English from the northwestern sea unexpectedly constructed ten-odd Western-style
ships and crossed the waters to Luzon. They wanted to occupy

the land, [but] the padre (a religious man) presented them with gifts and requested their withdrawal.[34] Thereupon the English departed. . . I think the padre was a Catholic priest. [These] Westerners all believed in Catholicism. Each [state] used this kind of person [i.e., priests] to manage its affairs. Still, that the English suddenly were willing to recall their forces *does not mean they believed in the padre's* [religion]. The Spanish have already possessed Luzon for two or three hundred years. Their merchant ships have circulated freely, and wealth has been accumulated in a foreign storehouse. *But now the state's power is related to its dignity* [rather than to actual military power] ; *if the eastern and western boundaries are seized by the English, then half of* [Spain's territory] *will be lost.* [Spain] is now in decline, but it is still a large Western state. Although she is fighting her last battle to the death, and although Britain is strong, how can Britain suddenly destroy [Spain's] base? *To cede territory other than gradually is to meet the enemy at his threshold; this is not* [good] *strategy.* That they could not steal Luzon was plain to the English [and they appear to have reasoned thus] : *"To coerce and then to wait for* [their] *entreaties before withdrawing troops would cause* [the Spanish] *to be in awe of our virtue. If we are willing to be yielding in our actions, later when our merchant ships come to the East and wish to use their territory as a lodging spot on the Eastern Route, they will be unable to refuse."* That Java has already been taken and then returned in line with this policy is clearly manifest.[35]

Leaving the Philippines, Hsu next discussed the various islands south of Luzon, first the Celebes and then the Sulus. For the Celebes he listed directions from Luzon, described the island, and mentioned the establishment there of Dutch forts in the north and south; he noted the place was originally a vassal state of Java. The products were said to be about the same as those of Luzon, but it produced the best sea slugs available. Always alert to native resistance and martial spirit, Hsu also took note of the ferocious Macassar natives, trained from childhood to use a short knife so expertly as to be able to fight off several tens of men. These people had not been "bound" by Holland; instead they related as elder and younger brothers according to treaty. To Hsu, worried by China's forced acceptance of an unequal treaty relationship with Western states, the message was clear: Europeans respected power based on the people; even a primitive state which possessed this attribute would be respected by Westerners. Hsu and his readers were beginning to see the need for closer and more effective ties between rulers and ruled without which China, for all its sophistication of culture and great heritage, would remain a weak and ineffectual giant.

> [Regarding the natives of Macassar], the Europeans call them "heroes of the Southern Sea." The people have martial spirits, yet they understand [the duties of] caring for their parents. *With several ten-thousands of this kind they are able to secure their frontiers; they can produce the sound of thunder* [i.e., cause their enemies to fear], *and they love their secluded, uncultivated island. It is not strange they are labeled as heroic.* If there really is this sort of people, how can the various European states suddenly accomplish their aims in the Southern Ocean?[36]

The small island state of the Sulu archipelago appeared in a similar manner. Hsu noted its position, its peoples, and its tributary relationship with China. He cited unsuccessful Spanish incursions, and listed items in the junk trade with Amoy: pearls, tortoise shell, sappanwood, nutmeg, lakawood incense, split rattan, and parrots. Again, the martial skills of the native peoples impressed Hsu, who continued to search for answers to the problem of China's coastal defense; here, in "self-strengthening" was a lesson, one with a compelling historical significance for future Chinese leadership.

> Since Spain and Holland have glared like tigers at the Southern Ocean, the various barbarian states have all suffered attacks [lit. "have been swallowed and bitten"]. *The Sulus are but small islands of protruding rock, but because they have earnestly fought a war of resistance for several hundred years,*

they certainly testify to the fact that even barbarian tribes are able to [practice] *self-strengthening (tzu-ch'iang).*[37]

Borneo next received the author's attention. Pirates infested this island, and it produced both gold and diamonds. The people were of various Malay tribes; the wealthy wore Chinese silks. They followed the Moslem religion and worshipped every seventh day. They ate no pork. Hsu noted here that all Malay peoples believed in Islam, which had originated in Arabia and then spread to Southeast Asia. In the mountains of Borneo were wild men who loved to kill people. When the Dutch first entered a harbor in Borneo, the local people were afraid of their cannon and fled deep into the mountains. But they took noxious weeds and poisoned the Hollanders' drinking water before departing.

The diamonds mined here were of five colors, but golden, black, and red were said to be most valuable and were much prized by Europeans. A large diamond was worth several ten-thousands of taels to Europeans. The small and coarse ones could be used for industrial purposes, so they too were of some value. In recent years many Chinese from Chia-ying, Kwangtung, had gone to Borneo to open mines. Many tens of thousands were already there, and their affairs were governed by elders who served for one or two years. Each year several junks came from Canton and Ch'ao-chou to trade; they gained immense profits. In addition to gold and diamonds Borneo produced lead, tin, Baroos camphor, nutmeg, pepper, sea slugs, swallows' nests, tortoise shell, kingfisher feathers, sandalwood incense, and split rattan. Hsu also included sailing directions from Amoy. The author quoted extensively from such works as the *Hai-lu, Hai-tao i-chih, Po-hai fan-yŭ lu,* and *Hai-kuo wen-chien lu,* the last considered by Hsu as the most dependable source for this "largest of the islands in the Southern Ocean." Among their numerous topics, these works dealt with the Dutch role on the island.[38]

It was in his lengthy discussion of Java, however, that Hsu included his most complete account of the Dutch in Southeast Asia. Between Java and Sumatra was the Sunda Strait, *"a route that must be followed by the various Western states* [whose ships] *come east.* "[39] He related that in the Ming dynasty Dutch warships had arrived at Bantam and had recognized the land to be suitable for forts. They first obtained land to repair their vessels, but gradually they enhanced their position until finally Bantam was destroyed.[40] The rest of Java then came under Dutch administrative control. Even Overseas Chinese worked for the Dutch to help govern the area, a fact of much concern to Hsu, who had worried about Chinese "traitors" in the coastal regions of Fukien.

> Java is a large state in the Southern Ocean and has had contact with China since the Liu Sung dynasty [420-479 A.D.] . . . *It sent tribute in baskets in strict* [observance of the regulations] *and was a strong vassal beyond the seas.* Then suddenly [Java's] doors and windows were blocked up by Holland . . . The precise date when Holland occupied Java's ports is uncertain, but it was approximately during the middle years of the Ming dynasty. *From that time on the seas off Kwangtung have not seen the sails of Java. An oppressor has horizontally blocked off the way, and there is no way to come. What a pity!* . . .[41] As regards the wealthy lands in the far south, Java is the richest. Holland used treacherous schemes to take her and thereupon attained wealth and power (*fu-ch'iang*). In the late Ming, four [Dutch] Western-style ships arrived and attacked Fukien and Chekiang. *Indeed,* [the Dutch] *were using Java as their den* . . . The products of Java are rice, sugar, coffee, and swallows' nests. Recently they have learned how to cultivate Fukien tea. Its flavor is quite good, but it is not very plentiful. *The neighboring barbarian islands use Java as an entrepot, and* [their] *articles of trade are all collected here* . . .
>
> The people of Fukien and Kwangtung who have emigrated to this place number several tens of thousands. Holland selects those who are able and virtuous to be *chia-pi-tan* [captains]. (This is the European name of an official equivalent to a *chou* or *hsien* [magistrate] in China.) They specialize in supervising litigation between Chinese. In recent years because Chinese have monopolized trade, new Chinese immigrants

have been prohibited . . . In Java [the Overseas Chinese] from Chang-chou and Ch'üan-chou are the most numerous, and some have been away from China for several generations. They speak the barbarian language, wear barbarian clothing, eat barbarian food, and read barbarian books . . .[42] The wealthy traders [among the Overseas Chinese in Java] make large profits, and there is none in poverty. By paying bribes to Holland they seek to be appointed as captains. If there is a dispute between Chinese, they all present themselves before the captain and bow deeply, but do not kneel. They call themselves "your servant." There is none who is not pronounced guilty or not guilty [by the captain], including those who commit grave crimes.[43]

Ku Yen-wu's account was cited for Java's history, and the *Hai-tao i-chih* for distances from Amoy and descriptions of the natives and the Dutch and their customs. Here were described Dutch churches and practices of the Westerners' religion, and Hsu found material on Dutch officials in Java and the adjacent islands as well as of Dutch intrigues with the local sultans (*shih-tan*). Hsu also detailed the case already cited in his description of Luzon regarding British strategy in Southeast Asia; he found that the economic interests of European states in Southeast Asia had been admirably supported by the strategic policies of these states.

During the Chia-ch'ing reign [1796-1820] the Dutch king was forced by France's Napoleon to flee to the wilderness to die, and the state was ceded by France. Because Britain feared that France would capture Java at the same time, in the fall of the fourteenth year of Chia-ch'ing [1809-1810], Britain attacked Batavia; but the Dutch headman maintained a strong defense and did not surrender. A year passed before [the British] came again. They surrounded [the island] and attacked with cannon. The Dutch headman withdrew, and the land was then taken by Britain. Annoying Dutch laws were eliminated, and traveling merchants could conveniently go there. *In this event Holland was swiftly destroyed by Britain.* Several years later Napoleon was defeated and Holland freed. [The Dutch] *king humbled himself and sent valuable presents to entreat Britain. Britain then retroceded Java. So* [now] *even if British ships consider Java as their primary* [port of call] *in the Eastern Route, Holland does not dare oppose.*[44]

Other islands in the area received Hsu's notice: Bali, Sumbawa, Sumba, Flores, and others. But only the smaller islands that had become important to Westerners merited more than a passing glance. Thus Timor was described in more detail: its eastern half contained ports belonging to Portugal, while the western half fell under Dutch control. The Molucca Islands also had fallen to the Dutch, as had half of the islands of the entire region. At all of the various ports the Dutch had built cannon emplacements, and these were well fortified.

In the Ming dynasty during the reign of Lung-ch'ing [1567-1572], Portuguese ships first reached Ternate in the Moluccas. Spanish ships met them there. They fought over these islands. In the T'ai-ch'ang reign [1620] Dutch warships expelled the two states, and Holland subsequently monopolized the profits of the Moluccas. But the products such as cloves, cardamon seeds, and other items which they sold were insufficient to cover the expense of defending [these possessions]. Further, they prohibited other states' merchant vessels. Therefore the profits have been very small and the islands have been out of the main stream for a long time.[45]

Hsu's account shifted to New Guinea (Papua), the world's second largest island, which appeared to the author *"in the shape of a tortoise with its head raised."*[46] The dense forests of this island hid black wild barbarians who killed people for meat. Since the Dutch had lost Australia, they had taken this island only as a second choice.

Jumping once again to continental Southeast Asia, the *Ying-huan chih-lueh* introduced the various vassal states of Siam along the Malayan Peninsula, and distances were recorded from Amoy.

The author was amused to find, contrary to Chinese preferences, that the people of this area were most happy if they had daughters, who were able to care for them when they were old. Men and women shared their wealth equally. There were no coffins; corpses were simply buried beneath trees. There was no ancestor worship. Products of these areas were swallows' nests, tin, ivory, and cotton. The local people followed Buddha, and they sailed small boats as fishermen.[47]

Several hundred Chinese came to these places each year to trade, and many Fukienese lived at the various ports. Here they traded goods and cultivated pepper. The Cantonese generally lived in the hills where they panned gold. Taxes were levied on all vessels regardless of size: a large one would pay 500-600 foreign dollars, while smaller vessels were 200-300 dollars. Heavy taxes were placed also on alcoholic beverages and opium.[48] At the extreme tip of the Malayan peninsula the port of Singapore, the "Lion City," was located, now one of the primary centers of Western activity in Southeast Asia.

> [Singapore] long ago was originally a barbarian area. In the twenty-third year of the Chia-ch'ing reign [1818-1819] it was taken by the British. *It occupies a key position between the Southern Ocean and the Lesser Western Ocean, and is a central market for the various maritime states.* The British made it a free port in order to collect merchant ships. Western-style ships which come here every year number several hundred. Oceangoing merchant vessels of Fukien and Kwangtung and the ships of the various states of the Southern Ocean also reach here from time to time. [In the port] *there is a forest of masts. Eastern and Western goods are all gathered here, and it is the primary port on the western shore of the Southern Ocean.* The value of the goods exchanged every year here exceeds several tens of million dollars (*yuan*). The English have built storied dwellings, but they are not numerous. Overseas Chinese from Fukien and Kwangtung number over ten thousand . . . Singapore was formerly a wild and isolated minor barbarian area which was unworthy of notice. But since

Britain established a port there, it *now occupies a strategic position between East and West.* When British ships come east they arrive at Singapore as if they were returning to their own land. Any lack in provisions can be filled there. In recent years the "Singapore" [written with different characters] frequently mentioned in China *was thought to be a large state with abundant lands and people; we did not realize it was only a coastal market place.*[49]

Located on the Malacca Strait ("Strait of the Red Hairs," *Hung-mao-ch'ien*) were two other British ports which attracted Hsu's attention.

Malacca was originally a vassal state of Siam, but it was occupied by Portugal in the early Ming. Subsequently it was snatched away by Holland. In the Chia-ch'ing reign [1796-1820] the area reverted to Britain, and it was then made a port. It is not as prosperous as Singapore. Northwest of Malacca is an island called Penang. There is a high peak in its center, and the scenery is magnificent. Here there live 54,000 people, of which one-fifth are from Kwangtung and Fukien. This place also is controlled by the British. A headman resides at Singapore to superintend trade for the three ports of Singapore, Malacca, and Penang. The products of these places are gold, silver, lead, tin, rhinoceros horns, ivory, pepper, kingfisher feathers, and various finely patterned mats.[50]

Coming to Sumatra, Hsu listed the island's important products. Those of the land: grains, rattan, pepper, betel nut, "dragon's blood" (a medicine), and Baroos camphor; of the mountains: gold, copper, iron, sulphur; of the rivers: gold dust; of the sea: ambergris. He noted that Sumatra had been a tributary of China since the T'ang and Sung dynasties. Here too the Dutch and British had taken ports, but in recent years the British had returned these in exchange for Malacca, so that all now belonged to Holland. Merchant junks from China came frequently to this island for trade.[51]

Hsu relied on Ku Yen-wu's account for Sumatra's earlier

history, but said that for recent developments only the *Hai-lu* could be considered detailed and accurate. He also sought out eyewitnesses. More than a century before the leadership of a "helmsman" had been celebrated in Chinese song, Hsu was able to appreciate the crucial significance of reliable experience in whatever class of society it could be found. "Recently when I was in Amoy," he said, "I met an old helmsman named Ch'en who was most familiar with the [routes] to and from the western part of the Southern Ocean. Formerly [he] had gone several times to Bangka [an island near Sumatra], so I inquired with him concerning its direction." [52] But Hsu found that Ch'en's information disagreed with that of the *Hai-kuo wen-chien lu*, so he then consulted the *Po-hai fan-yü lu* and found that this agreed with the old man's story. *"The old helmsman's words were true, not false.* This land produces tin, so the merchant ships of Amoy frequently go there to trade." A Western source was also used. This was the *Wan-kuo ti-li shu* (Book of geography for all the states of the world), probably the world geography written by Karl Gützlaff under a slightly different title for the Society for the Diffusion of Useful Knowledge in China. [53] This work recorded some generalizations about Chinese overseas which caught Hsu's fancy. He wrote: "The Overseas Chinese [in the islands of the Southern Ocean] are very numerous. *The people from Canton and Chia-ying* [Kwangtung] *are laborers; the people from Ch'ao-chou* [Kwangtung] *are farmers; those from Ch'üan-chou and Chang-chou* [Fukien] *are merchants. Those who make the greatest profits are the people from Ch'üan-chou and Chang-chou."* [54]

Hsu concluded his study of the Southeast Asian states with liberal selections from Ku Yen-wu's account. Here Hsu found a general appraisal of the area's development and a history of China's contacts with non-Chinese states. Ku mentioned early trade with Rome and India, for example. He dwelt at considerable length on Chinese "traitors" who dressed like barbarians and aided non-Chinese merchants. Hsu even included Ku's report that the "French" ate Chinese children! [55] Ku's material, with its detailed if often inaccurate information, provided a framework for Hsu's own conclusions which he inserted in the narrative.

The author's portrayal of Southeast Asia—in terms of its

peoples, products, relations with China, or even the position of Westerners—did not constitute a radical new view of that part of the world. This could all be found in works by other Chinese authors. However, Hsu's stress on the importance of trade as one of the foundation stones of modern state power appears to have been the statement of a minority view against the idea that only agriculture was fundamental. Hsu found that European trade was a phenomenon that had begun to undermine China's position vis-à-vis her tributary states, and it thus formed a fundamental part of his picture of Western impact in the new international world. Hsu was clearly disturbed by the course of events in Southeast Asia. Overseas Chinese in the employ of Westerners, for example, posed domestic implications to an official in China's coastal region. But in his concluding analysis Hsu showed that trade itself was a crucial mechanism in international relations. Although it was not generally admitted in China by officials and scholars, Hsu pointed out that commerce had long been an element of great importance in the tributary system of China. He hinted that China's failure to use trade more effectively as a positive device for international manipulation had been folly.

Hsu acknowledged that trade with the outside world indeed could be a complex and unpredictable matter, with problems upsetting to the Chinese order; but this had been the case even in earlier Chinese history.[56] Now with the stakes involving China's influence beyond her borders, he implied that China had no choice but to be an active participant in foreign trade. He hinted that the numerous Chinese traders in Southeast Asia should have been supported positively by China. Instead, the Chinese had allowed by default the gradual penetration of this region by Western states, which combined trade with state strategy and thereby gained wealth and power. Consequently, as a result of an opportunity missed, the Chinese currently faced an ominous menace on their own frontier.

Formerly the Southern Ocean was a dwelling place for pygmies; today it has become an inn for Europeans. If frost and ice have come several times, how can it not come again [i.e., it was a dangerous situation that could have been perceived]*? This state of affairs has developed gradually; thus it has now been over three hundred years* [since the problem of the Western threat first arose]... From the time Westerners first occupied the various islands *they have built strong forts and splendid storied buildings. Their ports of trade are prosperous; their vessels are very sturdy. They* [differ] *from the earlier barbarian tribes there who were wild and rude, for their manner is extremely persistent. Furthermore, the many* [recent] *events in China have resulted from an early planting of the seeds* [of trouble] *there.*[57]

In such passages Hsu hammered home to his Chinese audience that China could no longer sit tight and secure in its own world, oblivious to the great events outside which had begun to transform the East Asian sphere. China now had to rise to the challenge. With his treatment of Southeast Asia, as well as of the islands east of China, Hsu thus reviewed for his readers some of the undeniable realities of world politics in the mid-nineteenth century. Hsu's treatise was not, however, a document of defeatism. Rather, it suggested the need to deal with the new situation that China faced. Chinese officials had to rid themselves of the exaggerated Neo-Confucian bias against trade. Chinese leaders must be pragmatic; reliable information should be sought and used to form realistic policies.

Recently a leader in the lost cause of defense against Britain, Hsu also took a stand against aggression wherever he found it in Asia, whether it was the Mongols against Japan in past history, the contemporary growth of Japanese control of Liu-ch'iu, or the present European encroachment in Southeast Asia. Implicit throughout his presentation was a confidence that once properly informed of the Western threat and organized effectively with self-strengthening programs for a heroic resistance against the "persistent" Europeans, the peoples of China's "Southern Ocean" would overcome.

Chapter VIII

THREATENED ON THE INNER ASIAN FRONTIER

If Hsu's depiction of China's waning influence in Southeast Asia failed to shock even the most unrealistic Chinese literati, the message of Western influence penetrating the whole world became all the more plain in his treatment of India and other continental Asian states surrounding China. Woven into the very fabric of Hsu's geographical tapestry of the states southwest and west of China were innumerable threads of evidence which verified that the threat to China was global in scope.

India

The story of Western Europe's eruption on the world scene and spread over the globe had not been told effectively in Hsu's China. Prince Henry the Navigator, Vasco da Gama, and Afonso d'Albuquerque were generally unknown by name or deed. Indeed, even the subcontinent which had attracted Western explorers and traders was draped in ignorance, partially hidden, and remote. Hsu's detailed examination of India, based on Western sources—its geography, peoples, products, customs, and religions—presented to Chinese literati what was probably the most informed treatment of the region then available. Into this account Hsu added information about the coming of the West to India. India was to Hsu an example worthy of careful scrutiny. Because India had become the location of Western activities, Hsu noted that he would treat the area in detail.[1]

The author observed that because India had become a dependency of England, and since indigenous accounts of India were confused and obscure, he would rely on Western, and specifically English-derived, materials. Though he failed to identify these sources by name, he referred in several places to Abeel and even included an alternate map of India obtained from the American missionary.[2]

This exotic land of India, known to Hsu as the Five Indias—
Central, South, East, North, and West—had been variously recorded
in Chinese historical records as Shen-tu, T'ien-chu, Yin-tu, and
numerous other names and transliterations.[3] *"Because the people
there wrap their heads with white cloth, the Cantonese call this the
Small White Head state."*[4]

India's products, beside the "five grains," cotton, and the
opium poppy, were diamonds, topaz, green agate, pearls, coral,
medicines, fragrant woods, and delicacies of the sea; here there
were lions, tame elephants, and large birds. The author noted some
of the region's customs, and as in other sections, took a close look
at the women. Women were always of interest to Hsu because they
were yet another part of a particular culture's story. Indian *"women
hide their ears and nose with clothing, and they wear gold and silver rings;* on their wrists and ankles are bracelets and bangles."[5]

A short historical sketch was presented to the reader, identify-
ing India as the source of Buddhism. Contacts with China were
established during the Later Han dynasty. Hsu recorded that during
the T'ang period India had sent tribute missions to China. The area
had been conquered by the Moslems, subsequently attacked by the
Mongols, and later by Tamerlane of Samarkand. Finally, the author
noted, the Mogul state arose, with the various parts of India paying
tribute as its vassals. But then India faced maritime invaders, one
following the other.

For the first time in 1495 the Portuguese of Europe sailed
to Bombay on the southwest coast; here they carved out a
harbor and founded a city. Because merchant ships went there,
it became prosperous. Holland was envious, and attacked with
warships; they also took sites for ports and set up yamens.
*They became the strong and prosperous power of the Indian
Ocean for several decades.* Then the English came to the East,
expelled both of these states, and took their lands. The French
also came to set up ports on the southeastern coast of India.
In 1668 the English purchased land in Eastern India's Bengal,
and they built lodging places [at Calcutta]. Here they built
cannon emplacements and seventy houses; sails and masts

collected here like clouds. Goods were traded, and the port became increasingly wealthy. In 1752 the headman of Bengal [Suraja Dowla] destroyed their dwellings and imprisoned their people [for Hsu, shades of Lin Tse-hsu and Canton]. The British retaliated with a large force and destroyed Bengal; at the same time they attacked the various parts of southern and central India. These areas resisted, but their efforts were not united and they were defeated in confusion. *Of these* [states] *there were some that were destroyed; some that accepted* [British] *authority; and some that became vassal states in name only. From that time on, seven-tenths of India has come under British administration. Only the several remaining northwestern parts have not yet capitulated.*[6]

The British headman who governs all of India resides in [Calcutta]. There are 30,000 English troops and 230,000 native troops, called sepoys. The civil officials all come from Britain when they are children to learn the native language. They are promoted in the government and are very well paid.[7]

Hsu scanned the Indian subcontinent, looking first at Bengal, then at Assam, where he noted the British had recently been experimenting with tea cultivation; he viewed Madras, Pondicherry, Bombay. From this port came the infamous Malwa poison—opium. Piece by piece Hsu detailed the situation of the numerous "states" and famous cities of India. Here too the author presented such minor states to the north as Bhutan, Gurkha, and Kashmir. He recognized the British threat to Tibet, but he felt that at the time Bhutan and Gurkha were still acting as buffer zones. If they were absorbed by Britain, however, there would be no protection for Tibet. The conflicting interests of Britain and Russia in the border areas of Northern India came to Hsu's attention.[8] Likewise, India's role in world trade and trade with China interested the author.

Bengal [i.e., Calcutta] is the most flourishing of all the British ports [in India]; Bombay is next, followed by Madras. The merchant ships which come from Britain, as well as from the various other European states, number in the hundreds and thousands. Duties collected amount to over 10,000,000 [units], but because [the British] support too many troops, there is little left after expenses . . .⁹ Bombay . . . is a large British port, and there is a city with outer walls. The natives here are called Parsees. Their color is somewhat whiter; they are extremely good and honest by nature. Houses are abundant. The products are agate, large onions, cotton, [and others] . . .¹⁰ The products of Kwangtung and Fukien are often sold to the Moslem region [of Western and Central Asia] via India. But this is not strange. [Calcutta] and Bombay in India are large British ports. [Since] the products of Fukien and Kwangtung [are numerous enough to make] mountains, these goods go to the Moslem areas via the route the merchants know best [i.e., to India] and they are very conveniently transshipped from there.¹¹

Two other products were noted. Hsu recorded that cotton was first brought to China from India during the Yuan dynasty. This beneficial product, however, was followed in more recent times by the destructive poppy. *"But now the poison of opium also comes from this place,"* reported Hsu. "All of the various places of India are sources of this item, but the largest producer is Malwa. Two kinds of opium are found. That which is formed into a ball is the 'big opium' and is expensive; it is collected in Bengal and Madras. That formed into strips is 'small opium,' and it is cheaper. It is collected at Bombay. India's major products are only cotton and opium, but in recent years opium has been the primary one. Each year they export more than several tens of thousand cases. *How strange it is that of all the world this insidious thing grows only in a state* [which was the source] *of Buddhism."* ¹²

To be sure, Hsu had little use for Buddhism. That this religion had done so little for India was another reason for opposing it in China: "From the Sung and Yuan periods, *Buddhism gave way to Islam. Now the various states of India are eastern vassals of Europe, and they respect Protestantism* [lit. 'the teachings of Jesus']. *Buddhism is even more insignificant now.* [Buddhist] *intelligence shone in the morning, but the pure land has become dirty. Other peoples cannot help but think twice about the power of Buddha."* ¹³

But the sordid tale of India's fall to European power as an object lesson to China appears to have been foremost in the author's mind in examining this Asian state. He worried about what this Western control meant to China.

Only in the middle years of the Ming dynasty did the various European states begin to stay in India. The first was Portugal, followed by Holland, France, and England. Because they considered wealth to be important, they bought up pieces of land along the coast and set up ports. *The southern barbarians* [i.e., the Indians] *were stupid and did not examine into this early growth.* The English gradually installed cannon in all the ports; they sent soldiers to guard these places. *They supported these troops and plotted to wait for the right moment to strike. When the Bengal situation provided a pretext,* [the British] *attacked with their entire force. The various southern barbarian tribes were like chickens roosting in a row.* [To defeat them] *was like breaking up rotten wood. Of the various tribes of India at that time, the* [British] *barbarians destroyed eighty to ninety percent. How pitiful!* . . .

From the time that the British took India they have levied taxes to support their soldiers. Daily they are becoming more prosperous and powerful (*fu-ch'iang*). Their territory touches on the southern boundary of Tibet and on the western border of Yunnan. *But although the territory is almost contiguous, communications are not easy and stairs and ropes* [are needed because the border area is so rugged]. *Passage by sea from Bengal to Kwangtung requires twenty days.* In recent years British merchant ships from India have constituted sixty to seventy percent of all those coming [to China]. *Formerly India sought to be in contact with distant places, but was unable; now India wishes to cut off contacts, but is unable. It is certainly impossible to anticipate the way circumstances can change.* [14]

India provided a useful lesson for Hsu and for all Chinese leaders. The failure of the Indians to pay attention to the growth of Western power within their gates, giving the British a pretext to attack (as had Lin Tse-hsu in Canton), as well as the lack of a unified resistance, had doomed this populous state.

The Cradle of Non-Chinese Civilizations

Moving on around the Asian circuit Hsu came to the states of Western Asia. He briefly treated Afghanistan and Baluchistan. Persia and Arabia were described more fully, and in these two sections appears a wealth of material concerning place names, relations with China, products, relations with European states, customs, and religions.

Afghanistan was a "large state of the Moslem region." Hsu noted its location in relation to its neighbors and its rough dimensions. Because it had been attached to Badakshan, it sent fine horses as tribute on several occasions during the reign of K'ang-hsi (1662-1722). Although originally a part of Persia, it established itself as a state (*tzu li wei kuo*) in the Ming dynasty and expanded at the expense of Persia during K'ang-hsi's reign. The author included a short history of the state, followed by a list of its products, a discussion of its customs, and a list of its administrative units. The *Hsi-yü wen-chien lu* (A record of things heard and seen in the Western Region) was quoted. Hsu used this work by Ch'i Ch'un-yuan as one of his major sources for the various states of Western and Central Asia even though he frequently criticized its contents. Western maps and materials were also cited as sources.[15]

An even briefer discussion was all the author felt Baluchistan deserved. He did observe, however, that the people here were trained to fight; though the state was small it was powerful. Because it was situated near the British vassal states of India, they often fought, sometimes winning and sometimes losing.[16] It was unknown when this place first became a state; when Cheng Ho traveled to this area it had had a different name.

Hsu's book devoted a long section to Persia, however. Thirteen alternative transliterations for Persia were listed, and he noted that this large Moslem state, because of the custom of wearing turbans, was called "Big White Head State" by the Cantonese. Again he noted the state's location in terms of its neighbors, and it was

identified according to China's historical records. It had become a
state during the Hsia dynasty, and very early had been an active
partner in trade with China. Persia had often fought Greece and
Rome. Its early religion was the worship of sun and fire. But because Persia bordered on Arabia, it had been taken by Islam during
the early T'ang dynasty and remained a primary area for that religion ever since. Tribute had been sent to China during the T'ang
and Sung periods. During the Ming dynasty it had been the chief
tributary of China in the "Western Region."

Hsu's account listed the vicissitudes of the state in considerable detail. The capital was described, as was the palace. The land
was fertile and the climate warm, but there was little rain. Persia
produced good horses, dates, salt, copper, iron, gold, silver, porcelain vessels, amber, pearls, kingfisher feathers, and lions. He went
into some detail about the lions which for the most part were found
in the dense forests on the upper reaches of the Amu River: *"When
they are born their eyes are closed for the first seven days. The
natives catch them while their eyes are still shut. If they wait longer
[the lions] cannot be trained."* [17] Hsu was obviously fascinated by
such things.

Hsu considered Persians to be strong and healthy people. Men
and women were "all beautiful." The state still stressed military
prowess; when an enemy was killed in battle it was necessary to
cut off his ear for proof. But despite Persia's military heritage, the
state had in recent years suffered both at the hands of Russians
and British. [18]

After criticizing the mistakes of the *Hsi-yü wen-chien lu*, Hsu
cited a "Westerner's account" of ancient Persia. In this long section
of ancient history, much of it based on Biblical information, Hsu
treated the rise of Darius, Babylon's destruction of Jerusalem, the
fall of Babylon to Darius, and the return of the Jews to Judah. The
reader was introduced to Alexander of Macedonia, Greek armies,
and to later conquering Roman armies in Western Asia. It was clear
to Hsu that contemporary European military power and aggressive-
ness were not without precedent in the history of the West.

In this section, ostensibly dealing with Persia, considerable information is also found concerning the various religions that sprang from Western Asia. Mohammed (Mo-ha-mai), a man of Arabia, founded the religion of Islam in the early T'ang. He then conquered both Arabia and Persia. Persia and India served gods of fire (*huo-shen*) in ancient times, but those states to the west of Syria all served the god of heaven (*t'ien-shen*). The latter religion first began with Moses (Mo-hsi) in the early Shang dynasty (1766-1122 B.C.) when the "god of heaven sent down to Mt. Sinai (*Hsi-nai-shan*) ten precepts with which [Moses] was to instruct people. This was the beginning of resting and worshiping every seven days." Much more detailed information followed concerning the roots of Christianity, and Hsu observed that Catholicism relied on many ideas absorbed from Mithraism.[19] The reader was directed to look in the various sections of his book that dealt with Europe and Turkey for further details on both ancient European history and religion.

Arabia in Hsu's book was *"the state where Islam arose."* It was a place where traders traveled in groups to ward off bandits; where the most abundant product was dates, eaten both by man and beast; where famous horses were raised, loved, and nourished by their masters as if they were their own children. These magnificent horses could run five to six hundred li per day. This place had especially fine camels capable of carrying heavy loads for great distances. Coffee was also produced and was purchased by all of the Europeans.

Here Hsu presented a fairly accurate sketch of Mohammed's life and accomplishments, as well as the basic tenets of Islam. He noted that the Moslem calendar had begun with Mohammed's flight to Medina, just as the European calendar took the birth of Jesus as its point of reference. He observed also that the adherents of Islam from Southeast Asia, from the "Western Region," and from Africa yearly came by the several tens of thousands to Mecca and Medina to honor Mohammed.[20]

The impact of Western trading nations had been felt already in the area. Muscat had become an important port run by wealthy merchants who had signed a commercial treaty with the British and Americans. Aden (on Hsu's map mistaken for Socotra), a small island at the entrance of the Red Sea, now was occupied by the British. Hsu could not have missed the analogy with Hong Kong. Sea routes from Europe to China were described in this section, and Hsu observed that British "fire-wheel ships" now took mail to Europe via the Isthmus of Suez.[21]

Hsu asserted that during the Ming period Arabia had repeatedly sent tribute to China by land across Central Asia. Arabia had also been visited by Cheng Ho, who considered it as the most remote region of the Western Ocean. Hsu then included some most revealing and surprisingly liberal conclusions about the religions that sprang from this area. Such sentiment regarding Christianity, appearing in a book that was published almost simultaneously with the outbreak of the pseudo-Christian Taiping movement, would alone perhaps have been sufficient to damn Hsu in the eyes of Confucian conservatives. He wrote:

> Buddhism arose in India; it considered compassion as its chief [concern], with quietude and extermination [of desire] as its goal. The scholars of China investigated and explained its teachings. They then felt they had achieved awareness and were happy. Although the ten precepts of Moses were shallow, they were just and without defect. Jesus provided an inspiring example and exhorted men to be good. In this he did not go beyond the basic ideas of Moses. *The ideas of Chou Kung and Confucius were not translated into their languages. Intelligent and outstanding men of other lands arose, instructed people in their customs, and urged them to do good. Their intentions were no more wrong than China's. Therefore it was not necessary for them to grasp the rules of the Confucians.*[22]

Toward the end of the discussion of Persia and Arabia Hsu detailed the dimensions of the Roman Empire, known to China at the time as Ta-ch'in. He also devoted several pages to material that identified West Asian place names in Han dynastic records. This was a natural act for a scholar of the Han as was Hsu, but one that further legitimized Chinese interest in the outside world by showing

such concerns to be historically justifiable. Land routes from Europe
to China also attracted Hsu's interest; he concluded that because
of the Hsiung-nu the ancient Romans had been forced to come to
China by sea.[23]

China's "Western Region": Russia on the Horizon

Hsu looked with dismay at China's so-called "Western Region,"
composed of states and peoples that he observed had been from
Han times sometimes united, sometimes fragmented. The various
names for places and states were confusing and numbered in the
hundreds and thousands. This region of Central Asia was located
on Western maps west of Sinkiang and Tibet, southeast of Russia,
and north of Persia, Afghanistan, and India. It was a region with
geopolitical significance. In the West it generally had been known
as Turkestan (*Ta-erh-chi-szu-tan*), but was also called Tartary
(*Ta-ta-li*).

The author found that Europeans rarely traveled to this area,
so their records only summarized the general conditions of the
region without detailing the names of the various tribes and states.
There were, however, only six or seven places or tribes large enough
to be considered important. Those in the northeastern portion were
nomadic states; those in the southwestern part were states with
walled cities. These states and tribes resided in a buffer zone between Russia and China. "After the collapse of the Yuan dynasty,"
he said, "Russia established itself in the northwest. Its capital is on
the Baltic Sea in Europe. It gradually seized land *to the southeast,
reaching to the eastern shore of Asia's Black Sea. Then it continued
to seize land over to the area north and west of Asia's Caspian Sea.*"[24]

The peoples and states of this area, including the Kazakhs and
Eleuths, as well as Badakshan, Bolor, Kokand, Tashkent, Bukhara,
and others, were briefly described. But Hsu found reports of Anglo-
Russian rivalry in the area more compelling. He reported that in
1839, because Russia desired to seize territory in India, Russia sent
a leader to Bukhara to make war on the British possessions there.
British forces met the threat, and the two states negotiated a settlement. This incident, he noted, had been reported in 1840 in "an

English newspaper translated in Kwangtung."[25] The source told of the Russian menace to Britain's position in India and depicted Russian moves into Central Asia in response to Britain's involvement in Afghanistan (in the First Afghan War, 1839–1842). Hsu also cited the account of the *Wan-kuo ti-li shu*.

Russia in recent years has expanded her territory. The state's southern border already extends to the western and northern shores of the Caspian. From the northern coast of the Caspian it has pressed straight on southeast into the heart of Tartary's Moslem areas [to places] such as Khiva. [These peoples] are scattered and weak; they are no match [for Russia]. [The Russian] *cavalry goes and comes as if there were no people there. Bukhara is relatively large, and it is in truth the key spot on the way to the East. Therefore Russia coerced and subdued [Bukhara] in order to move closer to spy on India.* The British came by sea to take India; Russia came by land to spy out India. *If we speak of being clever, then Russia is not equal to Britain; if we measure their strength, then Britain is not equal to Russia. The two states have been powerful enemies in the West for several decades. Who knows what rearrangements* [in the international order] *this will make in the future?* [26]

Depiction of South and Western Asia in Hsu's book thus brought more evidence to Chinese literati of the changes that had occurred on China's continental periphery as a result of the emergence of Western power. Weak states were unable to withstand the onslaught of the West. The analogy between what had occurred in India in the recent past and what might happen in China in the near future unless she moved decisively to organize more effectively was altogether too clear.

Hsu could see that China no longer (if ever) held a position that would allow her to play off one barbarian state against another in an arbitrary fashion. But he viewed Chinese understanding of the vigorous competition between Western states such as Britain and Russia to be of utmost importance. In the uncertain world of the future Chinese statesmen, with such knowledge, might play a role in effecting a power balance that would benefit the Middle Kingdom.

亞剌斯
地闌羈屬

大西洋海

瑞國

愛倫蘭

英羅巴

蘇格蘭三島

英羅

嗹國

荷蘭

普魯士西部

佛利比

日耳曼列國

士魯普

佛郎西

士瑞

葡萄牙

西班牙

海中地

塞爾牙

哥爾

沙丁尼阿

大剌分國

直布羅陀

加利非阿

海中

EUROPE

亞細亞界

烏拉嶺

烏拉嶺

亞細亞界

峨羅斯西境

峨羅斯都城

黑海

土耳其

亞細亞界

干地亞

居伯羅

Chapter IX

THE "BARBARIAN" BASE IN EUROPE

It was apparent to Hsu Chi-yü that China in the mid-nineteenth century faced a situation unprecedented in Chinese history. Western ships propelled by machinery rather than sail, cannon with surprising accuracy and range, information of remarkable detail and sophistication—all of these features bespoke a civilization technologically superior to China. Hsu consequently devoted much of his book to the evaluation of European states from which this new power had arisen. He related the early origins of these states and traced the history of their first maritime contacts with China and her sphere of influence. He showed how the Portuguese, Spanish, and Dutch had been the forerunners of the more recent and contemporary threats posed by Britain and Russia, and he examined the European institutional organizations that accounted for their wealth and power.

A General Picture of Europe

Europe was the name of the continent on the extreme northwest corner of Asia. This was the place called "Large Western Ocean" by the Chinese, and it amounted to only about one-fourth the land area of Asia. Hsu noted that although this continent was bordered on the east by the Ural Mountains, it was essentially a maritime area, for it was otherwise encircled by the seas. The land of Europe had been inhabited even before the Hsia dynasty (traditional dates, 2205–1766 B.C.), when its people roamed and hunted for their livelihood. These early peoples ate meat and used skins for clothing; their customs were similar to those of the Mongols. But in the middle years of the Hsia the various states of Greece became "Easternized," and the people learned how to cultivate and fashion implements. In the early Han the state of Rome in Italy founded a governmental system and opened up territory on the four sides to form a unified power in the Occident. This was the state called "Ta-Ch'in" in the Han histories. But when Rome fell after the

Han, *"Europe became fragmented into warring states* (chan-kuo)*."* [1]

During the T'ang and Sung eras when the Islamic states were powerful, they often invaded Europe. The various European states hurriedly sought to save themselves. *"This was when the method of* [using] *cannon was discovered in China, but the Europeans did not know* [the technique]*."* [2] Hsu related that at the end of the Yuan dynasty a German who had worked for the Mongols for the first time copied China in making cannon, but still the Europeans did not know how to use them. Finally, when Tamerlane attacked the areas of West Asia, some Europeans joined him as soldiers and at last took gunpowder back to Europe. Thus, Hsu pointed out that the contemporary European superiority in armaments had its origins in China and that such knowledge had come to Europe in relatively recent times. Such information must have been encouraging to Chinese who worried about Chinese chances of catching up with the West.

The various states analyzed the [gunpowder] and practiced [making it], so that finally *they grasped its mysteries. They also followed* [the basic idea] *of cannon and made fowling pieces which they used to attack enemies, so that in one hundred battles they were one hundred times victorious. They employed huge war vessels to cross the sea. They explored the West and discovered the whole continent of America; in the East they obtained India and the various islands of the Southern Ocean. The influence of the* [European] *states has covered the Four Seas. Now there are ten-odd states, including large and small* . . .

Of all the European states only Russia trades with China by land routes in the northwest; it does not use the maritime route. Of the ones coming to Canton, the British ships are the most numerous, amounting to six-tenths of the total. Most of the Spanish vessels come from Luzon. Their ships are outnumbered only by those of the British. They transport little else but rice. The next most numerous are those of Denmark and Holland, followed by Sweden. The merchant ships of France only number two or three at most, or one or two at the least. The items brought are woolens, clocks, and a variety of valuable goods. Portugal is the same as the "Ta-Hsi-yang" at Macao. Its merchant ships come very infrequently. Ships from the two German ports of Hamburg and Bremen sometimes arrive. Belgium now wishes to open trade, but their ships have not yet come. Italy, now divided into four states, has not sent merchant ships. Islamic Turkey and the small new state of Greece do not trade [with China].[3]

In this general introduction to Europe Hsu recorded the areas of the various states, noted their governments, populations, revenues, expenditures, and the size of their armies and navies. For example, Russia was governed by a king (*kuo-wang*). Its land area equaled 3,020,000 square li; population was forty-one million. Its annual revenues amounted to 5.2 million dollars of foreign silver. (This Hsu noted varied in value from 7.2 mace for the "heavier" silver, to a range of from four to six mace for the "lighter" variety.) The dynasty's (*kuo-chia*) debts were 200 million dollars. There were 600,000 soldiers normally, but during any war their number was increased to one million. There were thirty-six war ships.

In contrast, Britain was governed by a woman ruler (*nü-chu*). Its area was 300,000 square li, with a population of twenty-two million. Its annual revenues were 228 million dollars, while its debt amounted to 3.5 billion dollars. Normally the state maintained 90,000 soldiers, but this increased to 370,000 in time of war. The navy possessed 610 war ships, but during the war this number also increased to over a thousand.

For each state of Europe, including Turkey, Hsu outlined such statistics. In his comments on this information, however, the author revealed he did not understand the method Westerners used to calculate land areas, for the system was very different from that of China. Also, in the numerous books he had consulted, the numbers given for revenues, populations, size of armies and navies, were all different; the author therefore concluded that the figures were not to be taken as more than estimates.

The so-called "debts" of the states were owed to the people. Hsu explained that in the West when states were involved in war they summoned the gentry (*hsiang-shen*) to an assembly (*kung-hui*) and ordered them to plan for military expenditures. Funds were then borrowed from the rich merchants and great traders in return for an annual interest payment. *"If* [these funds] *are exhausted and the revenues of one year are insufficient to repay* [the debt], *then taxes are increased to obtain a surplus. Half of the* [instances] *of the states' succumbing to the rebellion of angered people is due to this cause."*[4]

Hsu located the European continent according to one of the eight compass-points in the *pa-kua* (Eight Trigrams) system of divination. Thus Europe was located to the northwest of China. And Europeans therefore were endowed, according to the theory of the Five Elements, with the principle of metal which was associated in this theory with the direction west.[5] The land was fertile; its products abundant.

Hsu briefly outlined the history of European-Chinese contacts by sea. Then he described the people of the Western continent. "The people of Europe are *tall and dazzling white, with prominent noses and deeply recessed yellow eyes.* (There are also some with black eyes.)" He continued his account of the people: their hair styles, clothing, their general appearance. To Hsu Europeans looked only half like Chinese, but it was reported that if they lived in China for a long time, their hair and eyes would turn black. Men wore felt or cotton hats three or four inches high, and these were taken off when they met a guest. Both men and women loved cleanliness and bathed daily.

The people are by disposition [inclined to work with] minute details. *They are talented in dealing with ideas and making things. Their work in metal and wood is so ingenious that it is hard to believe. Their use of water and fire* [for power] *is especially marvelous.* Firearms were first invented in China, but other lands copied these and improved on them to make them wonderfully excellent. *Their work in making castings and the refinements of their* [cannon] *are dared by them alone. Their vessels are especially marvelous; their sails, ropes, and tools are all finely made. In surveying the maritime routes they record depths in every place without missing by a foot or an inch.* That they have come across 70,000 li to China is no accident.[6]

Europe's climate was examined and compared to China's. Hsu concluded it was a mistake to say Westerners feared cold places, for they warmed their houses and wore several thicknesses of felt; instead it was the "black barbarians" from India and Southeast Asia who could not tolerate the cold, for they were accustomed to warm weather.

This continent possessed all of the so-called five grains and various fruits. Europeans ate wheat flour that had been baked into cakes. Beef, mutton, and pork were eaten with knives and forks; chopsticks were not used. Europeans drank coffee with sugar. Olives provided oil. Liquor was made from grapes and other fruits and grains. Cotton was brought from India and America for clothing. "Fire-machinery" was used to weave cloth, so that the price of labor was very low. Forests were plentiful.

In this introduction Hsu questioned what had caused the rise of European power. He found that the various states of Europe were all adept at bringing in interest on their investments; capitalism was behind the growth of Western power. *"They regard commerce as the basis* [of the state]; *there are customs taxes, but they do not tax the fields."* The Europeans furthermore did not fear traveling to far places to trade, and they had established ports in all places. Thus as a result of their ability to build good vessels *"and also because the states depended entirely* [on trade], *they had no choice but to pursue it with all their might."* [7]

Hsu also presented more information on Christianity in his introduction to Europe, with additional details following in his treatment of the various states. All of Europe had been converted to Catholicism (*t'ien-chu-chiao*) during the Han dynasty. The "king" of the religion lived in Rome. But Luther founded Protestantism, "the religion of Jesus," (*Yeh-su-chiao*) in Germany during the early Ming dynasty, so that now half of the states followed each religion. They had fought over their religion, but in fact the Catholic god was Jesus; the books of the two were the same, but the interpretations were different. The religions seemed quite similar except that the Catholics "worshiped the cross and an image of Jesus" while the Protestants did not.[8]

The author noted some peculiarities of the Western solar calendar: it was without intercalary months and some months had thirty-one days, while others had only thirty or twenty-nine. He also determined that Prussia, Austria, and Russia used the same spoken and written language; these were all states connected by land. Others that shared a common language—including American states—were Britain and the United States, Spain and Mexico, Portugal and Brazil.

In his introduction thus appeared a curious blend of fact and fiction which characterized Hsu's account of the Western world. Yet, in spite of the book's errors, the author's general picture remained valid. One of Hsu's major discoveries, for example, was that European power was based on ancient developments.

The Ancient Roots of Western Civilization

Much of Hsu's record of Europe's development in ancient times appeared in the sections devoted to Turkey, Greece, and Italy. For each of these states the author included lengthy discussions of their history, or of the ancient states that had been located in the territory of the modern states.

Hsu treated the Turkish Empire in the European section of his book, since it was indeed a European power and its capital was located in Europe, though like Russia it was a state that straddled Europe and Asia. Hsu sketched the history of the area from ancient times to the nineteenth century. He portrayed the continued threat to Turkey from Britain, France, and Russia; he also showed how these European powers were divided among themselves over Turkey. Turkey was then examined in more detail according to its three divisions: Western (European Turkey), Central, and Eastern.

European Turkey was an area of the West that was still held by Asians. The Turks were a tribe *"whose temperaments are overbearing; they love to fight, viewing death lightly while stressing the importance of promises."* [9] Opium was not prohibited in this country. Its capital, Constantinople, held a magnificent palace; it was also an important center of trade. The embassies of the various states were located here. The European possessions of Turkey— Bulgaria, Bosnia, Albania, Serbia, Wallachia, and Moldavia—all received brief notices in Hsu's account. And he noted the importance of European Turkey in ancient Western history. "Western [Turkey] is the land where Greece arose, and this is the place where Western states began to emerge from darkness and mist [i.e., to form a civilization]. Constantinople was the eastern capital of Rome; it was comparable to Lo-i [Loyang] of the Chou dynasty. *Europe is far from China; it was not gradually transformed by the ritual and music* [of China]." [10]

Hsu presented Central Turkey, which he labeled "Turkey Minor," with only the barest geographical facts. His treatment of East Turkey, however, was rich in detail concerning ancient Western history and religion. He criticized early Chinese records of the region for their inaccuracy. For example, he viewed as sheer nonsense the *T'ang History*'s account of Syria as a country of amazons which imported males from Judea. This was the land where Jesus of the Catholic and Protestant religions was born and reared. Noah of Mesopotamia was *"the ancient ancestor of the* [people] *of the various Western states."* [11] Babylon had been the ancient capital of a large state, but had been destroyed over two thousand years before.

Reflecting Hsu's reliance on Protestant materials, his treatment of the ancient Middle East included numerous stories from the Old Testament:

At that time the king of Babylon had a strange dream, *and his heart was troubled. Without revealing the nature* [of the dream] *he ordered his officials to explain it. They would be rewarded if they hit the mark; otherwise they would be punished.* The officials were extremely frightened and were at a loss what to do. Daniel said, *"Your servant knows. The king has dreamed of a great statue standing before him. His head was of gold, his chest of silver, his waist of copper, his legs of iron, and his feet of iron mixed with mud. Suddenly a large rock fell upon it, and the statue was broken; a wind blew the pieces away. I believe this was* [the dream]." *The king was shocked and said it was thus; but what was the meaning?*[12]

Daniel of course interpreted the dream and became "prime minister" of the king, an ideal outcome for a man gifted with the ability to predict the rise and fall of kingdoms. Hsu continued his account with details of Babylon's history, noting the city's dimensions and observing that Verbiest had said it was one of the world's seven great engineering feats.

Hsu concluded his treatment of Turkey with a detailed account of Jewish history, with all events dated according to Chinese dynastic periods. Thus he introduced Abraham (Ya-po-la-han) from Canaan who lived during the Hsia dynasty. Several generations later there was Jacob, who had twelve sons, the youngest of whom was Joseph. The reader found here the story of Moses, "whose scholarship was superior," as he led his clan out of Egypt to Canaan. There he became their king and proclaimed ten precepts in order to instruct the people: "[These precepts] taught [the people] to serve their god (*shen-t'ien*), to respect their parents, not to kill, not to commit adultery, not to steal, not to lie, not to desire the belongings of others, and to worship every seven days. *This was the beginning of the West's religion.*"[13]

The author observed that Europeans had passed on the story that Moses received these precepts from their god on Mt. Sinai written in stone, but he concluded that this was merely a claim to gain the people's respect. Other Old Testament personalities were introduced: Joshua, Samuel, Saul, David, Solomon. Finally Hsu's book dealt with Jesus, whose "grave was often visited by Europeans" before the land was cut off by Moslems. The Europeans were therefore angry and they attacked the Moslems for over two hundred years; their soldiers wore crosses on their clothing. Hsu noted that he had often discussed the Jews with the "English official, Lay," from whom he learned that Jews were very talented in discussing literature: "The various kinds of books in Western states are translated and interpreted by Jews; therefore it is only the record of their [ancient] state that is detailed. European scholars who study abroad *do not go to Greece but rather to Judea* [Jerusalem]; *therefore it is a district of European culture.* It is also said that Jewish women are beautiful and entrancing; they are quiet and perceptive by nature. They are completely different from [the women] of other areas. *If one marries a Jewish girl, she will bring dignity to his home.*" [14]

But in spite of this characterization of the Jews, the author presented Greece as a center of ancient European civilization. Here the ancients of Europe began to leave behind their barbarism. While Protestant missionaries were writing accounts that linked the ancient Chinese to Biblical records and the story of the Tower of Babel, Hsu found the earliest stage of Western civilization to be coincidental with the most ancient era of Chinese culture, an age of mythical sovereigns and culture heroes known to traditional Chinese scholars as the Hsia dynasty: "In the earliest times Europeans dressed in clothing made of grass and ate only fruits and nuts; the darkness and mist had not yet broken. By the middle of the Hsia dynasty the various states in the East had already been transformed. I-na-ku [?] arrived in Greece at that time from Canaan; for the first time *the natives were taught how to build houses and to cultivate grain.*" With the coming of Shai-ko-lo (?) from Egypt in the middle years of the Shang, Hsu continued, the natives first learned to weave wool into cloth and to ferment grapes to make wine; they used olives to make oil and metals for knives. A written language was also brought to the natives, and Hsu stressed that this was the beginning of European culture. [15]

In this survey of ancient Europe Hsu included a long account of the early origins of Greek government. The various states of Greece entered into an alliance and established an assembly (*kung-hui*) which met twice a year. Each state sent two ambassadors to the assembly. It decided treaties of alliance, administered justice, developed future state policies, and directed military preparations. The separate states were thus brought together as one. Other states feared its power and left it alone *"to prosper in achieving wealth and power"* by trading in the Mediterranean.[16]

In ancient Greece Hsu discovered an appealing model which brought power to small states by means of effective organization; at the same time it brought great benefits to the people. In Athens, then a small and weak state, King Theseus (Te-hsiu) found that there were three classes of people: the nobility (*chueh-shen*), artisans, and farmers. The nobility oppressed the people (*min*), so that the artisans and farmers were poor and the state weak. The king was grieved over this. *"Thereupon he eliminated officers, reduced the number of offices, repressed the bullying nobility,* and assumed great personal power. *He benefited the people* (li min) *and induced traveling merchants to come.* The people of distant lands came there for trade; *the artisans daily perfected their craftsmanship and produced amazing things. The surplus was sealed up. Farmers' granaries increased daily and there was abundance."*[17] Such decisive gains for the farmers at the expense of a "bullying" class held much appeal for idealistic Confucians who believed peasants to be the basis of the state. For Hsu, who early in his career had opposed incompetent and abusive bureaucrats, here was evidence that China's governmental institutions—by his time replete with obvious imperfections—did not possess a unique claim of legitimacy in world history as a system that benefited the common people.

When Theseus finally died, his son replaced him and ruled like his father with even more beneficial results for the artisans and farmers. *"From that time the nobility had no power,"* says Hsu, *"but the influence of the common people (shu-min) was great."*[18] When this king died, however, the people deliberated among themselves, saying that another virtuous ruler would be impossible to find, so they abolished hereditary kingship and thereafter relied on an elder official called an archon to manage the affairs of state. Hsu related the various details of this system; he cited the oppressive legalism of Draco and the relief brought by Solon's reforms. These included the establishment of a deliberative hall (*i-shih-t'ang*) and a court of law; these administrative bodies supervised the affairs of government.[19] Thus, considerable information concerning Greece's governing apparatus and ancient history found its way into Hsu's account. To be sure, Hsu recognized the connection between these ancient forms and the contemporary European and American systems.

In a remarkable comparison with the Chinese view of non-Chinese, after treating the Persian Wars, Hsu noted that the Greeks had despised the Persians as "outside barbarians" (*wai-i*).[20] The career of Alexander the Great also caught Hsu's fancy as a Western example of military genius and success.[21]

Hsu identified Italy too as an ancient unified state; it was known during the Han dynasty in China as the Ta-Ch'in state. *"It extends into the Mediterranean Sea like a man's leg wearing a wooden shoe."* The author treated the Roman Empire: its rise, its geographical extent; and in clear harmony with events in Chinese history, its collapse resulting from the onslaught of "northern barbarians," a term which if used in the Chinese context came dangerously close to an act of disloyalty to the Manchus. He noted Napoleon's invasion of the peninsula and its division into small states after the Congress of Vienna. Its products were listed, including the production of silk. The author held a low opinion of Italians, who, he believed, were weaklings, thieves, and murderers, a view which makes obvious his heavy reliance on Protestant sources.[22] Hsu related that Rome was the residence of the "king" of the Catholic religion.

> Rome was an old city in ancient times, *and at its zenith it was famous as the foremost city in the West.* During the Liu Sung dynasty [420–479 A.D.] it was occupied by Visigoths, a northern barbarian tribe. *Consequently the king's palace was half destroyed; books and old documents were also swept away without leaving a trace. From this time the people accepted barbarian customs, but these were not their former*

[customs]. The Catholic religion was spread throughout the West during the Former Han dynasty. The belief of the people of Rome was especially strong. Thus when the state fell to the barbarians, the followers of the Catholic religion jumped at the opportunity to entice [others]. Their accomplices grew in number daily, and *great power came to them. The Franks destroyed the Visigoths, and their land then returned to a teacher of the Catholic religion called "king of the religion."* When the king died the rulers of the religion gathered together to appoint an old man to succeed him. *This is quite similar to the custom in Tibet of the lama sitting on a bed.* Their religion spread to all the states. If there were some unwilling to follow it, *they at once stirred up trouble, attacked with an army, and destroyed them. Or they taught the people to rebel against their rulers.* Thus the Franks became hegemons, and the king of the religion helped them to oppress [people].[23]

But during the Ming dynasty, Hsu again noted, a German named Luther founded another religion called the religion of Jesus, which he called the orthodox teachings. He condemned Catholicism for its heterodoxy. Half of the states of Europe followed his new teaching, so that the power of the pope was reduced. Nevertheless, the disciples of the Catholic religion were "like ants," and there were believers in even the most distant places. The people were lazy in farming, so there were wild and deserted lands in Italy. The mountains hid fierce bandits. For an old bandit fighter like Hsu, it was disturbing to note that the church provided such men with a sanctuary: *"If they are apprehended they hurriedly flee to a Catholic meeting place and* [the case] *is never again opened."*[24]

In recording the history of Rome, Hsu referred to "Western accounts." Romulus and Remus founded Rome and taught the people agriculture and warfare. At a later time the people, as in Athens, removed their king. *"They selected two virtuous men as high nobles and established an assembly to govern affairs. These high nobles were changed once a year. From that time the state had no king, but it daily became more powerful and prosperous."*[25]

Hsu traced the general background and events of the Punic

Wars. The reader found a detailed account of the expansion of the empire over the face of Europe and the shores of the Mediterranean; Julius Caesar, Brutus, and Mark Antony (Ma-erh-ko An-to-ni-yueh) all appeared in Hsu's book. He found that under Justinian, "the eastern king," administrative and legal reforms were carried out. *"At that time the state's people sailed to China and returned with silkworm mulberry, which they tried to cultivate; [the mulberry] grew there, and from that time production of silk arose.* (European production of silk dates back a thousand and several hundred years; but Chinese have not known this, for we thought it was all sold at Canton.)"[26]

The Eastern Empire faced not only a threat from Islam, but also from the rising power of Russia to the north. They met the northern threat by sending girls to marry Russian barbarians, an old Chinese device too; later they succeeded in bringing Russians under the influence of the Catholic religion. In this way they secured allies against the Arabs.[27]

Fully aware of the potential of political control through religion, Hsu resumed his account of Western religion, stating that the books written about religion by Westerners were numerous. He traced the development of Christianity from Moses, to Abraham, to David, and finally to Jesus Christ, noting that "Christ" meant "god." Jesus' father was named Yueh-se-fu; his mother was Ma-li-ya. Hsu recounted the Biblical tale of the birth of Jesus "in the fifth year of the reign of Ai-ti in the Former Han."[28] Jesus taught the people not to kill, commit adultery, steal, or lie. He called the god (*T'ien*) his father; he was the only son and had been sent to save the people of this world. Simon Peter, James, and Matthew were his famous disciples. He healed people, and his followers called him king of the Jews. But the Jewish priests disliked him. Finally, Judas, a disciple, sold out his master. Jesus was taken before the high official, Pilate, who judged him innocent. But the crowd was angered. He was nailed to a cross and died. The next day disciples discovered his corpse was missing, and they traveled to the various states to spread his teachings. Stephen heard and believed, but was stoned to death by the Jews; also there was Paul who had opposed

Jesus' disciples, but he later became a strong supporter and wrote many books.

Hsu admitted that he had often read books on this religion, undoubtedly those given him by Abeel.[29] He noted the continuities from Judaism to Christianity. Christians, he said, worshiped only their god; they did not worship their ancestors. They believed Jesus was a ruler who would save the world, and that their spirit went to the state in heaven (*t'ien-kuo*)—also the name of the earthbound Taiping kingdom—when they died. The author referred at length to the factional disputes within Christianity and noted that after Luther opposed the church the pope became very angry and ordered the various kings to kill Protestants, but that the new religion could not be stopped. *"From this time on rulers and people killed one another over religion; states attacked states because of religion for several hundred years . . .* I have said that Jesus established his teachings to save the world. *But the various states have endlessly destroyed and killed due to divisions in the religion. If Jesus knew this what would he say?"* [30]

Hsu argued, however, that China's recent problems resulted not merely from the Westerners' desire to spread their religion; this was simply one aspect of a complex European order which was now descending on the Chinese world. "Europe is a distant border area, and it was not reached by the teachings of Confucius. Jesus was born among them and forbade adultery and killing; he disregarded himself in order to save the world. *Other lands revere and believe in his principles. Even if there originally had been no so-called necessity of spreading his teachings to China, this would not have prevented the many problems* [of late]." [31]

Portugal, Spain, and Holland

Portugal was an early visitor to the China seas, Hsu noted, because the people of this state had made great progress in the period after the Yuan dynasty with navigational techniques for distant travel.

The Portuguese were skilled in reckoning with mathematical

*and astronomical instruments, measuring the movement of the
sun and the courses of stars. They used calculations to know directions and distances on water and land. In the early Ming period
their king sent men who were good at managing boats to sail large
war vessels to the south. They turned eastward from the western
coast of Africa, passed the eastern coast and pressed on eastward
to Malacca. From the straits of Sumatra and Java they traveled
extensively to the island states of Southeast Asia. Wherever they
went the Portuguese immediately left men to set up ports . . .
The Portuguese then established a port at Macao; this was the
first time that a European state had traded in Kwangtung.*[32]

Hsu sketched the ancient history of Spain and its development
up to the Ming dynasty, when Ferdinand and Isabella sent Columbus (K'o-lun) west in search of land. Spain thus discovered the
wealth of America. Magellan then sailed to Luzon and took that
island for Spain. This conquest further enriched the state. Hsu
traced Spain's history through the Napoleonic era, and noted that
Spain's colonies in America had rebelled against her control, now
leaving only Luzon and Cuba as colonies. He continued:

*The people by custom sail on the seas and they are talented
in traveling to distant places.* From the time they secured
America's Mexico, *the state possessed gold and silver and was
considered the wealthiest in the West.* Even today the states
of Europe use its foreign money; most of it is called "Luzon
dollars" . . . But in recent years it has become very weak. How
did it become so poor? [By relying on] *wealth without*
[proper] *rule, even the Ch'in and Sui dynasties could not avoid
destruction; how much more* [this is true] *of an unimportant
barbarian state (i-kuo).* "[33]

Hsu found Holland to be a small state in Europe. The country
was low and by the ocean, so the people naturally became talented
in dealing with the sea. They were able to build fine vessels. Therefore Holland became the first state of Europe to develop a vibrant
overseas trade. Hsu outlined Holland's development historically as

part of Europe's story of interstate conflicts. But in the early Ming period, he observed, Holland had sent vessels eastward to the seas of China and Java; the islands of that area were gradually taken and ports established. *"To cross 70,000 li of sea for trade was because the state, although small, was wealthy."* [34] Holland had often caused trouble along the coasts of Fukien and Chekiang and had even occupied Taiwan at one point until expelled by Koxinga. (Koxinga, foe of the early Ch'ing, was portrayed in Hsu's work as a patriot.) But later Holland's ports in the Indian Ocean had been gradually taken by the English and French.

> Holland is a flat land. There are rivers but no mountains; there are hills in the east, but very few. In the north are wild oats and sesamum indicum (shaped like a tick; purple-black; it produces oil and can be found in northern Shansi; it is not linseed). In the northwest is barley; in the central area are hemp and materials for paint; in the south wheat is grown. By custom [the Dutch] like to smoke tobacco, so they grow a great deal of it. The pastures are broad, fertile, and convenient for herding cattle. The cakes made of cow's milk are the very finest. [The Dutch] are also good at making two kinds of "fire spirits" which are sent to the various states; their woolens are the finest and are much valued in China. *The people are customarily simple and reliable; they endure hardships and are frugal in clothing and food. In earning a living they work extremely hard. There are no vagrants and no thieves. If there is profit to be found, they do not regard several thousand or ten-thousand li as too distant.* By nature they love cleanliness and constantly clean their houses. If there is dirt on the streets they must wash and sweep them entirely clean. Taxes are quite heavy. The gentry (*shen-shih*) settle [the state's] affairs (*ch'ou-pan*), and the king is unable to assume this responsibility. [35]

For Hsu, a Confucian, the frugal habits of the Dutch were admirable. Their talent for making money by hard work and persistence was also attractive to the former citizen of Shansi trading communities, where wealth was honorable. These Hollanders seemed to fit a Chinese ideal. Having noted ominously that the gentry had taken power away from the king, Hsu reflected on the usefulness of organization and careful planning even for so small a state as Holland: "[In recent years] *the various island states of the Indian Ocean have recognized Britain as their ruler, but the island states of Southeast Asia, with the exception of Spain's Luzon, all take Holland to be their master. Their land was originally* [as small as] *a pill, but they have planned the state's policies* [so as to affect places] *over 70,000 li distant for several hundred years without change. This can be called a* [state] *which is good at strategy."* [36]

Russia, France, and Britain

Russia, situated on the northern stretches of both Asia and Europe, as well as portions of North America, was the "largest state" in Hsu's new world. Six-tenths of the country lay in Asia, the author observed, while only four-tenths was in Europe. But both its new and old capitals were in Europe. "[Russia's] *prosperous areas and the proud, elegant cities are gathered together in the western portion. The land to the east, while broad and extensive, is deserted, poor, and sterile.* [Russia's] *treaties and wars have all been with the various states of Europe. The state's power is in the West, not in the East."* [37]

Russia before the T'ang dynasty, Hsu noted, was composed merely of scattered tribes which were vassals of the Huns. But in the T'ang period, a Russian leader gathered the tribes together and founded the state. Russians accepted the Greek Orthodox church. Later it fell to the invading Mongols. In the Ming period, with Swedish aid, the Russians expelled the Mongols. There was then a king named Ivan who enlarged the state's territory; his nature was wild and he loved to kill. Russia was still very weak, and Poland became a threat. The people, in their fear, sought a virtuous ruler to pacify the state. In 1775 Peter became king. Hsu was beginning to recognize outside models for China, so Peter was an appealing example. When Peter was a child his elder sister desired power and sought to take the throne. But Peter escaped calamity by becoming a monk. Then he was "selected" (*t'ui-li*) by the crowd. *"He humbled himself and summoned the brave and virtuous to aid in planning the affairs of state. He personally taught soldiers to ride and shoot; at the same time they studied fire arms, so that all became strong troops. Thus* [he used] *governmental discipline to reform the state's customs."* [38]

Consequently Peter pacified the state. He then traveled to the borders and opened ports on the sea. He had found that Russians were not trained to sail ships, so he *"changed his name and went to Holland. There he became the apprentice of a boat's master and learned this man's techniques in every detail before returning* [to Russia]. *"* Peter then directed his own ships in a war against Sweden and won. Sweden gave Finland to Russia, and Peter built a new capital on the coast, called "Fort of Peter." *"The plans to dredge out the waterways of the Baltic Sea were all managed by* [Peter]; *by winning wars and conquering territory he expanded* [the state]. *Russia's recent power in truth began with Peter."*

A queen named Catherine eventually replaced Peter; she was *"lewd and licentious, with many lovers, but nevertheless was brilliant in running affairs* [of the state]."[39] In this iconoclastic statement by a Confucian scholar who surely noted the similarity between Catherine and China's infamous Empress Wu of the T'ang dynasty, Hsu suggested that a ruler's virtue had little to do with a state's power. Catherine, by gathering craftsmen of other states by paying them well to teach her own people the various arts, supported learning and military preparations. Consequently she had prepared her state to deal with both Turkey and Poland. Hsu mentioned Catherine's successors and some of Russia's more recent conflicts before closing his introductory sketch of Russian history.

Hsu recorded the dimensions and location of Siberia and said it was a barren land which had never supported states. Because it was a land frozen nine months of the year, it was almost uninhabited. Due to the cold, people were unable to remain there very long. China, therefore, to Hsu's dismay, had not paid much attention to it. In the middle years of the Ming dynasty when Russia began to prosper, merchant ships went to the coasts of Siberia when the seas were not frozen and they exchanged "foreign goods" for skins. Gradually the Russians became more familiar with the land, and its abundance contributed to making Russia wealthy and strong (*fu-ch'iang*). The tribal leaders of the area who went to Russia saw their grand and imposing capital, with marts and palaces, and this caused them to submit to Russia as tributary vassals. A fortress was built at the mouth of the Amur River, and Russians came in exile to Siberia to populate the place. They invaded the eastern area as far as the Pacific, posing a threat to China by land as had the British by sea. In the reign of Catherine a minister named Bering had been sent to spy out the northeast. He discovered that Asia and America were not connected, but were separated by a strait of several tens of li. This strait came to be named the Bering Strait. Russians then crossed over and occupied a corner of America, as had the British on the opposite side of the continent. Hsu continued: *"The eastern portion of Siberia produces only furs; it is well stocked with such kinds of animals as fox, hare, sable, squirrel, and others. These are sold primarily to China. The western portion produces gold, silver, copper, and iron. But the iron is especially plentiful. Each year more than one million tons are produced. The various states of Europe depend on this* [as their source of iron].*"* [40]

The author carefully listed the names of Russia's cities, ports, administrative units, and minority groups, with some details following each topic. The geographical features of the country also appeared, as did information concerning Russia's customs, religion, history, government, and military. The author recorded that Russia by custom observed the teachings of the Greek branch of Catholicism. A "general ruler" of this religion possessed great power. The various teachers of the religion lived among the people, and there were 70,000 "temples" with 160,000 monks.

A prime minister managed the affairs of the Russian government. When a crisis arose the king summoned one hundred and twenty nobles to discuss and debate matters in a public meeting. There were eight ministries which were roughly equivalent to those of China. Usually clansmen managed border affairs. Each year, in addition to other miscellaneous taxes, the state levied taxes on the fields, amounting to 78 million ounces of silver. Russia maintained an army of 610,000 men, trained in cavalry and firing weapons, and possessed forty fine large ships to carry troops, thirty-five war ships, and twenty-eight ordinary ships also for troops. In addition there were another three hundred small ships, with 40,000 sailors in all. Military discipline was strict and punishments severe. Slavery existed in Russia, and each noble, official, or rich merchant kept several tens or hundreds. Over a million slaves could be found in the entire country, but many fled to become soldiers.[41]

Historical contacts between China and Russia drew the author's attention.[42] He summarized the territorial growth of Russia "in all directions" after Peter the Great's reign. It had become so large that no other European state, including Britain and France, could hope to occupy even one side. Moreover, the various states of Europe were unable to hold Russia in light regard. The situation in Europe, Hsu concluded, seemed very similar to that of the ancient Chinese states of Ch'i, Ch'in, Chin, and Ch'u during the Warring States period.[43]

But despite her navy and merchant ships, Hsu concluded that Russia still could not be considered the equal of the Western European maritime states in terms of naval power; thus its merchant vessels traveled only in the seas of the West and did not come east to Canton. Trade with China consequently was *"by land, not by sea."*[44]

Hsu also considered France prominent among the "powerful and large states of Europe." In ancient times it had been inhabited by wild barbarians, but with its conquest by the Romans and the beginning of agriculture, the customs of the people gradually changed. Hsu recorded the early history of France, noting a traditional rivalry between France and England. The reader was introduced to Charlemagne, Joan of Arc, the Henrys (Hsien-li) and the Louis (Lu-i) of French history. He noted the aid France provided George Washington which had "forced" England to make peace. The French Revolution and Napoleon's rise attracted his attention;

Napoleon "used soldiers like a god" and was "feared as a tiger," qualities which could be respected highly by Hsu, defender of the Fukien coast.[45]

Hsu described the geographical features of France, including its rivers and waterways. He found that France, like China, had constructed canals to crisscross the state, a fact which Hsu considered fascinating, perhaps because of his own family's identity in previous generations with the work of maintaining the canal transport system. *"The French have opened up many branches of rivers as canals,"* he said. "([They] are most clever in [devising] irrigation and waterway schemes. The state regards this as a special branch of learning.) *Vessels are able to reach every spot. They have also opened up many drains and ditches in order to conserve the water that leaks out. Because of this the land is the most fertile in the West."*[46]

Because French farmers worked extremely hard, even though France held a large population, food always exceeded the demand. The plentiful grape wine of France became its foremost product, one bottle worth several tens of foreign silver dollars; the total annual value of this product alone accounted for sixty million dollars of the state's income. "Hot wine" (brandy?), olive oil, turnips for sugar (sugar beets?), fine broadcloth, and camlets were some of the products of the state. *"They are able also to weave silks with designs."* Hsu noted that France annually produced a great quantity of silk, but could not satisfy the demand so additional amounts had to be imported from Italy, and he characterized the French as follows:

> *The people are clever in manufacturing. The majority of* [Europe's] *guns, fire-wheel carts, and fire-wheel ships are constructed here.* In the capital is a clock and watch factory which employs two thousand men; each year it produces 40,000 watches and 18,000 clocks which ring by themselves. *Their methods* [of production] *constantly change, and these are so cleverly ingenious that it is impossible to imagine . . . The people are customarily brave; they maintain a joyful*

expression on their faces, and they are proud and stubborn.
Every day they sing and dance. They do not worry whether
something is expensive or cheap. Their clothing is elegant and
they do not begrudge the expense. They like to travel and are
accomplished in entertaining people who have come from
distant places.[47]

Hsu thus took note of the growing industrial capacity of the West,
which more than any other factor, had accounted for the new
power of Europe. After the Opium War it was no longer possible
for a Chinese official who had kept touch with reality to ignore
the "ingenious devices" of the West or the methods by which these
things were produced.

Paris is situated on both banks of the Seine River. The city
wall is a square [enclosing] a large area with over 900,000
citizens. The king lives in a lofty palace with many floors, and
towers over gates are facing one another. *It is elegant, refined,*
and without comparison in the West . . . The streets wind in
and around, and numerous shops cluster together like a bee-
hive. People coming and going bump into one another in the
hustle and bustle which continues day and night . . . [Paris]
is the most prosperous capital in all of Europe. Inside the walls
is a large college (*shu-yuan*) which holds 360,000 printed books
and 70,000 manuscripts. Students from abroad are allowed to
live at the college and borrow books. Fourteen hospitals have
been built, and famous medical doctors have been attracted
to reside in them. Annually they treat 14,000 patients. *Those*
in the various states who study medicine all wrap up their
possessions and travel to Paris, returning after three or five
years when their studies are completed. In addition there are
many technical colleges wherein reside masters of the various
arts, *such as military science, canal engineering, and manufac-*
turing. Each of the students studies [the subject] *he desires to*
know.[48]

Hsu noted that the French had great respect for learning; the
best students became high officials. Two important boards, com-

posed of the nobility and gentry, convened to deal with matters of state *"such as determining punishments and making war; this board* [of nobles] *is ordered to deliberate and make plans.* The prime minister has no power, but merely announces the king's orders." France maintained a large army and navy, with 290 fully-equipped warships of various sizes, including several dozen "fire-wheel" ships. Hsu was particularly fascinated by France's love of military glory.

> *All of the people love military achievements. When the army is summoned their spirit is aroused and their faces become stern. When they are ready to go into battle, they use troops to confuse the enemy by heading straight out determined not to turn back. Even if the first ranks are made into a row of corpses, the ranks behind press on without stopping. When they are victorious the whole state shouts* [with joy]; *even though the wounded and dead number in the thousands and ten-thousands, they do not pity* [themselves]. *Instead they take their state's prestige and the entire state system* (kuo-t'i) *as their* [first] *pleasure . . . Their headmen are very ruthless and they are fond of devising means to understand military affairs. There is no method of naval and land warfare which they do not analyze. They also like to use the arts of politics* [to make favorable alliances]. *Thus in wars with the various other states they have been victorious nine times out of ten.*[49]

With such detail Hsu showed his Chinese readers that the military prowess that had stymied Chinese armies was not the sole possession of the British. Indeed, to a Chinese reader after 1860 such as Tung Hsun, witness of the combined military power of Britain and France directed against China, such material encapsulated in Hsu's book of the 1840's must have seemed prophetic.

France had also been active in occupying lands outside of Europe: in India, South America, and Africa. But Hsu noted that these possessions were not considered to be very important by France; if they were lost they would not be missed. All of the states of Europe depended on maritime trade, so that each year many merchant ships came to China, but those from France were the least numerous. Hsu reasoned that France was so rich and her people so talented in manufacturing that she had a sufficiently prosperous trade in Europe. There was no necessity for France to trade with China.[50]

Assuming that Ku Yen-wu's term, *Fo-lang-hsi,* referred to the French rather than to the Portuguese, Hsu concluded his coverage of France with long quotations from Ku's *T'ien-hsia chün-kuo li-ping shu*; these traced China's early relations with "France" and again included Ku's allegation that the "French" bought and ate children. This Hsu now concluded was untrue. Also apparently taken from Ku was an account of an ingenious method of sinking European ships, including a report of people who were able to stay under water for seven days and nights at a time. Hsu decided that all of this was pure fantasy.[51]

Hsu found Britain to be one of the most powerful of the states of the West. It was formed by the "three islands" of England (*Ying-lun*), Scotland, and Ireland. In ancient times the land was inhabited by native barbarian tribes of Celts. During the Han dynasty Julius Caesar occupied France and crossed the sea to "pacify" England. It thereafter belonged to Italy for several hundred years. Hsu traced the coming of the Britons, Scoti, Picts, Angles, and Saxons before the arrival of Catholicism; then came continued invasion by the Danes until by trickery Alfred defeated them and arranged a treaty of peace. Alfred, who as a youth often traveled to Rome to be with scholars, then opened up lands, summoned traveling merchants, and fostered centers of learning to translate books. His reign during the T'ang dynasty was a period of greatness.

During the reign of the next king, however, England fell upon bad times. For the first time Catholicism began to prosper and the priests secured great influence and power; indeed, their power became greater than that of the king. The problem of the Danes remained, and the king was forced to pay them annual bribes amounting to 17,000 catties of silver; this later rose to 24,000 catties, but the wars continued. For example, in the nineteenth year of the Sung dynasty's Chen-tsung reign (1016), the Danes attacked and destroyed London. Later a headman (*ch'iu*) named William, who had often acted as an official in France's northwestern prefectures, arose from the northern tribes of England. When the Danes destroyed England, William plotted to restore the state and he requested the pope's aid. Whereupon the pope gave the English land to him as a fief. William then attacked the Danes, occupied London, and finally became king.

Hsu recorded the names of Henry I and II; the latter had tangled with the Catholics, but after killing their representative the people were so angered that Henry, who feared the power of the pope, had to worship at the grave of Becket. The king extended his control to Ireland. His successor was a violent man who loved war and wanted to attack the Moslem tribes of Judea. On his return to England another state captured him for ransom. John, his younger brother, eventually took the throne, and again there occurred a clash with the church. "[John] *insulted Catholic priests, so the pope in Rome became angry;* [the pope] *renounced the English people and stopped their worshiping by closing down the temples. Marriages and funerals were eliminated, and the people were forbidden to drink spirits, eat meat, or cut their hair* [i.e., join the priesthood]. *The people were all angry and blamed the king. The king could not do otherwise but to pay tribute to the pope. Thereafter the king's power declined. The people themselves selected and recommended gentry to decide matters of government."* [52]

Hsu's brief account, after citing early attempts to reduce the power of the monarch, jumped from John to Edward III to Henrys IV, V, and VI; the Wars of the Roses received some notice. Finally during the Ch'eng-hua reign (1465-1488) of the Ming dynasty, Henry VII assumed the throne and pacified the state. This king, by nature skilled and clever, excelled in administration and was called a virtuous ruler. Henry VIII, whose nature was violent and boastful, succeeded him and married a Spanish princess for reasons of state. Hsu noted with interest Henry's appetite for young, beautiful women, some of whom he later killed. *"The surrounding states called him a ruler without principles."* [53]

Elizabeth, a woman ruler, later ascended the throne. She was virtuous, brilliant, and talented in governing. When Holland refused to follow Catholicism and Spain attacked her, the English woman ruler sent her forces to aid Holland. Spain then attacked England. Its warships sailed to English harbors, but suddenly a great wind whipped up the seas and wrecked half their vessels, while small English boats surrounded and destroyed the remainder. From this time on the state's power grew.

The author's account continued with England's succession of rulers, religious disputes, the unification of England and Scotland *"as one state,"* and the clash between the king and "gentry" which led to the death of Charles I. England defeated Holland under Charles II, but London's great plague and fire again weakened the state. In the twenty-seventh year of the K'ang-hsi reign (1688), the king of Holland entered London and took the throne as William III. This able king died without issue. But the king of Hanover in Germany was known as a virtuous ruler, so the people of the state summoned him to the throne as George I. After a period of adjustment to English customs, he brought harmony to the people. It was at this time that the English merchant ships sailed the Four Seas and England increasingly became prosperous and strong (*fuch'iang*).[54] She won successive wars against France. Good rule continued under George II, when England defeated Spain and took away French possessions in America.

The English had crossed the sea in search of new land in the middle years of the Ming dynasty, and they had secured the fertile land of North America; they sent citizens there to consolidate their position. They gradually developed this land so that Britain came to depend on it heavily. But because of many years of war, Britain taxed these lands so harshly that the Americans could not endure. A man named Washington occupied the land and summoned an army to resist British attack. The French had a hatred for Britain that went back for generations and they sent aid to Washington. Washington thus proved victorious and he established the state of America. At that time Britain was humbled and diminished in power; but then her trade with India increased and she became wealthier than before. Britain penetrated Southeast Asia and the various barbarian tribes there accepted her control. British vessels collected in trading spots to bring back wealth. *"Then* [Britain] *became the foremost of the states of the West."*[55] Hsu followed the rise of Napoleon and the subsequent threat to Britain, and he briefly portrayed the Battle of Waterloo. At the present time, Hsu found, the ruler of the state again was a woman, Wei-to-li-ya, who had become queen at the age of eighteen.

Following this lengthy introduction to Britain, Hsu described the country in detail and listed its products. "The three islands of Britain consider England as the ruler," and England was the place where the state had been established.[56] England's size and topography were described. Here flowed more than ten rivers, but these were all very short. The land was fertile. England was divided into fifty-two parts (*pu*). In one of these, Middlesex, the capital city of London had been established on the Thames River. This city was huge, but had no city walls. Its population was over 1,400,000. Here a large, stately palace was surrounded by official buildings. The city's streets crossed at right angles, and they were lined with stores. It ranked as the largest city among the Western states. In the center of this city stood the "temple" of Paul, a disciple of Jesus. Here a large college collected scholars; artisans who worked with iron came to another place in the city. London's port was very large and over one thousand merchant vessels of other states arrived there annually; in addition it received over three thousand British ships each year.

Scotland, north of England, had been a separate state in ancient times. But in the thirty-first year of Wan-li (1603) during the Ming, it united with England to form one state. The people here, known for their patience and frugality, had saved up what had been brought back as profit from their trade in the Four Seas so, though the land was cold and barren, the Scots lacked nothing.

Ireland, west of Scotland and England, inhabited early by aboriginal tribes, had come under England's control during the Southern Sung dynasty. The land was poor, but coal and minerals had been found there. The people possessed coarse natures, and they loved to drink spirits, they did not plan for the future. The Irish believed in Catholicism and wanted to be rid of England's control.

In addition to coal, Britain's natural products were, according to Hsu, "iron, tin, lead, swallows' nests, and sand," items that apparently found their way to Chinese ports on British ships.[57] Horses, cows, and sheep were very numerous; two varieties of wheat were grown. Although the land was fertile and crops were bountiful, Britain did not produce enough for her population and so had to import from other states.

But Britain's ability to pay for these imports was no mystery to the Chinese investigator. He observed that the state possessed a sizable industry. Over 490,000 people wove cloth on machines made of iron. These machines were run by "fire-wheels" which made them work by themselves. Consequently labor was reduced and the price of the goods could be kept low. Annually over 400,000 tons of cotton came to these places from India and America to be woven into cloth. In addition they produced woolens and silks, the latter found by Hsu to be inferior to those of France; they imported raw silk from China and Italy. Approximately 300,000 people worked in the production, again with various sorts of machinery, of guns, cannon, swords, and clocks. Each year Britain's total production of miscellaneous articles of trade amounted to something over 100 million ounces of silver. A world away from Marx, who published his earth-shaking manifesto the year Hsu finished the *Ying-huan chih-lueh*, Hsu noted that *"there is no place within the Four Seas their merchant ships do not reach; great profits come to the merchants, but the artisans are poor."* [58]

Hsu was intrigued with the governmental institutions of the state that not only had defeated China but also had been so successful in slicing up the global melon. The power of Britain—in India, Assam, Burma, Malacca, Singapore, Australia, New Zealand, Africa, and America—meant that the internal organization of this state merited particular attention. To reveal the direct connection between the state's domestic order and its influence as a world power, Hsu here reiterated the story of Britain's penetration of the non-European world, the details of which could be found in the portions of his book that specifically dealt with the various areas.

Hsu found that in the capital was an assembly (*kung-hui*),

divided into two sections called "House of Nobles" and "House of the Gentry." Two "prime ministers" directed the British government, one to supervise internal affairs and the other for external affairs. Additional high officials variously supervised the treasury, taxation, trade, justice, the state seal, the affairs of India, and the navy. Aides assisted each official. Representatives of the nobility and the clergy were gathered in the House of Nobles, while in the House of the Gentry were talented and educated men who had been selected by the common people (*shu-min*). When an urgent matter had to be discussed, the king ordered a prime minister, who in turn notified the House of Nobles, to summon the group for consideration of the problem. Regulations were followed to decide what could or could not be done. Then the House of the Gentry would be notified, and this body had to give its approval before any action could be taken.

Hsu reported that if the people had matters they wished to be discussed and considered, they first were required to make their case known to the House of the Gentry, from where it might be passed on to the House of Nobles to the prime minister and finally to the king. Also, if there were appeals from the common people they were to go to the House of the Gentry for investigation. The opinion of this body would then be submitted to the House of Nobles for a final decision. If a member of the gentry was guilty of a crime, he was judged by the whole group of gentry. He was not imprisoned with the commoners. The various regulations for punishments, rewards, and war were all decided by the nobles; but matters of taxation and money were determined by the gentry. Hsu noted that this form of government had been copied by many other European states. He also briefly described Britain's jury system and reported that Britain's annual revenue was over twenty million ounces of silver, which equaled its yearly expenditures.

Interested in military power, Hsu found that the army in Britain numbered 90,000 men; in India were another 30,000 British soldiers, plus 230,000 native soldiers. The state possessed over six hundred warships of all sizes, and over one hundred fire-wheel ships. The uniforms of British sailors were blue; those of the army were red. They honored the navy but had a low opinion of the army.

The instruments of British maritime power received close examination. Britain's largest warships carried one-hundred-twenty cannon; others were equipped with one hundred, ninety, seventy-four, and sixty. Medium-size vessels carried forty-four, thirty-six, and twenty-eight. The small carried only twenty, ten, or six. The large ships had three masts and were about one hundred feet long. They were sixty to seventy feet high. The large ships drew over thirty feet, while the smaller drew over twenty or ten feet. Copper sheathing one or two inches thick protected their hulls from barnacles.[59] Hsu was interested in keels, planking, nails, sails, and even the types of wood used to build the British ships, which he considered evidence of Western technical superiority. His earlier experience in Amoy preparing defense lines undoubtedly led to his fascination with Western cannon, which he described explicitly. Steamships were also introduced to the Chinese reader in some detail. Though the description of the engine probably puzzled most of his readers, who no doubt wished to know how it really worked, nevertheless Hsu's general picture of these "fire-wheel" ships with their paddle-wheels and belching smoke undoubtedly sufficed to anchor a vivid image in the minds of his readers. In a day and night these amazing ships could travel over a thousand li. Such ships had been constructed only during the last forty or fifty years. Because steam machinery had been used in Europe's mills, able persons had extended its use to propel vessels. The author noted that recently in America the device had been further applied to carts which ran on roads made of iron.[60]

Hsu thus recognized the revolution in transportation, resulting from such inventions, which was now bringing distant places and alien cultures closer together. The British, for example, now traveled in luxurious steamships from India to England within fifty days via Aden and the Red Sea (crossing 170 li of land at Suez to continue by ship in the Mediterranean) to Gibraltar and finally to the capital of England. "Fire-wheel ships travel very fast and do not fear the wind and waves."[61]

Hsu reported in his book that Westerners might further reduce
the distances between West and East by constructing huge canals
at Suez and Panama. This did not make him happy, for he realized
that China would then be subjected to increased pressures from
Western contact. "But while it is easy to construct canals connecting rivers, it is difficult to open canals between seas. Moreover, the
boundaries between two lands have been established by Heaven
and Earth to delimit East from West. Now that they desire to use
manpower to chisel through, would this not destroy [the distinc-
tion]?"[62]

Before concluding his treatment of Britain Hsu touched on
miscellaneous items and oddities. He described British uniforms
and the people's customs: marriage, division of inheritances between the sexes, monogamy, seven years' exile for crimes, and
British courtesies. "The British custom when guest and host meet
is to take off their hats [as a sign of] respect; each extends his right
hand and they mutually grasp [hands] as a ritual. Outside of kneel-
ing in worship to their god, they do not kowtow to their king."
He also found that "the men constantly obey the orders of their
women, and this is true of the whole state." In conclusion, the
author offered food for thought to Chinese who still regarded
Europeans as backward barbarians. "The British are tall and dazzling
white; their hair and eyes are either black or yellowish-red. *Their
clever schemes are precise; in their actions they firmly endure, and
their manner is brave and determined. Their resolution* [has made
Britain] *foremost of the various European states."*[63]

Other European States

In the extreme northwestern part of Europe were located the
two states of Sweden and Norway, "now united as one state."
"The shape of the land is like a palm-leaf fan hanging down."[64]
While this region held wild barbarian tribes in ancient times, in the
early Sung dynasty a headman brought the tribes together to build
cities and establish the state of Sweden. Similar events occurred in
Norway and Denmark.

As was true for all states examined by his book, Hsu recorded the historical development of these Scandinanvian countries: their religion, customs, systems of government, products, and military and naval power. Thus the Chinese reader found religious wars, a succession of rulers with strange-sounding names, such as Chi-li-szu-te-na (Christina), queen of Sweden who *"abdicated and went to study in Rome."* Hsu followed the history of these states up to the Congress of Vienna, when the ambassadors of the various states of Europe met to decide on future political divisions after the wars of Napoleon. That they had forced Sweden to return territory to Denmark perhaps served as a model in the minds of Hsu's readers at the end of the century, when China looked to European powers to pressure Japan out of the Liaotung Peninsula.

Sweden was extremely cold, and the north was barren land. Farming even in the south had always been difficult, so the farmers suffered from poverty. Trade in lumber, metals, and furs supported the state. Norway merited only passing notice. Her people were sincere and generous and they were known as good traders. Even Lapland appeared in Hsu's book; here in the winter *"the sun is not seen for seventy-five days, while in the summer there is no night and the moon cannot be seen for seventy-five days."* [65]

Hsu concluded that Sweden was the poorest state in Europe, unable either to cause trouble or to protect itself. Its merchant ships came only occasionally to Canton. Denmark also was only a small state. Because its merchant ships often flew a yellow flag, the Cantonese called it the Yellow Flag State. The author portrayed Denmark in much the same manner as Sweden. This state had fought England and Norway, but had suffered serious losses during the recent wars of Napoleon. It had lately however become a fairly prosperous trading state. Its products included grains, cattle, and horses, most of which went to Britain in trade. This state too was quite weak in comparison to the other European powers.

Austria's first merchant ships to Canton had flags picturing two eagles, so the Cantonese had called Austria the Double Eagle State. Hsu briefly traced the history of Austria. Because the king had married the woman ruler of Hungary, the two territories had united and Austria therefore had become a large state. The Chinese reader was introduced to Charles V. Hsu listed the numerous wars of Austria, many of which were fought in support of Catholicism. Poland had been carved up like a melon by Austria, Russia, and Prussia; thus Austria had grown even larger. Napoleon of France took the state and attacked its neighbors in all directions. After these wars all of Europe's ambassadors came to Austria's capital to deliberate. All of the states defeated by Napoleon had their boundaries restored. Later Austria became involved in a long war with Turkey.

The state produced mercury, cinnabar, and iron. It possessed broad and fertile pasture lands which each year produced cows, horses, and sheep by the "billions." Fine cloth and glass were also produced. Vienna, a city of 300,000 people, was the location of a large and elegant palace. The king did not follow standard rules of decorum, but went out among the people. Because of this the people were close to him. Austria's cities had colleges, some of which held 70,000 volumes.[66]

Hsu viewed the Austro-Hungarian empire, with brief comments for each section. For example, he described Venice as the largest port of the Mediterranean in ancient times. Ten thousand vessels gathered there, and *"it controlled the seas for over a thousand years."* Now, he observed, Venice had declined and there was little commerce. He also presented an historical sketch of Hungary, which Hsu explained had been occupied in ancient times by a Western branch of the Hsiung-nu. Hungary produced gold, silver, copper, grain, fodder, timber, cattle, swine, and wine.[67] In conclusion Hsu observed that Austria was the foremost of the various German states. Of Europe's powerful states Austria was, however, only fourth; it followed Britain, France, and Russia.

Hsu found Prussia, also a large state in Europe, inferior to Austria in terms of state power. Cantonese had labeled this state the Lone Eagle State *"also because of the picture on the flags of their merchant ships."* Following a short outline of Prussia's history, Hsu found Prussian resistance after Napoleon's victory of great interest.

The Prussian people were unhappy with French administration and thought of their former rule. *Because the people hated the French, the king entered an alliance with other various states to attack* [France]. France's armies were dispersed and they abandoned [Prussia's] land. Prussia regained its original territory. The king then repaired the state's administration. *He encouraged the farmers and artisans, established centers of learning, and gave aid to traveling merchants. Therefore the common people* (pai-hsing) *felt close to him. The people of neighboring states all clamored to emulate him.* [Prussia] *became an illustrious state in the West . . . The people are regulated so that when they come of age workers enter the trades and the cultivated enter their studies. Otherwise their parents are punished. The men who are over twenty all enter military studies for three years before returning. Because in the autumn of each year they are drilled and inspected, rewarded and punished, the soldiers of the state are numerous and strong.*[68]

The Prussians believed in Protestantism. Berlin, the capital, measured thirty-six li on each side, with fifteen gates, twenty-two markets, and a population of 220,000. Inside the walls were orphanages, hospitals for sick travelers and for the poor, colleges for the military and liberal arts, and armories. The king's palace was 460 feet long, 270 feet wide, and 100 feet high. The various residences of officials were clean and constantly kept in good repair. Schools were also provided for the various trades. *"Iron work is the finest,"* wrote Hsu, *"the workmanship is as detailed as if it were made of gold or silver. The porcelain is especially good; it is strong yet delicate, and it is not inferior to that produced in China. Yet it is very inexpensive."*[69]

After surveying in no little detail the many divisions of Prussia, the cities, products, and trade, Hsu offered a short conclusion:

The Europeans all call Prussia a perfect state. Although it does not equal Austria in power and size, *in terms of its governmental policies, making it a friendly neighbor who does not grab and attack, it is far superior to Austria.* Frederick William III suffered at the hands of strong neighbors, but he turned defeat into achievement. *His custom was to support learning and spread wealth out over the land. In regulating the army he used the idea of ancient* [China] *to make soldiers of farmers.* How can [we] consider them as wild barbarians and disregard them?[70]

Hsu's coverage of the remaining German states, while complete in geographical scope, added little of interest. He discussed the various states historically and showed their place in recent European developments. Short notes of their governing apparatus, products, and other information were included. But some of the author's general conclusions are noteworthy. Hsu's positive view of the German states quite probably reflects the influence of the Pomeranian Protestant missionary and publicist in Canton, Karl Gützlaff, as does the author's distaste for Catholic Germans:

Those who live in the northern [German states] are all strong and healthy; they are pure and good by nature and they love to study the arts. The Southerners' habits are wasteful; their day is spent in drunkenness and overeating, and they have no plans for the future . . . Germany occupies the center of Europe, *and its eminence* [in Europe] *is like that of China* [in Asia]. *The people are intelligent, with broad and penetrating* [minds]. *They are considered as nobles in the West. The separate areas have set up ranks of nobility similar to the feudal ranks of the* [Hsia, Shang, and Chou dynasties]. A local leader is made king [by the various states]. Although Austria daily extended her territory, it did not retain the name of ruler of the German states. *Instead several tens of minor nobles pass on their lands to descendants; that the various large states do not plot to swallow or bite them is because* [the German states] *have retained the ideas of the ancients.* Also, the founding fathers of the states of France and England were all Germans. When a [ruling family] of one of the several states of Europe dies out, that state at

once summons a German noble or the eldest son of a prince
to be king. Large states like Britain, and small like Belgium
and Greece have all done this. In [Germany] *is stored the
kingly spirit of the West.*[71]

But Switzerland appears to have been even more attractive to
Hsu. The people there enjoyed a government without bothersome
restrictions; their custom was to be dependable and honest. The
state had had no wars for several hundred years. It did not have a
king, but instead a local official was selected by various areas to
manage the affairs of state. This arrangement had been followed
for over five hundred years, and the state had suffered no disturbances. Switzerland was the envy of all Westerners, as it appears also
to have been at least to one Chinese.

> *Switzerland is the Shangrila* [lit., "Plum Blossom Fountain"]
> *of the West. It punishes oppressive and avaricious officials*
> [lit., "large rats"] *by prosecuting and removing them* [from
> office]. *The lords and subordinate officials rule independently
> without trouble. The nobles each are accustomed to maintain
> strong armies, but there is nothing of consequence* [for them
> to do] *and they are entirely ignored. How can this not be
> considered rare?* The American, [Doctor] Cumming, often
> traveled to this land and praised the wonderful scenery and
> pure customs. What a pity it is in a far-off border region so
> that it was not gradually refined by [China's] uniform rules
> of propriety and music.[72]

Hsu's portrayal of the European world thus revealed to Chinese
readers some of the basic features of the states that now appeared at
China's gates. Though Hsu's account was marred by the inclusion of
superstitious Eight Trigrams theories regarding the effect of geographical location on human behavior, his use of Western-derived materials
provided more explicit information, and even statistical details, than
had been available before in an appealing and well-integrated presentation. From Hsu's book emerged convincing evidence that Western
states possessed many admirable, even desirable, features.

Hsu admitted that the high cultural level of the West had been attained without the benefits of China's ritual and music. He even compared the development of European nations with states in ancient China. Europe of the nineteenth century, fractured into small political units, appeared to be similar in some respects to the China of the Warring States period (403-221 B.C.) on the eve of the first empire. In an attempt to outdo its neighbors each European state, according to Hsu, sought wealth and power—an idea in China closely linked with Legalist thought, the ideology that had brought at least temporary success to the ancient empire builders of the Ch'in (221-206 B.C.). Basing their growth on ancient political, economic, and social systems, many of these Western states had recognized the utility of trade and had made it the basis of their income and power, thereby automatically reducing the tax load of farmers. Powerful "gentry" governed most of these states and some states had even eliminated their monarchs. Thus competing for hegemony in Europe, the various states had sent out ships to explore the world and discover new markets as sources of wealth that could be translated into power.

The Protestant states of Europe, full of dedicated, hard-working, frugal, and ingenious people, greatly excited Hsu's interest. In such states the evils of Catholicism, which had proved so bothersome in China, had been rejected. These states served as the home bases in modern times for the development of industry and new modes of transportation as well as appealing forms of political organization which reduced the gap between the people and their leaders.

The major states of Europe now shared the benefits of efficient organization. Even a backward state such as Russia had quickly caught up with its Western competitors by learning their methods to achieve power. With each state aiming at specific political and power-oriented goals, the people felt a close identity with their state and fought with a patriotic zeal that made even small states strong. These states possessed colleges, technical schools, libraries, good hospitals—all institutions suggestive of higher cultural accomplishments—and large cities with impressive palaces and public buildings. Such features in Western states indicated a cultural level closer to that of China than to the Inner Asian or Southeast Asian examples that theretofore had appeared as typical forms of non-Chinese or Chinese-inspired culture.

The wealth of these Western states was so great (resulting in large part from the rapid production of goods by machine) that at least one, France, required no trade with China! Indeed, silks from France and Italy, tea from India, cotton for cloth from India and the United States, and European-produced porcelain were all as good as China's and, because of more efficient production methods, could be sold more reasonably.

For Hsu's readers, who in later years began to search for models outside of China, his introduction to European states provided appealing suggestions for further study. Whether they looked at Hsu's ideal states of Prussia, Austria, and Switzerland, or at the more powerful states of Britain, France, and Russia, Chinese intellectuals who studied the *Ying-huan chih-lueh* in the 1860's and later (as well as Japanese readers of the 1860's) discovered a variety of intriguing organizational forms.

European nations thus began to serve as models for Chinese in search of modern political forms and the secrets of state power.

Chapter X

DESPAIR IN AFRICA, HOPE IN AMERICA

The three final chapters of the *Ying-huan chih-lueh*, all comparatively short, rounded out Hsu's world with the presentation of the African, North American, and South American continents. North Africa, identified by the author as a part of Europe's Mediterranean basin, had supported some of the ancient cultures that had served as bases of Western civilization. "Black" Africa to the south was of comparatively little interest to Hsu. Here, in addition to his geographical information, he simply found more examples of European movement into regions replete with resources but weak in organization and state power. As additional evidence of the rapacity of some Western states, he described the slave trade that centered on this continent.

In contrast, Hsu was excited about America. Here he found a potential center for a third world power that might balance European strength and reduce its pressure on China. The space allotted in his work to the United States far exceeded that for any other country (10,128 characters compared to 7,488 for the nearest competitor, Britain). The disproportionate attention to this nation in Hsu's treatise indicates the author's reliance on a more complete source (Elijah C. Bridgman's history) as well as his fascination with the unique system he found in this nation, so much of which seemed in harmony with old Confucian values.[1] Hsu, indefatigable foe of the British also was enthralled with American success in the face of British military power.

The Dark Continent and European Power

Africa appeared to Hsu as a broad continent about one-third the size of Asia. Though large, it was half covered by deserts. Hot and inhospitable in many parts, Africa had been the home of a famous ancient state in the north—Egypt. But now Islamic peoples controlled the northern regions. To the south lived tribes of "black barbarians," and in these regions the Portuguese had established ports. Here were also ports belonging to Britain, France, the United States, Holland, and Denmark.[2] The black people of Africa, variously called Negroes or Hottentots, were purchased as slaves by many states.

Hsu reviewed the many states of North Africa. He found that in Egypt, a state established during the early Hsia dynasty, the earliest roots of Western civilization were formed.[3] The author cited Biblical material to explain the ancient origins of the people of Egypt. In the earliest times, after a great flood, there was an old man named Noah with sons Shem, Ham, and Japheth. Ham's son, Mizraim, during the Hsia dynasty, founded a state in North Africa. Here he taught the people to build dwellings; he established a government with officials and devised a system of writing. Several generations later came Abraham, who saved his people from enemies; from that time on they learned methods of military preparations. Thus the civilization of the area grew increasingly sophisticated. Meanwhile Europe was still inhabited by aboriginal barbarians, but toward the end of the Hsia period civilization was carried to Greece. Neighboring peoples all submitted to Egypt, and thereby learned her arts.

But Egypt eventually lost its power to Greece and Persia, later becoming a dependency of Rome and falling several centuries afterward before the onslaught of Islam. Turkey took Egypt; Napoleon seized the state. But after Napoleon, Egypt returned to Turkish domination before establishing itself as an independent state. This caused a large war involving, beside the two belligerents, Russia, Britain, and France. Finally Egypt became an "outer tributary" of Turkey.[4]

Hsu noted Egypt's mummies and the pyramids, one of Verbiest's Seven Wonders. He described the destruction of the state's libraries when Islam struck. *"In the capital was a large repository holding 700,000 books, said to be the West's literary collection. When the Moslems attacked they used these books as fuel to cook food."* [5] Hsu compared this to Ch'in Shih Huang-ti's burning of the books in ancient China.

Carthage, Phoenicia, the great Sahara, Tripoli, Tunisia,

Algeria, and Morocco were all treated in Hsu's examination of North Africa. But beside his interest in mundane geographical arrangements, climate, products, and customs, the author continued to stress the two themes of ancient cultures of the Western world and recent encroachment by European states on these early centers of Western civilization.

Hsu considered Phoenicia the West's first maritime merchant state. Before China's Hsia dynasty the people there did not travel from place to place; but in the middle years of that dynasty the wise men there for the first time fashioned boats and carts. With these they traded what they possessed for what they did not and thus became prosperous. Greece had learned the methods of Phoenicia, so that eventually she controlled the Mediterranean ports and became a *"wealthy state with a strong army* (kuo fu, ping ch'iang)."[6]

Sea power as a component of state power had been as important in ancient times as in more recent days. In the long wars between Rome and Carthage, for example, the Romans were unable to resist Carthage's superior fleet. One of the Carthaginian warships fell into Roman hands. They copied its plans and built a hundred like it in three months; then they learned how to navigate these craft.[7] Thus, by copying the devices of the enemy, a state could once again compete and even emerge victorious.

Central Africa appeared no less inhospitable as a region than the North African area. The winds caught the desert sands and blackened the skies. It was unbearably hot, with little water. Travelers often died of thirst or were covered up by the sand. On the deserts travelers all used camels, however, which they could kill in emergencies to drink their blood or the water in their humps. Here, in Kordofan, Darfur, and the Sudan, the inhabitants were all Islamic black barbarians. The area furthermore was afflicted with disease so that people from outside could not survive. If visitors were not killed by pestilence, the natives themselves would oblige. The many British explorers who had been sent there had all died.[8] Little was therefore known of the place.

In the northern section of East Africa Islamic tribes lived

intermixed with the black barbarians. But further south there were only the blacks. These natives gathered gold dust and medicinal herbs for a living. Many of the people here had also accepted Islam. In Mozambique the Portuguese had established several settlements; but Hsu observed that because Portugal had become weak, little commercial activity centered on such places. Now the Portuguese only sold "black mouths" as slaves. Hsu wrote that such slaves were found in each of the various barbarian residences in Macao. He condemned this trade in humans, and explained that only weak and poor states like Portugal now engaged in it. Most of the slaves of the Europeans came from West Africa. When the ships of the various states arrived there to buy them, they transported two or three hundred each trip like goods or cattle. The continent of America had received an unusually large number of slaves, and they were used to irrigate gardens, plow fields, plant coffee, and make sugar.[9]

European states all desired to take control of African territories, but because they feared malaria they dared not go inland. They set up ports along the coast, and these were gradually being developed. In Senegambia, for example, the French had established three ports along the coast to trade with the black barbarians. They had installed cannon emplacements here for protection and each year about thirty merchant vessels came from France to trade. British ports also were located here. Commercial houses in charge of the trade had been established, and British warships patrolled these waters against slavers.[10]

In Guinea the British likewise had a commercial foothold; but they also had opened up centers of learning in order to "change the black barbarians with the teachings of Jesus."[11] Even the United States had recently taken land to the south of the British which they called Liberia. Slaves lived there, and they were taught the arts of civilization. In the area were also ports of Holland and Denmark.

Having briefly treated the various states and places of South Africa as well as the islands off the continent's coast, where he found further evidence of European penetration. Hsu concluded his short chapter on Africa with a general summary:

The continent of Africa, if viewed according to the directions of the Eight Trigrams, is in the southwest. *Its atmosphere is heavy and murky; its people are stupid. Consequently, even though since the beginning of the world there have already passed thousands and ten-thousands of years,* [the people] *are simple and sorrowful, appearing as* [if they were living] *in the most ancient times.* [They] *were unable to develop* [a civilization] *by themselves.*[12]

America: New Nations against Europe

Hsu discovered in America an extraordinary situation. This huge land which formed two continents and stretched nearly from pole to pole, though originally an underdeveloped area that had been colonized by the European powers, now supported states strong enough to throw off European domination. This new world had given birth to George Washington, who founded the United States. Latin American states had followed his example; Hsu noted that only the poorer lands of America still remained under European control.

In addition to purely geographical information on the United States, the author devoted considerable space to descriptions of the nation's political system, commerce, finance, military power, transportation facilities, education, religion, and history. He also noted some of the explorers, the process of colonization, and the story of the American Revolution—with special attention given to the role of George Washington. Hsu presented a kaleidoscope of information about the United States to Chinese readers of the mid-nineteenth century.

In his descriptions of the twenty-six states of the union, the author in all cases followed a similar pattern. He located each state by citing all of the states that bordered on it. A description of the basic topography and climate followed. In most cases Hsu briefly sketched the state's history.[13] He listed products and natural resources, dealt with the state's commerce, and introduced the name of the state capital. If there were famous colleges in the state, Hsu mentioned them, though not by name. The administrative system of the first state in the list, Maine, was cursorily described; for the systems of other states, Hsu offered only short comments, usually simply stating that the state's system was identical to Maine's. The author presented population figures last, as well as miscellaneous comments.

Hsu used Chinese analogues to introduce the geography of the United States. For example, twenty-three states were compared in size, directly or indirectly, to four standards familiar to the Chinese: Chekiang, Fukien, Chihli (Hopei), and the size of an average hsien in China. According to this method, Hsu noted that New Hampshire was one-third the size of Maine, which he had already compared to the size of Chekiang. Though such comparisons were valid only in the broadest sense, they served to clarify his information for Chinese readers.

In his introductory notice of America Hsu located the continent and presented a general description of the area:

Explaining [America's] situation in terms of the globe, *the three continents are on the east, while America is on the west. The three continents are on the face of the globe, while America is on the back of the globe.* America is a continent [by itself] and is not connected with the other three continents. It is divided into two lands, northern and southern. *The northern land is in the shape of a flying fish. The southern and northern parts look like the thighs of a man wearing billowing trousers; they are connected by a narrow waist in the middle.*[14]

From the beginning of the world [until recently] America had no contact with other continents. *Its original inhabitants possess the five senses, the members and trunk of the body. They are similar to Chinese* [in appearance]. *Their complexion is purplish-red, like copper, or like the color of palm fiber. They cut their hair, leaving several inches remaining; this is gathered on top the head and bound together in a topknot.* This region originally had no cows, horses, sheep, swine, dogs, or cats. When the Spanish first arrived and came ashore riding horses, *the natives observing from the shore thought horse and man were one, and they all fled in terror.*[15]

During the Hung-chih period of the Ming dynasty [1488-

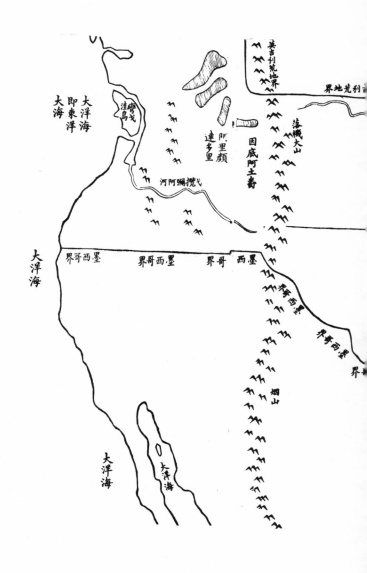

THE UNITED STATES AND LANDS TO THE WEST

界地荒利吉英
界地荒利吉英
湖爾力必蘇
界地荒利吉英
界地威利吉英
關沙河

因底阿士蕎

干遜
威士
華呀
衣
休侖湖
密執安湖
密執安
湖蘇比利
界地屬利吉英
界地屬利吉英

奧倫諾爾

英釐安納

阿海倭
湖阿塵衣副安
伊釐湖
爾約紐
賓夕爾勒
尼安

淮溝的
紐罕什爾
緬

士麻薩諸
得羅
得嘉
島

因底阿士蕎

河釐爾蘇密

密蘇爾釐

阿甘色
伊的阿
西納田
理馬
蘭阿
來阿
尼爾阿
勿爾言
開倫
新折爾西
拉華得

得
密士失必河
密士失必
阿拉巴麻
若耳治
那爾勒
北喀
南喀
爾勒
那爾勒

大西洋海

得撒界
魯西安納
得撒界

佛勒爾勒

加勒海

1506] a Spanish officer named Columbus sailed a great vessel westward in search of new land. He arrived at the archipelagoes of the Caribbean Sea, and he [then] knew there was the spacious land of America. He first took hold of Colombia . . . [Later] the Spaniard Cortez learned of Mexico's abundant wealth. He led troops to attack Mexico and snatched away the country. He then expanded to the south. The Spaniards gradually spread and settled in each country of western South America, like the gnawing of silkworms.

The climate of each state of [the United States of] *America is agreeable. The North is like Yen* [Hopei] *and Chin* [Shansi], *but the South is similar to Kiangsu and Chekiang. The sea-coast is long and level; there are no deserts and little malaria.* (The South has a little, but it is not very severe.) The land is level and fertile; it is suitable for the five grains. Cotton is of the highest quality and is the most abundant product. Both England and France obtain their cotton here. All varieties of vegetables and fruit are [grown] here. Tobacco is also very good, and it is carried in trade to distant places. The products of the mountains are coal, salt, iron, and zinc . . . South and North America are several ten thousand li in length, but the essence [i.e., best land] is that in the United States. *The favorable climate and fertile land are almost as good as that of China.* The English crossed ten thousand li of sea to get the place, and this can be called obtaining the pearl [i.e., hitting the bull's eye]. They developed it for more than two hundred years, and it quickly achieved a prosperity which has overflowed into the rest of the world.[16]

An investigator in search of effective state mechanisms, Hsu was excited by the appealing, and even unique, features of this rich nation.

The government of [the United States of] *America is very simple* [i.e., there is no red tape]. *The taxes are also light.* Every year a census is taken. Every two years out of 47,700 people, a person distinguished in ability and knowledge is selected (*hsuan*) to live in the capital to participate in the country's government. In the capital where the general commander (*tsung-t'ung-ling*) resides, the states have established an assembly (*kung-hui*), and each state selects two virtuous scholars (*hsien-shih*) to be in the assembly. They participate in deciding great matters of government—such as making treaties and war, and [regulating] commerce, taxation, and stipends. Six years is the length of office. Each state appoints six judges to take charge of penalties. They are also recommended and selected (*t'ui-hsuan*) to fill the office. If there is one who is unjust, the multitude (*ch'ün*), after deliberation, dismisses him.

[The Americans] have not established titles of king and count, and they do not follow rules of succession. *The public organs are entrusted to public opinion (kung-lun). There has never been a system of this sort in ancient or modern times. This is really a wonder . . .*[17]

From among the commanders (*cheng-t'ung-ling*) of each state, a general commander is recommended, *and he alone governs the affairs of making treaties and engaging in war. Every state obeys his orders.* The method used to recommend and select him (*t'ui-che*) is the same as that used to select the commanders of the various states. The term of office is four years, but if he holds a second term, it is eight years. From Washington to the present, the country has been established sixty-odd years. (Washington died of an illness in 1798.) There have been altogether nine men as general commander. The present general commander was recommended by Virginia . . .[18]

[The District of] Columbia is situated at the tail end of the western branch of the bay of Maryland [i.e., Chesapeake Bay]. It is northwest of Virginia and it straddles the boundaries of the two states [of Virginia and Maryland] for forty li. It is the capital of the United States. Formerly, after Washington defeated Britain, he lived in Columbia. It was set aside to be the governing place of the general commander. The gentry (*shen-ch'i*) of the Union all gather in this place to discuss the state's policies. Because the city was founded by Washington, and because he was *the founding father (ch'uang-yeh chih tsu) of the Union, it was named Washington.* Here is the general commander's palace, a hall for discussion of affairs of state, and civil and military yamens . . .

To the west there is a different city called Georgetown; here there is a college and an armory where cannon are cast. On the opposite shore [of the Potomac] is another city called Alexandria, where there is an armory and an orphanage. There are 43,000 inhabitants . . .[19]

Each of the former territories [i.e., colonies] were separately established as states. Each state has one commander and an assistant commander to assist him. (There are states with one assistant and some states with several.) The term of office is four years. (There are also states which change the office every year or every other year.) The crowd (*chung*) comes together to discuss the matter, and if they all say he is worthy, the commander holds office for another four years. (After eight years they are not allowed to continue in office.) Otherwise the assistant commander will be selected as governor. If he is not in harmony with the expectations of the people, they carry out [an election by] recommendation and selection (*hsing t'ui-che*). *The country and city elders write out the surname and given name* [of their choice] *and cast this into a small box. When that has been done, the box is opened to see who has the most* [recommendations]; *that person is established in office, regardless of whether he is an official or a commoner. A commander who has retired from office is as before equal with the common people* [i.e., there is no difference in rank] . . .

The United States (*Ho-chung-kuo*) are all in the east. When Washington founded the country there were only ten-odd states. Later the various states nearby came into the [Union] one by one. There were also some that were divided, so there are altogether twenty-six states. The land that has not been developed in the western region is inhabited by aborigines. In the newly-developed land, hunters first killed its bears, deer, and wild cows [bison]. People without occupations were permitted to develop the wild land. When forty thousand people were gathered together, a city was founded and the land was called a territory (*pu*). These places are in addition to the states. Today, beside the states, there have already been added three territories. The capital, Washington, where the general commander resides, is not included in the number of states and territories . . . By 1840 the population was somewhat over 17,169,000 . . .[20]

In the United States the [annual] revenue from taxes is about 40,000,000 dollars. The salaries of the civil officials total 4,760,000 dollars. The salaries of army officers and soldiers equal 4,300,000 dollars. Naval officers and sailors receive 4,570,000 dollars. Miscellaneous expenses are 3,800,000 dollars. The cost of land development is 13,000,000 dollars. Although the general commander controls the finances, *his own salary is set at 10,000 dollars, and he cannot get even a copper more for his private use* . . .[21]

The set number of professional soldiers of the United States does not exceed ten thousand, and these are distributed to various forts and passes. Beside this, with the exception of scholars (*ju-shih*), doctors, and astronomers, *the farmers, laborers, and merchants from twenty to forty years of age can be conscripted by the officials. They are issued* [identification] *cards. They serve as a militia.* Food and weapons are provided by the individual. *In peacetime each works at his own occupation, but if there is war, they all enter the ranks together.* Various ranks of officers have been set up, *but these offices have only rank and no stipend. Every year while the land is not being worked they gather for exercises.* This militia is something in excess of 1,700,000 men. *This is like the method used by the ancients* [of China] *to make troops of the farmers.*[22]

[When Washington retired from office, he] left only twenty war ships and ten thousand professional soldiers. *Yet the land is very extensive and the natural resources are abundant. Each section of the country is in agreement to unite at a command, so all the great states maintain cordial relations with it and there is not one which dares insult it. From the time of the treaty of peace with Britain, sixty-odd years have passed and there has been no war.* Its merchant ships come to Kwangtung every year, but their number is less than those of Britain . . . Because its ships fly a flag with flowers [i.e., stars] the people of Kwangtung call it State of the Flower Flag (*Hua-ch'i-kuo*). (Its flag is square, with alternating red and white [stripes]; in the right corner there is a separate square of black on which are placed white spots picturing the Big Dipper.) . . .[23]

There are many small rivers and these have been connected to build canals. They also build fire-wheel carts, using rocks with melted iron poured on them for the road in order to facilitate their movement. In one day they can travel over three hundred li. Fire-wheel ships are very numerous. They move back and forth on the rivers and seas like shuttles; this is so because the land produces coal. (Fire-wheel ships must burn coal, for the power [generated] from wood is too weak and cannot be used.) . . . The states all believe in the Western religion [Christianity]. [The people] enjoy discussing scholarly matters, and colleges are established everywhere. The scholars are divided into three categories: 1) those who study astronomy, geography, and Christianity; 2) those who study medicine to cure illnesses; and, 3) those who study law to manage trials and imprisonments . . . [24]

In his treatment of the United States, Hsu pursued the theme of George Washington in the Revolutionary War and as president. He viewed Washington as comparable to the Chinese ancients who made their names in the *san-tai* (that is, the Hsia, Shang, and Chou dynasties). That Washington and his countrymen had made a paper tiger of the British lion evoked much interest from Hsu, who so recently had witnessed China's defeat by Britain. For Hsu, as for so many later Chinese modernizers and finally even revolutionaries —such as Tsou Jung, Chang Ping-lin, and the editors of the *Min Pao*, journal of the T'ung-meng hui—Washington's charisma crossed cultural boundaries; he became a hero with universal appeal.[25]

When England acquired the land of North America, they drove out the aborigines and occupied their fertile land. People from the three islands [England, Ireland, and Scotland] were sent to fill the land, and they hurried to it like water rushing to a pool. Unemployed French, Dutch, Danes, and Swedes also crossed over the sea. The land gradually developed, and it turned out to be a fertile place. The British had a high official reside there and maintain it. Cities were laid out along the coast, and taxes were used to enrich Britain. Trade flourished and gradually became very abundant. *Because of this, sudden wealth and power were achieved* . . .

During the Ch'ien-lung period Britain and France went to war; this war lasted for several years without a final decision. Many ways were devised to extract money, and taxes doubled. According to the former regulations, the dealers in tea were to pay a tax, but the British issued an order that the purchaser also had to pay a tax. The Americans were unable to endure this. In 1775 the gentry all gathered together in a board and wanted to deliberate with the resident headman (*ta-ch'iu*). The headman drove them away and directed the levying of taxes even more vigorously. The crowd was enraged and threw a ship's tea into the sea. They plotted to raise troops to oppose the British. There was one named Washington who was from another part of the United States. He was born in 1731. At the age of ten his father died, and his mother raised him. *At an early age he had great ambitions, and he was naturally gifted in both civil and military affairs. His bravery and eminence surpassed all others.* He was a military officer for the British. Just at the time when a war was being fought with France, local southern barbarians (*t'u-man*) plundered the southern area. Washington led troops to oppose them . . . The British general did not record his achievement. The people of his native place wanted to choose Washington as chief (*ch'iu-chang*), but *Washington feigned sickness and declined; he returned to his home, closed the gates, and did not go out . . .* [26]

When the people rebelled against Britain, they insisted that Washington be the commander-in-chief. This situation arose very suddenly so that weapons, powder, provisions, and fodder were all lacking. But Washington encouraged the people with his patriotic zeal. When the arrangements had been made, they besieged a large city. Suddenly a great wind arose, and the vessels were all scattered. Washington jumped at this chance and took the city. Later the British army assembled in great force and attacked. Washington's army was defeated and frightened; it wanted to disband and scatter. *Washington, with a sense of duty, gathered the remaining army together,*

*and again they fought and won. The bloody war lasted for
eight years with recurring setbacks, but* [the people] *were
repeatedly roused to determination. Washington's resoluteness
did not diminish, and the British army was becoming old.*
France raised an entire army of men which crossed the sea
[to America]. The French army and Washington's army
attacked the British from both sides. Spain and Holland also
checked the advance of British troops and encouraged Britain
to make peace. Britain was unable to withstand, so a treaty
was made with Washington. The boundary of the neighboring
country [Canada] was delineated. The northern region of cold,
barren land still belonged to Britain, but the fertile land south
of the border was all given to Washington. This was in 1782 . . .

*When Washington had settled the country, he handed over
his military authority and desired to return to his fields.* The
people were unwilling to part with him and chose him to be
the state's ruler (*kuo-chu*). Washington then said to the people
that *it was selfish to take a state and pass it on to one's descendants; he said it was better to choose a person of virtue
for the responsibility of governing people* . . .

*From the time when Washington made peace with Britain
and ended the war, he devoted special attention to agriculture
and commerce. He issued a command that if from that time
on any commander plotted to seize another state's port, to
strip away fat from the people, to begin military operations,
or to cause hatreds to arise, the people should punish him*
(chu) . . .[27]

As for Washington, he was an extraordinary man. *In raising
a revolt, he was more courageous than* [Ch'en] *Sheng or* [Wu]
Kuang.[28] *In carrying out an occupation, he was braver than
Ts'ao* [Ts'ao] *or Liu* [Pei].[29] *When he took up the three-foot,
double-edged sword and opened up the boundaries for ten
thousand li, he did not assume the throne and was unwilling
to begin a line of succession. Moreover he invented a method
of selection* (t'ui-chü). [He believed in] *a world to be shared
by all people, and he swiftly carried out the traditions of the
san-tai* . . .[30] He governed his state with reverence and respected
good customs. He did not esteem military achievements; he
was very different from [the rulers] of other states. I have

seen his portrait. His bearing is imposing and excellent Ah! Can he not be called a hero?[31] . . . *Of all the famous Westerners of ancient and modern times, can Washington be placed in any position but first?*[32]

Indeed, for Hsu the idealized Washington fit an ancient Confucian ideal expressed in the *Analects*: "Tzu-kung said, If a ruler not only conferred wide benefits upon the common people, but also compassed the salvation of the whole State, what would you say of him? Surely, you would call him Good? The Master said, It would no longer be a matter of 'Good.' He would without doubt be a Divine Sage. Even Yao and Shun could hardly criticize him."[33]

Latin America

Central and South American states also appeared in the last chapter of Hsu's record of the world. Hsu reported that Mexico produced two-thirds of the West's silver money, and that many of the other states of the region were famous for gold and silver mines. Indeed, it was the wealth of the area that had from the first attracted the rapacious Spanish. The author found that even on this isolated continent of America an ancient state had achieved a tolerable degree of civilization. "In ancient times in North America, [where] the United States is and to the north, there were only scattered wild barbarians who had not formed tribes (*pu-lo*). Only in Mexico did a state arise in early times. *It had a walled city, temples, a king, and officials. They developed a pictographic writing system, and there were laws and regulations.*"[34]

This ancient state, Hsu observed, had fallen over a thousand years before, so little was known about it. But in the early reign of Hung-chih (1488–1506) of the Ming dynasty the Spanish sent Columbus in search of new land and he learned that Mexico was a source of gold. Consequently Cortez later came with soldiers to attack Mexico. This state was unable to resist Spanish cannon, so Spain defeated and occupied Mexico. Spain thus became wealthy. But after Washington rebelled against Britain and declared the independence of the United States, Mexico imitated him. In 1810

Mexico rebelled against Spanish control.[35] Mexico had then become
a leader of all the Spanish possessions, and this, according to Hsu,
spelled the end of Spanish power in America. Guatemala, for example, had already followed Mexico by rebelling against Spain.

In the pages devoted to Latin America Hsu described the
various states and islands according to the pattern established
throughout his book: the geographical setting, a short historical
sketch of the state or area, products, peoples, religion, government.
As already noted, the author took great interest in the reports that
Westerners would cut a canal at Panama to connect the Atlantic
and Pacific Oceans. "Westerners say a canal connecting the oceans
can be opened in this land. *If so, the oceans of the East and West
will be mixed together as one, and it will become ever so much
easier to sail westward to China's eastern border.*"[36]

Hsu recognized the immense economic potential of Latin
America. In addition to the area's production of precious metals
and stones, the author reported that this largely undeveloped and
underpopulated land already supported a variety of crops as well
as livestock. Many important ports now attracted ships from other
places to trade. Truly the Europeans who had emigrated to these
new lands of America were men of vision.

In his presentation of Africa and the Americas, Hsu reiterated
earlier themes—the movement of European power with its strong
organization into strategic and economically desirable positions in
Africa where weak native peoples were unable to resist; the great
benefits brought to Europeans in their discovery, due to superior
navigational techniques and mercantile incentives, of America's
wealth; the continued and growing threat to China of European
domination of the globe, with the specter of Western maritime
hegemony even more fearsome if the maritime routes were connected at Suez and Panama.

Yet for Hsu the American story was also an optimistic one,
for it was the story of a triumphant resistance movement against
European domination. Begun in the United States against Britain,
it was a cause already emulated by various South American states
against Spain. Thus Hsu, Confucian soldier against European

penetration of East Asia, spotted the United States as an anti-imperialist force and potent power worthy of detailed examination. Just as thirteen decades later Chinese leadership would find the United States a useful balance against Russian pressure, Hsu in the 1840's saw the new United States as a model for resistance to, and overthrow of, British colonial power.

Consequently Hsu was fascinated with the mechanisms of state power in this new and unique polity. Organization in line with high ideals that harmonized with ancient Chinese utopian views had brought the United States wealth and power—power to the people, a strong militia, and dedicated leadership working for the good of the people and the state rather than for the enhancement of personal or dynastic power.

Even federalism, with its fine balance between national and local control, caught the keen eye of this Chinese official. Aware of China's problems in balancing the needs of the central government with those of local interests, Hsu was struck by the vision of effective cooperation between national leaders and the "local gentry" who were supported by the people. For some of Hsu's readers such as Tseng Kuo-fan, the United States' system may have appeared particularly attractive because it suggested the possibility of modern state power through the enhancement of local control and initiative. Indeed, the father of nineteenth-century regional leaders in China religiously consulted Hsu's book in the 1860's and became known as an admirer of the United States.

Taught by his Confucian code to be the first to worry about questions concerning the polity, Hsu broadened the boundaries of his knowledge of the world after the Opium War. He found that Western states increasingly dominated the outside world. He thus attempted to deal with this threat to his state and culture by mollifying Westerners in order to provide time for China to learn the nature of their power and copy it. But his efforts to conciliate these aliens and explain the sources of Western power made him a subversive in the eyes of chauvinists. A decade after the Opium War they forced him from office. Hsu's return to positions of influence would have to wait till the truth of his message had been proved by another disastrous war with European states. Unfortunately, in terms of his status and influence within Chinese officaldom, for Hsu Chi-yü to publish the *Ying-huan chih-lueh* was to perish.

Chapter XI

RETURN TO CHINA'S HEARTLAND

After his removal from office and return to Wu-t'ai district
on December 21, 1852, Hsu presented a written notice to his
ancestors' spirits on January 2, 1853. In this document, delivered
to his ancestors of four generations while he offered sacrifice at the
family tomb, Hsu apologized for laying aside his mourning obligations while holding office since 1830. He then reviewed his career,
noting that as taotai first of Yen-Chien-Shao and then of T'ing-
Chang-Lung, "the barbarian miasma had just then become really
terrible. But through bitter hardships, I protected the border area
so there was no mishap."[1]

I, Chi-yü, respectfully obeyed my ancestors' instructions,
and I have lived a hard life [lit., "drinking ice and eating
bark"]; I have been incorrupt; I have tried to act with care
and diligence; I have used my strength to plan ways to save
[the dynasty]. Luckily, for the nine years I served in the
border areas [after the war] there were no disturbances. The
barbarian situation there became tranquil. But unexpectedly
things suddenly changed, and I was showered with criticism
each day. I solidly maintained my opinions and was unwilling
lightly to open hostilities on the border. Thereupon I was
attacked and criticized by sixty or seventy percent of the
censors on the review board. But the holy ruler pitied my
stupidity, and I was demoted to become subdirector of the
Court of the Imperial Stud.[2]

He concluded this document by apologizing to his ancestors, for
he could not now make a name to honor them; but he had nevertheless been incorrupt and had managed to leave office while still
in possession of his moral integrity.

Hsu, who had fought a losing battle in the maritime region
and was determined to give no pretext to powerful enemies, thus
retired to the Shansi of his past from the hugger-mugger of border

and court politics. Having floated with the conciliators along China's coast, he returned to Shansi's conservative elite, a group dedicated to values Hsu still shared despite his more realistic approach to foreign affairs. He moved back into a microcosm within China's culture island, and looked forward to peaceful years without worries or the responsibilities of office. For the next thirteen years Hsu would peek out at the world from this natural fortress of Shansi, which protected his Chinese heritage at least temporarily more effectively than had the emperor's batteries in Fukien and Kwangtung.

Like his ancestors who returned from official life to their homes in Shansi, Hsu hoped to revert to at least a part-time eremitism. Indeed, the title of his collected works, taken from the name of his study—*T'ui-mi-chai* (lit., "Retire to secrecy study")—suggests the intent of escapism. He observed that after twenty years in government service his "nerves were ruined," and that he returned home "with a worn-out spirit."[3] The contrasts between Fukien and his native Shansi were sharper than they had ever been before in his mind, and in numerous ways his home province awoke ideas which had been suppressed while he had been an official in the coastal march. Now he hoped to devote his time to scholarly interests, especially to resume his study of the Han dynasty and to do research in local history and geography.

Hsu's first project on returning to Shansi was to provide his family with lodging. He later noted that while serving in various offices under two emperors, he had been "working for the dynasty (*kuo-chia*) in its time of need." "I spent my fortune to help save the situation, as was only right. Although I was an official in the provinces for over ten years, the posts I had were extremely bitter. I carried out my duties, but did not provide my family with land."[4] He stated that he could not have bought a house for his family with the meager funds saved from his entire career on the coast. Even his friends chided him, saying, "In this world there is none so poor." But luckily he had been assigned to superintend the provincial examinations in Szechwan before his final dismissal, and he returned with over four thousand ounces of silver in his "bag."[5]

He had been able as a consequence finally to obtain a place at Tung-yeh-chen in Wu-t'ai district, his ancestral home, to "hide myself." "I built and thatched several rooms in which to come to roost." He also bought ten-odd *mou* of land "as a place to bury my family's bones." But with only this "bare house" he was unhappy and depressed. Since he was forced to earn money for his family's livelihood, he at last decided to begin tutoring.[6]

But the peaceful retirement Hsu hoped for was not to be. Soon after he settled at Tung-yeh-chen, rebels besieged Shansi. When the Taipings moved north in 1853 and attacked Huai-ch'eng (Tsinyang), Honan, the governor of Shansi, Ha-fen, ordered troops sent from T'ai-yuan to defend Tse-chou in the southern part of Shansi. But before this force arrived, the rebels had already crossed the Yellow River and occupied Yuan-ch'ü. Ha-fen thereupon moved to Yang-ch'eng to be closer to the action. The financial commissioner, Kuo Meng-ling, sent a memorial to the court requesting aid as soon as possible. Hsu, under the financial commissioner's seal and as a prestigious member of the local gentry, also memorialized. He cited numerous failures of the governor's defense organization and requested the replacement of Ha-fen by Wang Ch'ing-yun of Fukien.[7] When Ha-fen's position was taken by Heng-ch'un later in the year, Hsu, as a retired official and respected member of the local gentry, received orders to lead the local militia of T'ai-yuan and to defend Wu-t'ai.[8]

In this capacity Hsu was required to collect funds from the local gentry. That Wu-t'ai district was especially poor or niggardly, or that Hsu proved insufficiently persuasive, resulted in the collection of only about two thousand taels. Hsu complained that officials were more effective in collecting such funds.[9] In a letter to "three gentry" of T'ai-yuan, Hsu urged them to donate liberally and included a subtle threat. Though referring to himself as "younger brother" and saying he was much indebted to them, Hsu cited the example of the district of T'ai-ku. He had been requested, he related, to write letters to prominent gentry all over Shansi to ask for funds. But after two months the district of T'ai-ku, one of the Shansi banking centers, had produced only about forty thousand taels. Yet "this was a large district." So Hsu had discussed the problem with the financial commissioner, Kuo Meng-ling, and a prefect was sent to several districts to collect funds. In five days this prefect had collected over ninety thousand taels from T'ai-ku alone! [10]

With the 1853 rising of the Nien rebels in the area southeast of Shansi in response to the Taiping invasion of the area, Governor Heng-ch'un ordered Hsu in the spring of 1854 to direct the militia in the entire southeastern region of Shansi, still known at that time by the ancient name of Shang-tang. [11] This territory encompassed the two prefectures of Lu-an and Tse-chou, as well as the independent department of Liao-chou. Hsu thus journeyed to these places in 1854, when nearly sixty years old, to prepare a defense network against invasion from the south and east.

Later in 1854 Hsu's original nominee for governor, Wang Ch'ing-yun, replaced Heng-ch'un, and Hsu communicated with him at length, advising on the best methods to suppress the area's rebels and bandits. [12] He wrote that "at present south of the Yellow River to Yunnan and Kweichow . . . there is not one hundred li [square?] of territory which is peaceful." [13] But his own province was still comparatively peaceful.

Hsu ordered the civil and military officials of the region to collect maps of the various passes under his jurisdiction, so "at one glance the situation could be understood." And he directed reconnaissance operations against the rebels, at one time sending a "gentry" agent, Wu Lai-yü, to Kaifeng to size up the situation. [14] Knowledge of the enemy was crucial to Hsu, whether against coastal invaders or Chinese rebels.

Transportation in Shansi was a hardship Hsu continually complained of in his writings. The walled cities of the area were connected by imperial roads for passage of the uncomfortable two-wheeled springless carts of North China, but most of the region off the main routes could be reached only on foot or on the back of a small horse, donkey, or mule. The wheelbarrows of the plain proved impossible on the steep, narrow, unpaved mountain paths. Two years of work in the rugged southeast of Shansi thus were difficult for Hsu, now well past his prime. He found riding in the horse carts too unsettling; he preferred to walk on his tours of inspection. But after walking ten li or so he would lose his coordination. "How could this useless, feeble old man not be tired?" He thought of himself as "slow and cowardly;" "In charge of barbarian affairs in Fukien it was also because of this that I earned the emperor's displeasure." For whatever other reasons, but ostensibly because of bad health, in the eleventh month (December 9, 1855-January 7, 1856) of his second year in this service, Hsu resigned. He finally was able "for the first time to return home and wear ordinary clothing [i.e., to remove his official garb]."[15]

Hsu reported later in 1863 that he was in such poor health on leaving his duties in Shang-tang that he began to collect all the information he could locate on various types of exercises, "even from the *History of the* [Earlier] *Han.*" These included *t'ai-chi-ch'üan*, which he then practiced every day. "So now while my feet and arms are still weak, they are not limp; while my ears still are not good, I am not deaf; while my eyes require glasses, I can still write small characters." In later years he admitted he regularly took tonics which extended his teaching career by several years. "Only I still cannot tolerate cold or hot, or riding in horse carts."[16]

After his return to Wu-t'ai in 1856 the gentry of T'ai-yuan, capital of Shansi, invited him to teach at the Chin-yang Shu-yuan. He thanked them but did not accept the position. Instead he responded shortly thereafter to the invitation of "the officials and gentry" of P'ing-yao in the Fen Valley, one of the primary trading cities of Shansi, to be master of the Ch'ao-shan Shu-yuan.[17] He noted that because this school was run by gentry and not officials he was happy to be there.[18]

Before this time it is difficult to pin Hsu down to specific connections with Shansi merchants and bankers. No concrete evidence is found, for example, of close relationships while Hsu was a high official in the coastal region. Yet, in nineteenth-century China there was often an affinity of interests between officials and traders; it would be surprising indeed were there no contacts between Hsu the official in tea-rich Fukien and his wealthy Shansi provincials who played such an important role in the tea trade.

That Shansi bankers were involved in the opium trade, however, must have caused Hsu, unalterably opposed to its import and use, to be sensitive in his choice of contacts with this merchant community.[19]

The love of Shansi people for money was proverbial in the China of Hsu's time, and thrift was developed into a fine science.[20] Even Ku Yen-wu, a long-time resident of Shansi on whom Hsu relied so heavily in compiling the *Ying-huan chih-lueh*, had noted in the early Ch'ing period that the methods of the Shansi merchants were amazing. Rumors existed that Ku himself, famous scholar and founder of the *ching-shih* (statecraft) school, had close connections with Shansi banks and merchants.[21] Money and wealth were so honored in Shansi that a local proverb had it that if a Shansi man possessed three sons, the cleverest would become the head-servant in a yamen, the next would go into business, while only the fool would become a scholar.

Shansi merchants were the principal traders in the commerce with Russia, in addition to maintaining connections all over China and Tartary.[22] It has been estimated that in the early Ch'ing period their trade with Mongolia and Russia already amounted to about twenty million taels per annum. To secure this influence Shansi traders traveled as far as Moscow and across the camel caravan routes to Central Asia. Many of their activities in this widespread enterprise depended on private connections with officials.[23] And since the primary centers of trade in Shansi were the cities, or those nearby, where Hsu Chi-yü's father spent his last years, it is apparent that Hsu himself was not unfamiliar with these trading communities even before he attained high office.

Repeatedly in his *Ying-huan chih-lueh* Hsu revealed the crucial significance of mercantile activities as an ingredient of national power. Furthermore, when he was directing the defense of the Shang-tang region, he often showed empathy for certain merchants and repeatedly wrote of his concern for "traveling merchants" who were suffering at the hands of the rebels. But Hsu's merchant connections become clearer during his retirement as a scholar in P'ing-yao. As he admitted in a letter written in 1863, he knew many rich families in P'ing-yao and Chieh-hsiu. He revealed that because their sons had been his students, he had not been forced to borrow money. Evidently merchant friends in Fukien now aided him in his time of need. "The gifts I received from good friends in Fukien were not [sent] because I told them I was poor." Hsu went on to say, however, that he did not value money; rather, he was concerned only with the two characters meaning "moral integrity." He would wait for those who outlived him to decide whether he deserved these two characters on his coffin. But his further admission that he was no longer willing to hold office and manage dirty affairs suggests a degree of financial security. "After all, I am an independent fellow."[24]

During this time Hsu composed an essay to honor the mother of Chi I-chai, scion of a prominent trading family of Chieh-hsiu. Chi now headed an important Shansi firm, possibly a bank, which had branches in "several tens of locations" from north to south in China, "with half its wealth located in Hunan-Hupei and the other half near Peking."[25] Hsu had been the teacher of Chi's youngest son "for many years," so the relationship was close according to traditional Chinese reckoning. Hsu had great admiration for this merchant who used his wealth to support government programs against the Taiping rebels despite heavy business losses, as well as for his generosity as a philanthropist. The merchant had often said he did not mind donating money to the government "to repay my country (pao-kuo) in time of need," and Hsu therefore regarded him as a patriot.

The Ch'ao-shan Shu-yuan where Hsu took up residence in 1856 had been founded in 1701 and originally enjoyed an endowment of over 290 mou in fields to support the school, plus another sixty-odd to provide funds for scholarships.[26] But the school had fallen prey to hard times and gradually most of its land was lost. In the early years of the Tao-kuang reign (1821-1850), however, a local official organized the gentry of the district to re-establish the school and the support of merchants was secured.

On assuming his new position Hsu apologetically noted that he had been away from scholarship for a long time as an official;

but since as a child he had been surrounded only by books and had studied very hard, "even though I have not studied for years, when I now look at these books it all comes back to me."[27] As director of the school Hsu managed to improve the facilities, expanding beyond the original three halls and fifteen rooms; perhaps because of his successful administration, when later he complained of old age and mentioned retiring to his native place, "the officials and gentry would not hear of it." Consequently he remained for nearly a decade.

Hsu admitted that he took this teaching position because he wished to nurse his illness, but also because he needed to support his family of "eight mouths." Hsu's family now consisted of two concubines, a daughter and an adopted son, in addition to family servants. Lacking a son, Hsu was the last of his line and had been overwhelmed by melancholy. While supervising the defense of the Shang-tang area he continually complained that he was already sixty *sui* and was still without a son. Finally he asked the family elders for permission to adopt the second son of his cousin, Chi-hsun. Chi-hsun had accompanied him for years while he had been an official and was willing to give him the boy who was just five *sui*. Hsu knew he was required by family regulations to take a child from within the family, but he did not want one too old or unable to read. Thus Chi-hsun's son was ideal, for Hsu could supervise his education; moreover, he appeared to be a bright lad. Having secured clan approval, Hsu asked Chi-hsun to send the boy as soon as possible to his yamen since he wanted to begin the boy's education.[28]

He named the young boy Shu (Tree) when he adopted him at the age of six *sui*. Hsu put the boy under the care of his two concubines, at least one of whom he had purchased in Fukien. In the education of his son Hsu was completely dedicated to traditional methods and the established curriculum of Confucian scholarship. But the boy proved somewhat less than brilliant. Even though his adopted father began his education full-scale when he was eight *sui*, employing a tutor for him and not allowing "the naughty kids of the clan to join in with him," Hsu regretted that his son did not have a particularly keen intellect. "He is rather dull in reading."

Yet intellect was not everything in Hsu's opinion. "I have not allowed him to go out, so he still has not learned bad habits; he is pure and naive, and cannot tolerate people who argue." "In this way he is very much like me, but that is only natural for a flower which has been attached to another tree." By the age of eighteen *sui* Shu had just finished his studies of the Five Classics and *Tso chuan* (Tradition of Tso). He was then given the *Historical Records* and *History of the* [Earlier] *Han*, as well as Han-style writings of the T'ang and Sung and short essays based on the Four Books. In 1863 Hsu wrote that his son had spent the past year practicing the eight-legged essay style. His essays "were not bad, but lacked maturity." "He is not yet old enough for the examinations, but when he is I shall not order him to take them immediately. If he writes well and passes I shall not insist that he take the higher examinations. I simply want him to understand the principles (*li*), to be a good person, and understand some books. It is enough for him to continue the family line."[29]

Continuation of his family name obsessed Hsu. At fifteen *sui* his son had already been given a wife. "His wife is also well-behaved, but the grandson I look forward to holding every day has still not come." That Hsu's hopes were realized is uncertain. While his grandson, Chi-wu, aided in collecting his writings, it is not clear whether he was born before his grandfather's death.[30]

In addition to his adopted son, Hsu had had two daughters. The first was born in Fukien by his concubine from the family of Ma (Foochow Mohammedans?), whom he purchased there. This daughter had been betrothed to the Chang family of Hsin-chou, west of Wu-t'ai city, but when she was fourteen *sui* she suddenly died of smallpox. Hsu's life was brightened somewhat, however, when in the seventh month of 1857 (August 20–September 17), the concubine from Fukien gave birth to another daughter. She too contracted smallpox when only a month old. In 1863 Hsu wrote that she was already seven *sui*, but looked like a boy. She was very intelligent, however, and her father had been teaching her to read. "What a pity she is the daughter of a concubine," he said. "When she was born her mother dreamed of pine roots sprouting [note that Chi-yü's style (*hao*) was 'Pine-tree shrine'], so we named her Sung-ya (Pine-sprout). The *wa-wa* wailing of the baby was a lucky sign, but I still had to chant the poem, 'a weak girl is not a boy!' " [31] During his years teaching at P'ing-yao this daughter "broke [his] depression" when she was with him. By 1863, when she was six years old, Hsu had already promised her to the young son of a *chin-shih* scholar, Liang Yung-chou, of Ting-hsiang, a few miles southwest of Wu-t'ai city.

Hsu's disappointment with the scholarly progress of his adopted son was to an extent compensated by the rapid development of his favorite student, Chao Ssu-wei, son of one of Hsu's father's students who, many years before, had helped Chi-yü to compile his father's collected writings. Hsu taught this brilliant boy for nearly a decade and felt that of all his students Chao alone was capable of carrying out his tutor's teachings. His education was most strenuous, with traditional China's characteristic reliance on a precocious child's ability to memorize.

The tough discipline of Chao's education under Hsu's direction indicates the latter's continued loyalty to the old values of Chinese culture. Even in an era and world that had begun to challenge the validity of such values, Hsu prepared this boy to grasp the supreme delights of Confucian scholarship and ready him for the responsibilities of statesmanship. By four *sui* the child had copied the *Erh ya*; by six he had memorized four of the Classics, the *Classic of Songs, Documents, Changes,* and the *Spring and Autumn Annals*; by nine, now under Hsu's tutorship, he had mastered the Four Books and the Five Classics and was well into the *Tradition of Tso*, histories of the Han, T'ang, and Sung dynasties, as well as various styles of ancient and modern poetry; by twelve he had been introduced to Hsu's father's writings. But suddenly he fell ill at eighteen. His mother pleaded with the youth to take opium to kill the pain, but the young scholar, reflecting Hsu's own hatred for the drug, replied, "With such a sickness how can opium save my life? I will not lose my uprightness. If I take opium and still do not avoid death, I shall have lost my uprightness. Mother, do not grieve!" When the youth died shortly after in

1864, Hsu's heart was broken, for he felt he had lost more than a son.[32]

During these years of teaching at P'ing-yao Hsu found it diffi-cult to forget his past as an official. "I am now a useless person in an uneventful place." He recalled how he had loved to travel to famous places in China. By boat and by cart, he had covered the sights of fifteen provinces in his lifetime, an ideal of tourism he shared with the more energetic members of the scholar class such as Ku Yen-wu before him. Hsu admitted now, however, that such travels no longer attracted him; he was tired and looked forward only to home life and leisurely writing about his past experiences. He surrounded himself with tattered books, and every day he ground his ink to write several pages. He ate "simple, coarse food, and lived in a cold room." "But Heaven's treatment thus of such an ordinary person cannot be considered ungenerous." He noted that now he was neither official nor gentry in P'ing-yao, but just a teacher. His days were spent in teaching and studying, and he did not receive visitors often. In 1860 he wrote that he was "sick and exhausted; I shut myself up in my study, and in addition to correcting essays I read several chüan of old books and thus pass the year."[33]

Hsu completed much of the writing that appears in his col-lected works during this period. One of these articles strongly de-nounced Buddhism, citing other Confucian critics such as Han Yü, Chu Hsi, Wang Yang-ming, and Lu Hsiang-shan. He was clearly aware of the religion's usefulness as a Machiavellian tool for politi-cal control, and therefore approved of Ch'ing support of Lamaism and Buddhism in Tibet and Mongolia to help pacify border areas. In China, however, he argued that because most rebels had not been Buddhist-inspired, it was useless to support monks who were not potential leaders of uprisings. Hsu's position regarding Islam, Taoism, and Catholicism, all of which he opposed on the ground that they caused religious controversy, was similar to his view of Buddhism. Since Protestantism was not included in his list of dangerous religions while Catholicism merited specific mention, it may be that Hsu's historic encounter with Protestants on the

China coast, his interest in their literature, and the power he identified with Protestant states caused him to withhold judgment on this particular "religion."[34]

Hsu also carried on research dealing with the geography of Shansi during these years.[35] In addition to studying and recording ancient place names of the region and equating them to the modern names, Hsu began a new gazetteer for his district of Wu-t'ai (which was completed only after his death).[36] His interest in border states, now purely academic and verging on antiquarianism, continued; he painstakingly identified the names of border places in the Han period with their modern equivalents, and he revealed a lively interest in China's inner Asian neighbors, concluding that "our glorious dynasty is not limited by borders."[37]

In retirement Hsu began to write poetry at the age of sixty *sui* but always modestly recorded that he was not a good poet. Nevertheless, each time he wrote verses the local people would hustle to pick them up to chant. Hsu admitted that in this poetry he often dealt with his subject in a manner which seemed provocative to his Confucian peers; when he portrayed historical personalities in his poems, for example, he revealed even their extra-marital affairs without condemning their behavior. Still realistic, he remarked that conservative scholars would be surprised that he failed to censure such activities, but that he felt such behavior was simply ordinary. In spite of his claim that he ignored the news during these years, Hsu was much attracted to poetry that touched on "current affairs and extraordinary events."[38] While in P'ing-yao Hsu also wrote many prefaces for collections of poetry, as he had done even as an official.[39] Now students often requested that he teach them his style. When a young student, T'ien Feng-lu, asked Hsu to teach him poetry, Hsu modestly replied that he was not an accomplished poet, "so that he was asking a blind man for directions." Nevertheless, T'ien became his student. As was typical for retired scholar-officials, Hsu was attracted during these years to philosophical Taoism, though he hated the religious Taoists. He found the ideas of Lao-tzu particularly appealing.[40]

Considering the degree of latitudinarianism found in his

Ying-huan chih-lueh, it is curious that the eight-legged essay, infamous to later reformers, was his real love. As in Fukuzawa Yukichi, early advocate of Japanese modernization, in Hsu can be seen a mixture of public iconoclasm and personal conservatism. He revealed that he had always enjoyed reading *pa-ku-wen*; even though he had spent many years writing "sloppy" memorials, he was still able to criticize and correct this kind of essay. He confessed that he was not particularly talented in writing such formal essays, but that he had spent many years in the Hanlin Academy trying to improve. Instead he enjoyed writing things quickly to cover all the points—such as composing letters dealing with current affairs—without worrying about style. Yet he loved to read and discuss *pa-ku-wen*, and during his years as a professor at P'ing-yao he specialized in teaching the composition of this form. While at P'ing-yao Hsu wrote several prefaces to collections of eight-legged essays and style books, such as the one he adopted as a text for his students.[41]

Despite the escapist tendencies in this period of his life, Hsu nevertheless could be found periodically dabbling in the world of affairs. In 1857-1858 he communicated with Heng Fu, governor of the province, regarding the suppression of bandits and rebels.[42] Other letters were written to officials in the area concerning problems of pacification. In 1858 Hsu wrote that "my upper teeth are gone, and I suffer from a coughing sickness which has become very severe in recent years. If it is cold, or if I do manual labor, I begin coughing without being able to stop." For several months on end he was forced to stay inside and work by the stove during the winter. In 1858 he heard there was a grain shortage in the capital and that bannermen in charge of grain transport had committed suicide. In spite of his illness Hsu was moved to write a short treatise entitled *Ch'ou yun Hsi-mi ts'e-lueh* (To devise a policy of importing Western rice; i.e., rice transported by Western ships).[43] When this treatise came to the attention of a certain censor surnamed Lu, however, it served as the basis for new accusations against Hsu.

For a long while thereafter he was depressed. People wondered why, as a retired official, he was still willing to become involved in such things. Hsu complained that people thought he was stupid. He thought these people failed to understand him; they simply saw him as another poor scholar seeking to earn a living at the end of his life. They felt it odd he did not realize he had been cashiered. "But they do not know that in my mind are the [four] characters, 'even in death I shall be unable to close my eyes [because there is something left unfinished].' "[44] Hsu was so upset that he was not allowed to make recommendations to the court that he wanted "to go to Tao-kuang's resting place and smash my head." That the court had stupidly involved China in another war with powerful Westerners put a dagger into Hsu's pragmatic soul; in viewing his government he would agree with the words of Confucius: "To have faults and to be making no effort to amend them is to have faults indeed!" He stubbornly resolved that although his body was weak and old, "this hot blood of mine is not cold; my small heart is not dead, and in it lies a determination to spit out many words concerning security policies. If I say these things in the morning and die in the evening I shall have no regrets."[45]

Upon later reflection, however, he wrote that he did not blame "the Board of Revenue's criticism, because my ideas would have been difficult to achieve." Furthermore he admitted that one should not make recommendations without holding office. He felt sorry that he had not followed the admonition of Confucius that "if you are not in office, do not plan policy." Therefore after having written his recommendation, Hsu later "felt ashamed" and decided to "shut my mouth and not discuss current affairs; I do not any more read the *Peking Gazette*, for [if I do] my stomach is on edge and my spirit is quite unsettled. Instead I wish to be an old scholar living in great peace, content to spend my years thus." One glance at the *Peking Gazette* would cause him "to toss and turn all night without being able to sleep."[46]

But the outside world refused to leave him in peace. In 1861 Hsu bemoaned the fate of his cousin, Liang Wen-ch'ing, the brick-maker in Peking. After 1853 Liang's business had been in trouble due to cutbacks in official purchases: "But in the eighth month

(September 15–October 13) of 1860 the barbarians invaded Peking. The battle ground was so near his home by the T'ung-ho kiln that the cannon blasts burst the window paper."[47] His son had forced him finally to leave on a cart for Shansi, and the kiln was subsequently occupied by foreigners. After the peace Liang found that all had been lost.

Hsu's position far from the foreign menace at P'ing-yao, however, brought him a salary of three hundred taels per year, to which was added another three hundred gained from tutoring private students; an additional two or three hundred ounces were realized from the sale of his writings (epitaphs, prefaces to clan registers, and such), "following the practice of famous people of ancient times."[48] Hsu lamented that beyond the money required for basic necessities, the rest was "seized" as by a bird of prey for work on Shansi defenses. With the general breakdown of order in China as a result of the years of rebellion, even Shansi by 1860 faced a crisis. Hsu was now being pressured for funds just as, a few years earlier, he had put the screws to others.

In letters written in 1860 and 1861 he admitted that the situation in Shansi was terrible but that he just could not afford to donate more money. He apologized, saying that he had been unable to give very much even when he had been involved in defense work in Shang-tang. At that time his income of sixty taels per month had been barely enough to pay for the expenses connected with his duties. He felt ashamed that he could not have given at least a thousand taels as did some of the former officials who lived in the vicinity of Wu-t'ai city. He realized that the need now was even greater than it had been when the Taipings had threatened Shansi, but he simply possessed no more funds. He planned, however, to pawn two trunks of furs worth about three hundred ounces for his donation but cautioned that this would take him some time.[49]

In the winter of 1861 bandits threatened Hsu's home town of Tung-yeh-chen, seven miles southwest of Wu-t'ai city, a village with about a thousand households and over two hundred shops.[50] The people were terrified, so Hsu once again stepped forward to help organize local militia forces against these bandits and restore order. The following year he returned to his teaching post at P'ing-yao, but soon received an order from Governor Ying Kuei to again direct the Shansi militia to defend the region against the Nien rebels.[51] Hsu did meet with Ying Kuei in the fourth month of 1862 (April 29–May 27) along with two other prominent gentry in the area; but his health did not permit him to lead the forces again and he recommended several others. He argued that four men should be chosen to bring central direction to the militia. One of these was a certain Wang Ch'un-yeh, whom Hsu cited for his role in the San-yuan-li affair (now often cited as an early example of Chinese nationalism) outside Canton years before. "When the British barbarians attacked Canton, the soldiers in the righteous uprising at San-yuan-li killed several hundred [sic] of the barbarian soldiers. The death of the British leader, Bremer, was caused by Wang."[52]

The following year Hsu dejectedly observed that "of the eighteen provinces there is not one that is not in ruin; there is only this little bit of land [in central Shansi] that can be called complete."[53] Even at this time Hsu retained some responsibilities with the militia in P'ing-yao. When he became very ill in the early fall of 1863 he wished to resign his teaching post and return north to tutor in Hsin-chou, but because of his obligations to the militia he was unable to leave suddenly. He again became very depressed at the thought of his nation in ruin in the twilight of his life, and was preoccupied with the thought of death. He received a gift of burial clothes from his close friend, Wu Lai-yü, now a magistrate in Szechwan, which pleased him immensely. But he later gave these to another friend's family when that friend died; the son of this man in turn sent a new set to Hsu.[54] In a letter to his old friend from Fukien, Liu Yao-ch'un, Hsu wrote that already seventy or eighty percent of his friends had died; only twenty or thirty percent remained, but over half of these were near death. "And we two have no way of escaping either."[55]

The author of the *Ying-huan chih-lueh* was thus allowed neither to neglect current events of the outside world nor the pressing task of maintaining internal order. In the early reign of T'ung-chih (1862–1874), after China's second disastrous war within two decades against two of the strongest European nations, Britain and France, Hsu viewed the situation in China as especially desperate.[56] "China is scarcely a whole country." It was open to the penetration of foreigners. "Only Shansi is relatively safe behind its mountains and rivers." And yet so many Chinese officials and military leaders had given their lives to save the situation. In Hsu's opinion, the only hope now was to locate virtuous and able high officials who would be able to promote and nourish China's original spirit in order to settle the minds of the people and develop realistic policies vis-à-vis the outside world. Such men had to be experts in both the civil and military arts.

In 1864 Hsu wrote that the Nien rebels from Shantung and Honan had their "tongues hanging out" and their mouths were watering to get the riches of the five districts of P'ing-yao, Chieh-hsiu, Ch'i-hsien, T'ai-ku, and Yü-tz'u in the Fen valley, all centers of Shansi trade and banking. Because successful defense would now be most difficult, he had decided finally to send his family back to Tung-yeh-chen where they would be safer. In a letter to a relative in Wu-t'ai he said to expect his family to arrive after five or six days' travel, along with seventeen or eighteen chests of books and clothing. He would come later by himself if escape became necessary. Later Hsu wrote that he was nearly seventy *sui* and found his responsibilities in P'ing-yao too demanding. Again he planned to resign and return to the north in order to tutor at Hsin-chou. He noted he was already familiar with poverty but felt lucky to be able still to read the words of Confucius' disciples, Tzu-kung's "do not flatter" and Tzu-lu's "do not seek."[57] However Hsu was not to be left in his now somewhat fragile Shansi bastion for the remainder of his life. Already in 1863 Hsu saw some hope of change in Peking with the double regency of Tz'u-hsi and Tz'u-an. "The fog lifts," he said, "and the sun is seen."[58]

With the emergence of an exceptional group of reformers in the court of Peking, the court had ordered an investigation of dismissed officials and Hsu was finally reappointed to the fifth rank and ordered to Peking. But once burned and hardly able to forget, he begged illness: a coughing sickness, headache, an inability to ride in carts. To be on the safe side he reported that Governor Ying Kuei knew of his state. "It is not that I wish to be a recluse, but I really have no alternative." He protested that he had no thought of taking office again even after this investigation. But unexpectedly in the intercalary fifth month of 1865 (June 23-July 22) he received an imperial summons to court. "I could not but try my best to control this sickness and went to the capital." On November 20, 1865, the emperor issued an edict to the Grand Secretariat appointing Hsu Chi-yü as a member of the Tsungli Yamen, with the third rank, to help supervise the affairs between China and foreign states.[59]

On this prestigious board for foreign affairs, Hsu joined many of the T'ung-chih Restoration's leaders: I-hsin, Wen-hsiang, Tung Hsun, Hsueh Huan, and others. Concurrently he was appointed expectant subdirector of the Court of Sacrificial Worship, one of the supervisors of all sacrifices performed by the emperor. Taking such posts when he was over seventy *sui*, Hsu thought, "would make people laugh at me for acting like an old woman who dreams of sex."[60]

Although it appears that Hsu's final role in Peking was that of a Restoration figurehead, an example of a Chinese leader who had seen the light before others and had suffered the consequences, he was nevertheless pleased with his return to officialdom. Consistent with his earlier views on foreign policy, Hsu adamantly supported the acquisition of further information about the non-Chinese world; he continued to suggest the treatment of problems in foreign policy according to realistic and tactical, rather than grand strategical, formulae. This attitude is revealed clearly in a letter written to one of his colleagues of the Tsungli Yamen, Hsueh Huan:

> The situation with the various barbarian states has still not changed very much; there are always complications. Luckily all of the gentlemen who share my duties are very familiar with the barbarian situation. If we know the articulation points of [the foreigners'] joints [i.e., where they will bend], we will then conduct our affairs knowing how to deal [with

them]; and peace will be achieved for the time being. As for hoping to devise a foolproof method [by working hard once] which will function externally by itself, of this I am skeptical and cannot guarantee it.[61]

Hsu continued to move in Ch'ing officialdom. On July 17, 1866 he was appointed director of the Court of the Imperial Stud. Then, in an edict responding to a request by Prince Kung, he was ordered on February 25, 1867, to become the director of the newly-formed T'ung-wen kuan. This institution was established in 1862 to train Chinese in Western languages and Western knowledge in order "to borrow Western methods to verify (*yin-cheng*) Chinese methods."[62] The court had selected Hsu as an eminent scholar whom the students could admire and respect. At the same time the court relieved him of his duties with the Court of the Imperial Stud. He would thus be able to devote all his energies to his new assignment, held concurrently with his office in the Tsungli Yamen.

On October 21, 1867, Anson Burlingame concluded his stay in Peking as United States Minister with the presentation to Hsu of a copy of Gilbert Stuart's portrait of George Washington.[63] Hsu received the gift during an elaborate ceremony that was attended by members of the Tsungli Yamen, with S. Wells Williams and W. A. P. Martin acting as interpreters. On this occasion Burlingame praised Hsu's *Ying-huan chih-lueh* as well as the author's laudatory account of Washington. Burlingame noted that this view of the first president of the United States by a literatus of an ancient heritage was the source of great pride for the people of America. He urged Hsu not to recall the long years of forced retirement caused by his attempt "to make Washington and the countries of the West better known," but rather to rejoice in the "poetical justice" of his new position of influence and power where he could support the views which years before had resulted in his censure.

You passed in review the great men of the countries of which you wrote, and placed Washington before all the rest. You not only did this, but you placed him before the statesmen and warriors of your own country, and declared that he recalled the three dynasties whose serene virtues had shed their light along the ages for 4,000 years . . . [Now] you have been placed at the head of an institution whose purpose is to advance the views for which you were censured, and to instruct your people in the language and principles of Washington. By doing this you will please all the nations, for Washington belonged not to us alone, but to the world.[64]

Hsu responded in his note of thanks that Washington had become "an example and guide to mankind. His merit thus becomes a link between [the] ancient worthies and the men of all succeeding ages."[65] As a lasting tribute to the cross-cultural attraction that Washington held for a Chinese scholar-official, American missionaries in China contributed a granite memorial stone from Fukien to the Washington National Monument. On this stone Hsu's characterization of the American hero, taken from his *Ying-huan chih-lueh*, was inscribed in Chinese.[66]

Recognized at last for his more realistic vision of the non-Chinese world which fortress China now faced, Hsu finally retired from office "due to old age" on March 27, 1869. He returned to his native place for the last time. In 1873 Hsu celebrated the sixtieth anniversary of his *chü-jen* degree and was awarded the ruby button of the first rank. He died a short time later in the seventh month (August 23–September 21) at the age of seventy-nine *sui*.[67]

As a geographer Hsu Chi-yü had been able to depart somewhat from his cultural moorings in order to support a more rational approach to the outside world. Yet, in spite of all that he did to raise questions about the old Chinese order (and even about the Manchu dynasty), in his personal life he remained tied to the ideals of his culture. He was happy to be able to end his days in his native province of Shansi, where he found comfort in the Confucian world that had produced him.

Chapter XII

CONCLUSION

As a vicarious explorer of the unknown and uncharted expanses theretofore so dim in the Chinese record, Hsu Chi-yü became Marco Polo, Columbus, Balboa, Tasman, Cook, and Bering for many Chinese readers of the 1850's and 1860's. Because it was linked to the results of Western explorers, Hsu's book too opened up new passages, described straits never before seen by Chinese, and introduced new lands and peoples. Neither Chang Ch'ien of the Han nor Hsuan-tsang of the T'ang, for all their greatness as Chinese explorers, possessed such a broad vision of the world. From north to south, east to west—from Boston to Tierra del Fuego, from Naha to London—all fell under this Chinese geographer's eye. The Four Seas of China, which so neatly counted and therefore defined the world's waters, expanded and grew until they covered most of the globe— an idea no less difficult for continental China than for medieval Europe to accept. To this sea Hsu's official duties had brought him, and from this sea had come new information and ideas.

Just as our first view of the earth from space has changed our perspective in recent years, Hsu's use of Western maps radically altered his view of the world. The acceptance of this new world image and the documentation that supported it made Hsu one of the first nineteenth-century Chinese to borrow knowledge from the West. Hsu used this information to attempt, like Richard Hakluyt, a general summary of all that was known to him about man's habitat and the human race beyond China. A geography of marvels succumbed to a geography of facts. And just as in the West the increase of geographical knowledge had planted seeds for a renaissance, for a larger intellectual vision, so too Hsu's work brought new concepts to Chinese readers.

When Hsu wrote the *Ying-huan chih-lueh* he manifested an independence of outlook and tenacity of purpose that set him apart from the generality of late-Ch'ing bureaucrats. The same boldness that allowed him to criticize the Mongols, despite their association with the Manchus as northern invaders, also caused him to re-examine China's position in a changing world. Yet Hsu was no traitor to Chinese tradition. On the contrary, his borrowing from Western knowledge even at the price of personal censure reflected an intellectual honesty that was born of three important streams of Ch'ing thought. An advocate of the school of statecraft, Hsu stressed the importance of effective policies to strengthen the state. An empiricist who recognized the need to evaluate information from a broad range of sources and examine it critically, he realized the importance of collecting useful facts whatever their origins. Moreover, dedicated to the thought of Wang Yang-ming, Hsu believed in the unity of knowledge and action.

Combining a pragmatic concern for China's protection and survival with an intellectual and psychological framework that admitted the universal qualities of knowledge, Hsu was able to fit information pertaining to the outside world to his base of Chinese knowledge. In so doing, he took a crucial step toward China's modernization.

By the time Hsu traveled to Peking in 1843 to report to the Tao-kuang Emperor before assuming office in Fukien as financial commissioner, the seeds for his book about the world outside China had already taken root. The scholar from inland Shansi had gone as an exponent of an agrarian tradition to the maritime provinces of Fukien and Kwangtung where he heard and saw what was becoming inescapably obvious: an unprecedented force was threatening China. Having failed to protect China by military means and yet condemning the recklessness of Lin Tse-hsu, he joined the conciliation clique at the end of the Opium War. Now he hoped to buy time to buttress his state through the conquest of ignorance.

As a Confucian realist encouraged by his fellow officers and the emperor, during the following years Hsu pieced together information concerning the nature of the outer world and the character of Western power. The product of intercultural contact on China's maritime frontier, Hsu's book attempted to broaden the base of Chinese knowledge; it revealed clearly that China was not an island unto itself.

Hsu became an Oriental Galileo. He challenged orthodoxy and offered a bold new perspective on the world, with shocking implications to conservative Chinese views. Maritime countries, previously seen as weak, distant, and inconsequential barbarian states now emerged as the masters of the largest part of the earth's surface. China controlled less than one-half of the Asian continent, itself only one of the four in the world. This geographical fact, the expansion of *t'ien-hsia* ("all under Heaven") far beyond lands known to China, raised additional questions for Hsu. What now were the realities of China's position on this planet? How did China fit into the new order of states which he now found displayed on Western maps? Why had China, a large state with claims to ancient truths, fallen behind small Western states in terms of efficient organization and power? Such queries were all implied within Hsu's book which went beyond objective geography to probe the nature of Western power as well as to reveal China's tragic weakness in the world. The old dogma of Chinese superiority, which in its exaggerated form supposed all states of the world to be inferior to China in all ways, needed to be challenged before the Chinese could realistically appraise the secular world beyond the confines of Confucian ideology.

The *Ying-huan chih-lueh's* new view of the world differentiated between the rude and untamed non-Chinese (the "wild barbarians") and those non-Chinese who had accepted the obvious benefits of civilization; this did not differ from an earlier view. The latter category, however, was now divided into two distinct groups: those non-Chinese states that had received the basic premises of Chinese civilization through historical and tributary contacts and those that were based on non-Chinese civilizations (Indian, Islamic, and Europo-American). Hsu thus revealed a world with a pluralism of cultures and civilizations, all of which had developed semi-independently according to individual patterns, but always with cross-cultural influences. He admitted the legitimacy of these non-Chinese civilizations even though they lacked the truths of Confucius and sons.

Lessons were to be gained from an examination of the evolution of Western civilization. How had the Westerners of ancient times, who wore clothing of grass and ate fruits and nuts, emerged from the "darkness and mist" of barbarism? In Hsu's view there appeared to be a normal developmental pattern which followed that of China itself as traditionally understood. First there appeared intelligent men, the culture heroes, who taught people to cultivate grain, to build dwellings, to weave clothing, to make wine, to fashion metal for tools and arms. Ancient states arose upon this rudimentary economic and technological base, and writing systems emerged along with the institutions of government. Religions developed, urging people to be good. Then came the Roman Empire which, like the Ch'in, expanded its control over large areas and brought civilization to the less advanced peoples of Europe. Even after the collapse of the centralized Roman Empire (which fell to the "northern barbarians," as had so many Chinese dynasties), the various states of the West continued to experiment. They improved and perfected their systems because of mutual competition, just as the states in China had done during the period of the Warring States.

Western civilization, which now threatened China's order, thus possessed a long history and traced its origins to non-Chinese sources. Old truths, myths, and clichés about the non-Chinese world were undermined by this new information. The Chinese were shocked to discover that Western states were eminently successful political units with no desire to become tributaries of China; instead, they appeared as potent competitors. These states had established themselves without the blessings of China's emperors (*tzu li wei kuo*). They were therefore qualitatively different from the states that paid homage to China within her tributary system. Though Hsu wrote in praise of the supreme position of Chinese culture and the Manchu dynasty, it was all too obvious, unfortunately for his career, that his information concerning the non-Chinese world did not support such a view.

Recognizing the need to identify the sources of Western power, Hsu went beyond the mention of ships and guns to reveal such aspects as an advanced technology, efficient political and economic organization, and educational systems that provided both practical and theoretical learning. Thus in Hsu's book are seen the beginnings of concern for the problems of modern states. How could China become wealthy and powerful too? Tacit admission of China's weakness was underlined by the description of the sources of wealth and power in other states—the essential ingredients of the new global politics.

Western states possessed a technology "capable of harnessing water and fire." This superior technology had been invented by Westerners who were, according to the author, "resolute and enduring"—a conception radically different from the popular belief in China that all Westerners were "changeable." Western states now used machinery to propel their ships, their carts, and to produce cloth. These machines reduced the cost of labor while still producing goods of quality. With the use of new forms of power and with accurate, scientific techniques in navigation and cartography, Westerners had extended the influence of their nations into all of the power vacuums of the world: Russia had penetrated Siberia, the Western European states had invaded the Americas, Africa, Australia, New Zealand, the islands of the oceans, and the various islands of Southeast Asia. China, however, had neglected to respond effectively to these developments even in Southeast Asia.

Tracing European formulae for power Hsu explored the developments of ancient Greece. He noted that the people, meeting in an assembly (kung-hui), were directly involved with the business of government. Later even monarchy was eliminated. The state lent strong support to the merchants because customs taxes augmented state revenues. This aid to merchants lightened the tax load of the artisans and farmers. Greece thus became a powerful maritime commercial state, following the even earlier example of Phoenicia. All modern maritime states of the West, according to Hsu, learned from these ancient models and selectively copied them. Such strong commercial and economic structures could support a powerful military. Western states even borrowed money from the great merchants and the wealthy, paying them interest, in order to efficiently meet unforeseen demands on the state.

Hsu attempted to introduce simple foreign political concepts.

He was particularly attracted to aspects of social and political equality and government for the people (in tune with a Mencian ideal), which he found in the United States, Switzerland, and in other Western states. These institutions offered effective devices to cement the bonds between man, his society, and state. Some of the Western states had succeeded so thoroughly in securing the loyalty and support of the people (*min*) that they were happy to die for their state. Such manifestations of Western nationalism appear to have held great appeal for Hsu. Although the author did not label this Western phenomenon "nationalism," he clearly recognized the significance of the people's commitment to the betterment and protection of their state. Hsu found that all of the prosperous and strong Western states also used assemblies of "gentry" to aid in directing the state. In countries like Holland these even held power over the king. Furthermore, Western soldiers were provided with good clothing and sufficient food by such systems. Hsu noted that even a small state like Holland which supported such state policies had become rich and secure.

Since successful leadership was another ingredient for securing wealth and power, Hsu was also interested in historical personalities like Alexander, Julius Caesar, George Washington, and Napoleon. Such leaders had combined military skills with a talent for civil administration.

While few concrete recommendations can be found in the book—perhaps because Hsu did not wish to compromise its "objectivity"—his use of historical examples from beyond China suggests the direction he had begun to take. For example, one of China's obvious weaknesses was the lack of an effective navy. How had Rome solved a similar problem when Carthage threatened her with superior ships? The answer was to obtain such a ship in order to copy the design and techniques for its construction.[1] History spoke for itself. Here was a model from another time and place for Chinese to follow. Furthermore, the author found that Peter the Great (a popular example for later Chinese modernizers) and even the notoriously lewd, but talented Catherine had recognized the usefulness of learning from abroad.[2] Artisans from other states had been employed to teach Russians. Consequently Russia had become powerful. This was a potent argument for the self-strengtheners like Feng Kuei-fen, and one suspects that they may have been inspired at least partially by Hsu's work.

Hsu anticipated reformers who legitimized borrowing from the West by declaring that much of Western knowledge had been derived from China in the past. He suggested that Western cultures and civilization had benefited from ancient Chinese ideas. Later development, however, had been conditioned by the particular circumstances of environment and by the genius of the local people. States of the West had therefore supported the natural growth of a mature civilization. Significant discoveries in technology also had been imported originally from China, such as the production of cannon and gunpowder, but Western genius had extended Chinese principles for casting cannon to make light firearms. Western military capabilities had developed in this manner to a progressively higher level.

China's weakness and military failures were inexcusable to Hsu the realist. Seeing that entire civilizations as well as states were engaged in a global contest, he regarded success in this competitive struggle as the all-important goal. He had no respect for Indian leaders, who he felt had passively accepted subjugation from the West. He strongly implied that China too had made a grievous strategic error by not organizing and supporting Chinese traders and the Overseas Chinese of Southeast Asia against the inroads of Western commercial interests. Hsu insinuated that Chinese capitalism should have been used by the state against Western capitalism, for the globe was gradually being bound together by international trade and China should have been prepared to play her legitimate role.

Even though Hsu's book offered few definite solutions to the growing dilemma posed by the emergence of a new international order, it raised many of the basic questions that Chinese, such as Yen Fu, would attempt to solve in the following decades.[3] Indeed, Hsu's pioneering work deeply influenced a whole generation of nineteenth-century thinkers. As a subtle manifesto for change and reform, it laid some of the basic ideological foundations for the self-strengthening movement of the 1860's. When Hsu stated that even the Sulus were capable of practicing self-strengthening (*tzu-ch'iang*), he implied thereby that China should be able to do much more. Hsu may even have been responsible for the revival of this ancient term from the *Book of Changes*, a work to which his father had devoted his last years of study. The slogan, "self-strengthening," was later popularized by Feng Kuei-fen for a whole generation of Chinese modernizers.[4] Hsu's book also provided much of the necessary information about the outside world for leaders of the T'ung-chih Restoration and helped prepare this leadership for entry into a Western-directed international world.

The popularity of the *Ying-huan chih-lueh*, after it was reprinted by the Tsungli Yamen in 1866, and its impact on Chinese developments may be indicated by a few examples. Tseng Kuo-fan frequently used the book, becoming so convinced of the usefulness of world geographical knowledge that in 1868 he constructed three rooms in Nanking to hold a model of the world.[5] Tseng was impressed by Hsu's portrayal of Americans, whom he considered "simple and honest." Tseng was so taken by the idealized image of America that one leading Chinese historian has labeled him as the "first pro-American official in China's political history."[6] Another Restoration figure, Tung Hsun, wrote a laudatory preface for the 1866 reprint and thereby helped make Hsu a darling of the reform movement. K'ang Yu-wei read the book twice, once in 1874 and again in 1879 or 1880 after he had traveled to Hong Kong, where his interest in the outside world had been renewed by the sight of Western-style buildings and admiration for the city's efficient administration.[7] K'ang's student, Liang Ch'i-ch'ao, read it in 1890 and later stressed the importance of this year as the time when he began to feel "anxiety over the signs of strength and the signs of weakness among foreigners and Chinese."[8] In 1897 and 1898 both K'ang and Yen Fu called upon the Kuang-hsu Emperor to support a reform program fashioned after the model of Peter the Great, an example of modernization leadership for Hsu in the 1840's.[9]

After the collapse of the Ch'ing dynasty Hsu continued to

serve as a source of inspiration. He was taken as a model for modernization by a fellow provincial from Wu-t'ai, the "model governor" of Shansi, Yen Hsi-shan. Yen revealed that his earliest feelings of contempt for the Ch'ing government arose as a result of Hsu's persecution for revealing new truths.[10]

Hsu Chi-yü and his book have not been forgotten even in today's China. In the current anti-Confucian campaign Hsu has been resurrected as a nineteenth-century "Legalist," whose admirable realism in foreign affairs made him the victim of a reactionary Confucian backlash. A visitor to Peking in October, 1974, observed Hsu's book prominently displayed in an anteroom off the private chambers of Tz'u-hsi; a note indicated that the Empress Dowager had used the pioneering work regularly.[11] Workers were also seen busily reading and punctuating the *Ying-huan chih-lueh* in the Institute of Nationalities. Apparently Hsu still serves as a symbol in Peking for a rational, moderate approach to foreign relations.

Although there are differences between Hsu Chi-yü and today's Chinese statesmen who seek to use him as an example of realism in foreign policy, Hsu and his twentieth-century successors have all viewed China within a world of stronger states. For Hsu the historical analogy with ancient China was compelling. When he surveyed Europe's competing states in the nineteenth century he recognized a situation comparable to the Warring States period, an era that had produced the powerful state of Ch'in. He could not forget that the ruthless state of Ch'in had used its military power to conquer all of China's contending states. The question for Hsu and his China, as indeed for modern China's leaders, was how to avoid the fate of ancient Ch'i, Chin, Yen, and Ch'u in the new world of the future.

WORKS CITED IN THE *YING-HUAN CHIH-LUEH*: TITLES, AUTHORS, AND LOCATION IN THE 1848 EDITION

An-nan chi-ch'eng 安南紀程 (Record of a journey to Annam) Ts'ai T'ing-lan 蔡廷蘭 1.29b

Ch'ien Han shu 前漢書 (History of the Former Han dynasty) Pan Ku 班固 3.41b, 42b, 57b; 6.28, 37; 8.23

Chih-fang wai-chi 職方外紀 (A record of foreign places from the Chih-fang office) Ai-ju-lueh 艾儒略 (Jules Aleni) 2.42

Chung-shan chih 中山志 (An account of Chung-shan) Chou Hai-shan 周海山 1.21b

Fan-hai hsiao-lu 汎海小錄 (A short record of an ocean voyage) Yuan Wang-yun 元王惲 1.20a-b

Hai-kuo wen-chien lu 海國聞見錄 (A record of things heard and seen among the maritime states) Ch'en Lun-ch'iung 陳倫炯 1.1b, 17, 28, 31; 2.3b, 5a-b, 13b, 14, 31b, 37, 42, 45; 8.8b

Hai-lu 海錄 (A maritime record) Hsieh Ch'ing-kao 謝清高 2.3b, 12, 14, 22b, 26, 29, 31; 3.20, 24

Hai-tao i-chih 海島逸志 (An informal record of the islands in the sea) Wang Ta-hai 王大海 2.3b, 5b, 13b, 14, 16b

Hou Han shu 後漢書 (History of the Later Han dynasty) Fan Yeh 范曄 1.17b, 20b; 3.41b, 42b, 43b; 6.5

Hsi-Tsang chih 西藏志 (Account of Tibet) 3.8, 14

Hsi-Tsang chih fu-lu 西藏志附錄 (A record appended to the account of Tibet) 3.15

Hsi-yü shui tao chi 西域水道記 (A record of rivers and routes in the Western Region) Hsu Sung 徐松 3.55b

Hsi-yü wen-chien lu 西域聞見錄 (A record of things heard and seen in the Western Region) Ch'i Ch'un-yuan 七椿園 3.19b, 30, 30b, 31, 34a-b, 54, 55b, 56; 4.11a-b, 12, 21b, 28a-b, 29; 6.3b, 5, 11b, 28b

Hsin-chiang chih-lueh 新疆識畧 (A short record of Sinkiang) Chu Ch'ing-fan 祝慶蕃 3.55b

Hsin T'ang shu 新唐書 (New T'ang history) Ou-yang Hsiu 歐陽修　3.16, 42a–b

Lü-sung chi-lueh 呂宋紀畧 (A brief description of Luzon) Huang I-hsien 黃毅軒 2.6b, 8

Ming shih 明史 (History of the Ming dynasty) Chang T'ing-yü 張廷玉　1.18; 2.12, 14b, 26; 6.16b

Po-hai fan-yü lu 薄海蕃域錄 (A record of the maritime barbarian regions) Shao Hsing-yen 邵星巖 2.5b, 9b, 11b, 31b

Shih-chou chi 十洲記 (A record of the ten continents) Fang Kuang 方廣 1.20

Shui-ching chu 水經注 (Commentary on the Water Classic) Li Tao-yuan 酈道元 3.57

Sung shih 宋史 (History of the Sung dynasty) T'o-k'o-t'o 托克托　3.16; 6.16b

Szu-i k'ao 四裔考 (Barbarian tribes on the four sides), from *Huang-ch'ao wen-hsien t'ung-k'ao* 皇朝文獻通考 (An encyclopedia of the historical records of the imperial dynasty) 2.22b; 3.31b, 34b, 55b

(Ta-Ch'ing) i-t'ung chih 大清一統志 (Gazetteer of the Ch'ing empire) Chiang T'ing-hsi 蔣廷錫 3.55b

T'ai-wan wai-chi 臺灣外紀 (An unauthorized record of Taiwan) Chiang Jih-sheng 江日昇 6.47b

T'ang shu 唐書 ([Old] history of the T'ang dynasty) Liu Hsun 劉昫 6.9a–b, 10b, 16b; 8.17, 18

T'ien-hsia chün-kuo li-ping shu 天下郡國利病書 (A critical account of the world's divisions and states) Ku Yen-wu 顧炎武 1.17, 25, 26, 27, 30b, 32b; 2.15b, 26b, 28, 33, 34, 38b; 3.11; 7.12, 14

(Wai-kuo) ti-li pei-k'ao (外國) 地理備考 (A reference for the geography of foreign states) Ma Chi-shih 馬吉士 (Marques?) 7.18b, 29b

Wan-kuo ti-li shu 萬國地理書 (Book of geography for all the states of the world) Karl Gützlaff (?) 2.31b; 3.55

Yuan shih 元史 (History of the Yuan dynasty) Sung Lien 宋濂 1.18

Appendix B

LOCATION OF MAPS IN THE 1848 EDITION OF THE *YING-HUAN CHIH-LUEH*

1. The Globe, Eastern Hemisphere	1.1b-2
2. The Globe, Western Hemisphere	1.2b-3
3. Asia	1.9b-10
4. China	1.12b-13
5. Japan and Liu-ch'iu	1.15b
6. Annam, Siam, Burma, and Laos	1.23b
7. Islands of Southeast Asia	2.1b-2
8. Islands of the Pacific and South Pacific	2.39b-40
9. India	3.1b-2
10. Old American Map of India	3.3b-4
11. The Four Moslem States West of India	3.27b-28
12. Moslem Tribes of the Western Region	3.47b-48
13. Europe	4.1b-2
14. Russia	4.14b-15
15. Western Russia	4.16b-17
16. Sweden	4.30b
17. Denmark	4.35b
18. Austria	5.1b-2
19. Prussia	5.9b-10
20. German States	5.15b-17
21. Switzerland	5.26b-27
22. Turkey	6.1b-2
23. Greece	6.17b-18
24. Italian States	6.27b

202

25. Holland	6.41b–42
26. Belgium	6.49b–50
27. France	7.1b–2
28. Spain and Portugal	7.15b–16
29. The "Three" British Islands	7.31b
30. England	7.32b
31. Scotland	7.33b
32. Ireland	7.34b
33. Africa	8.1b–2
34. Egypt	8.3b
35. North America	9.1b–2
36. South America	9.2b–3
37. British Possessions in North America	9.7b–8
38. The United States of America	9.12b–13b
39. States in the Southern Portion of North America	10.1b–2
40. States of South America	10.8b
41. Brazil	10.9b
42. Islands of the West Indies	10.20b–21

NOTES

Abbreviations Used in the Notes

ABCFM   Foreign Mission Archives of the American Board of Commissioners for Foreign Missions.

CCCY   *Ch'ing-chi chung-yao chih-kuan nien-piao.*

CR   *Chinese Repository.*

CSK   *Ch'ing-shih kao.*

HPCC   *Pei-chuan chi, hsu-chi.*

IWSM   *Ch'ou-pan i-wu shih-mo.*

NPM   National Palace Museum, Taipei, Taiwan.

SKCC   *Sung-k'an hsien-sheng ch'üan-chi.*

WTHC   *Wu-t'ai hsin-chih.*

YHCL   *Ying-huan chih-lueh.*

Introduction

1. *SKCC* 3:6b; 3:4, 7b.

2. One of these "experts" was the son of Liang A-fa, the famed early Chinese convert to Protestantism. This boy, Atih [A-te], had studied under the tutorship of Elijah Bridgman from 1830 or 1831 to 1839. Bridgman noted at the time his concern and anxiety over the boy's employment by Lin, whom he never forgave for "ruining" the lad. ABCFM, *South China Mission*, v. la, no. 55 (Macao, 9/7/39).

3. Taken from an unpublished manuscript by Bridgman. "The Men of China," (1853), chapter entitled "Commissioner Lin"; Elijah Coleman Bridgman Papers, Amherst College Archives.

4. For two recent studies of Wei Yuan and his work see Jane Kate Leonard, "Wei Yuan and the *Hai-kuo t'u-chih*: A Geopolitical Analysis of Western Expansion in Maritime Asia." (Ph. D. dissertation, Cornell University, 1971); and Peter MacVicar Mitchell, "Wei Yuan (1794-1857) and the Early Modernization Movement in China and Japan." (Ph. D. dissertation, Indiana University, 1970).

5. See J. D. Frodsham, *The First Chinese Embassy to the West* (London, 1974), pp. viii, 38, 40, 41, 69.

6. Professor Roy Hofheinz of Harvard University, during his October, 1974, visit to the People's Republic of China, found that both the *Hai-kuo t'u-chih* and the *Ying-huan chih-lueh* have been identified as "Legalist classics."

7. A very brief summary of Hsu's work has been published recently. See Fred W. Drake, "A Mid-Nineteenth Century Discovery of the Non-Chinese World" in *Modern Asian Studies*, 6.2:205-224 (April, 1972). Also see Dorothy Ann Rockwell, "The Compilation of Governor Hsu's *Ying-huan chih-lueh*," *Papers on China* 11:1-28 (1957). In addition see Samuel Wells Williams's review of the *YHCL* in *CR* 20:169-194 (1851).

I. A Scholar-Official from Shansi

1. Arthur W. Hummel, ed., *Eminent Chinese of the Ch'ing Period (1644-1912)* (Washington, 1944), I, 309. Hsu's *tzu* was Chien-nan; his *hao* was

Sung-k'an. Lu Hsun noted in the introduction to his most famous short story the uncertainty of his main character's surname, personal name, place of origin, and general background. Lu Hsun, "The True Story of Ah Q," *Selected Works of Lu Hsun* (Peking, 1956), I, 77-81. But he nevertheless created in modern Chinese fiction the unforgettable Ah Q, symbol of Chinese society in the early years of the twentieth century. While reading "The True Story of Ah Q," one not only forms a concrete image of a complex if weak individual, but also senses the impact of a whole society and tradition upon this man. Dealing with real men in Chinese history rarely achieves such results, with notable exceptions like Arthur Waley's study of Yuan Mei. All too often biographical treatments of Chinese succumb to the very idiosyncracies of Chinese historiography that Lu Hsun satirized in his introduction to Ah Q's "true story." For Hsu, as in the case of many other important officials of nineteenth-century China, a paucity of information is encountered about the non-official man who remains obscure behind the facade of officialism. A picture of such a figure—as a complete man and not just a bureaucratic creature—and his role in society as a whole generally does not emerge from the hypo of Chinese historical materials. The standard biographical sketches of Hsu Chi-yü are disappointingly inadequate. Thus, unfortunately only a fragmentary portrait of Hsu can be pieced together from his collected writings and other miscellaneous sources. For a discussion of Chinese biography, see Denis Twitchett, "Problems of Chinese Biography," in Arthur F. Wright and Denis Twitchett, eds., *Confucian Personalities* (Stanford University, 1962), pp. 24-39. Also, see pertinent comments in Ho Ping-ti, *Ladder of Success*, pp. 267-268; as well as Nivison, "Chinese Biography."

2.   Albert Herrmann, *An Historical Atlas of China* (Chicago, 1966). See the various maps pertinent to Shansi, especially pp. 2-8 for the period before China's unification. Also see Donald G. Gillin, *Warlord; Yen Hsi-shan in Shansi Province, 1911-1949* (Princeton University Press, 1967), pp. 6-8.

3.   George B. Cressey, *Land of the 500 Million* (New York, 1955), pp. 38, 268; see Ho Ping-ti, *Studies on the Population of China, 1368-1953* (Cambridge, Mass., 1959), p. 283, Appendix II. The figure listed for Shansi in 1850 is 15,131,000. The *CR* 11:617 and 620 lists 14,004,210; *CR* 11:626 (1842).

4.   Samuel Wells Williams, *The Middle Kingdom* (New York, 1883), I, 96; Cressey, p. 267.

5.   Professor Eric Widmer of Brown University was my informant on pidgin Russian.

6.   *CR* 14:280-288 (1845).

7.   *WTHC* 1:16b-45 shows maps of the area; G. M. H. Playfair, *The Cities and Towns of China* (Shanghai, 1910), pp. xvi-xvii. Also, see *CR* 11:617-626 (1842).

8.   Samuel Couling, *The Encyclopaedia Sinica* (Shanghai, 1917), p. 609; *Shan-hai t'ung-chih* 1:26b-27; Williams, *Middle Kingdom*, I, 96; Immanuel C. Y. Hsu, *The Rise of Modern China* (New York, 1970), p. 35.

9.   Most of the information on Hsu's family is found in sections of the *WTHC*. Since Hsu compiled three of its four chüan, the material it contains relating to his ancestors was undoubtedly known to him and thus may be assumed to follow family documents closely. For a more detailed account of Hsu's ancestors, see Fred W. Drake, "Hsu Chi-yü and His *Ying-huan chih-lueh* (1848)," Ph. D. dissertation, Harvard University, 1970.

10. Hummel, I, 309. Hummel errs in showing Ching-ju's *tzu* as Tung-chih. *WTHC* 3:59-60b, 71; *SKCC* 2:26-27. Hsu Chi-yü held this doctor in particularly high regard. As a boy Dr. Li had studied Confucianism, but after failing in the examinations he began to study medicine. Hsu especially admired him because he gave equally good care to rich and poor, high and low, with no regard to their particular status. Without complaint he would come at night and in the dead of winter if called, apparently a noteworthy exception to the rule even in nineteenth-century China. *SKCC* 4:6b, 23a-b.

11. *HPCC* 17:3b. See Hsu's epitaph in *WTHC* for this: *WTHC* 4:6b. *SKCC* 1:23; 4:28b.

12. *SKCC* 1:19.

13. *SKCC* 4:22-23. The surname of Chi-yü's maternal line was also Hsu, written with a different character. The "two Fangs" are Fang Pao (1668-1749) and Fang Tung-shu (1772-1851), two leaders of the T'ung-ch'eng School. See Liang Ch'i-ch'ao, *Intellectual Trends in the Ch'ing Period* (Cambridge, Mass., 1959) pp. 76-79. A later admirer of this

school was Tseng Kuo-fan. See Mary C. Wright, *The Last Stand of Chinese Conservatism, The T'ung-chih Restoration, 1862-1874* (Stanford, 1957), pp. 59-60.

14. *SKCC* 4:11b-12.

15. *WTHC* 4:4. *SKCC* 2:5-6b, 9-11; 4:27.

16. *CSK, lieh-chuan* no. 209, 10. This refers to the teachings of Lu Hsiang-shan (Lu Chiu-yuan) and Wang Yang-ming. See Chan Wing-tsit, tr., *Instructions for Practical Living and Other Neo-Confucian Writings by Wang Yang-ming* (New York, 1963), pp. xxxiii-xxxiv. Wang Yang-ming's appeal to later Chinese leaders such as Liang Ch'i-ch'ao, Sun Yat-sen, and Chiang Kai-shek, as well as to Japanese modernizers like Sakuma Shōzan, Saigō Takamori, and Ōkubo Toshimichi has been generally recognized. However, the significance and attractiveness to some post-Opium War leaders of Wang's dynamic philosophy for action is often overlooked. See, for example, David S. Nivison's otherwise brilliant treatment in "The Problem of 'Knowledge' and 'Action' in Chinese Thought since Wang Yang-ming," in Arthur F. Wright, *Studies in Chinese Thought* (Chicago, 1953), pp. 112-145.

For Hsu, in later life an official perplexed by bandit, rebel, and border problems, Wang seemed a fellow spirit from an earlier age. Hsu's wartime headquarters, Chang-chou, Fukien, had been coincidentally the center for one of Wang's famous antirebel movements. Indeed, Wang's work and interest in border defense made him a compelling model from within the Confucian heritage for Hsu Chi-yü. Wang had advocated the collection of knowledgeable personnel for use in emergencies, the use of geography for both tactical and strategic purposes, and the use of merchants to enrich border areas which suffered economically. Echoing the ancient military manual, *Sun-tzu*, Wang also stressed a knowledge of the real strengths and weaknesses of the enemy and in 1519 became a pioneer in the story of Chinese modernization by ordering Chinese artisans to copy Portuguese guns that were brought to China two years before. Furthermore, Wang's belief that every human was related to a grand unity of life—that all men were brothers—as well as his emphasis on sincerity in the search for knowledge, may have contributed to the openness, found so remarkable by Westerners, that Hsu manifested in his dealings with them. Chan Wing-tsit, pp. 284-292. Wolfram Eberhard, *A History of China* (London, 1950), pp. 263-264. Eberhard presents the interesting argument that Wang's philosophy served the interests of the despot against the Chinese gentry, but that

it failed due to the lack of a strong middle class to act as a counter-
balance to the gentry.

17. Bachelors were *chih-shih* degree-holders who were given the high honor,
after a court examination and audience with the emperor, of joining
the Hanlin Academy. See William F. Mayers, *The Chinese Government*
(Shanghai, 1897), no. 473. Despite the claim in Hsu's epitaph that he
scored in the first class (see *WTHC* 4:6b), Hsu was probably in either
the second class or the top of the third class of the year's graduates
who were given the rank of bachelor. See Mayers, no. 477; H. S.
Brunnert and V. V. Hagelstrom, *Present Day Political Organization of
China* (Shanghai, 1912), no. 629C. Bachelors continued their studies
in the Department of Study of the Academy. See Brunnert and Hagelstrom, no. 201. After later examinations held by a palace commission
these scholars could be retained in the academy, and they would become either compiler of the second class (rank 7A) or corrector
(rank 5B). See ibid., nos. 200B and 200C; *WTHC* 4:6b.

18. Mayers, no. 208. Brunnert and Hagelstrom, no. 200B; *SKCC* 2:7b.

19. *SKCC* 2:4b-6b. This was written looking from a "snowy window"—
probably of the Ch'ao-shan Shu-yuan at P'ing-yao—on February 7, 1861.

20. Hummel, I, 582-583; *SKCC* 2:7b.

21. *CSK, lieh-chuan* no. 209, 2741/352:7b-9. Note the similarity of Feng
Kuei-fen's view over two decades later on the weakness of the Ch'ing
system. See Kwang-ching Liu, "Nineteenth-Century China: The Disintegration of the Old Order and the Impact of the West," in Ho Ping-ti
and Tang Tsou, eds., *China's Heritage and the Communist Political
System* (Chicago, 1968), Book 1, pp. 124, 177.

22. *CSK, lieh-chuan* no. 209, 7b. Censors were not restricted in their jurisdiction only to the province to which they were assigned. Shensi circuit
included Shansi. See Hsieh Pao-chao, *The Government of China, 1644-
1911* (Baltimore, 1925), pp. 89-90; *SKCC* 1.10-12b; *WTHC* 4:6b. For
the two most important of these early memorials, see *SKCC, shang*:
6b-13.

23. *WTHC* 4:6b. Brunnert and Hagelstrom, nos. 848, 966, 967.

II. The "Intractable Barbarians"

1. Hsieh Pao-chao, pp. 303-304.

2. *WTHC* 4:6b; *HPCC* 17:3b; *SKCC* 4:24b; Playfair, p. v.

3. *WTHC* 4:6b; *SKCC* 2:1b; 3:1-2.

4. *SKCC* 3:20-22, for the long letter written by Hsu to Wu's son. *CCCY*,
   pp. 121-122, 170-171; Teng T'ing-chen, "Teng T'ing-chen kuan-yü
   Ya-p'ien chan-cheng te shu-hsin," in Ch'i Ssu-ho, ed., *Ya-p'ien chan-
   cheng* (Shanghai, 1954), II, 590. See *IWSM:TK* 12:15b-16 for Teng's
   memorial (seen August 13, 1840) which reported that Hsu, taotai of
   Yen-Chien-Shao, was to be sent to work on coastal defense.

5. *SKCC* 3:7b, 20b; *WTHC* 4:6b; *HPCC* 17:3b; Playfair, p. v.

6. Ibid., p. 212; Charles R. Boxer, ed., *South China in the Sixteenth
   Century* (London, 1953), Appendix IV, pp. 341-343.

7. John Francis Davis, *China During the War and Since the Peace* (London,
   1852), I, 155. There was legitimate concern from the Chinese side over
   the potential danger of Western and coastal Chinese collaboration.
   David Abeel, for example, told on December 30, 1843, of a visitor who
   had come "to make arrangements for an attack upon the present Tartar
   dynasty, he himself being a descendant of the last dynasty which was
   overthrown by the present usurpers. He said if we would assist him,
   10,000 men should be raised, and without destroying a single life they
   would march to Changchau, and thence to Fuchau, the capital of the
   province, and wherever we went the authorities would be panic-struck
   at the sight of a few foreigners, and fly in every direction." *CR* 13:235
   (1844). Consider, for example, the kind treatment received by Abeel
   and Lowrie at Chang-chou in 1843. *CR* 12:523-533 (1843).

8. See Wolfram Eberhard, "Chinese Regional Stereotypes" in *Asian Survey*
   5.12:596-608 (1965).

9. Chang Hsin-pao, *Commissioner Lin and the Opium War* (Cambridge,
   Mass., 1964), pp. 209-210; John K. Fairbank, *Trade and Diplomacy on
   the China Coast: The Opening of the Treaty Ports, 1842-1854* (Cambridge, Mass., 1961), I, 81.

10. *CCCY*, p. 122; *SKCC* 3:4b; Chang Hsin-pao, p. 213.

11. *SKCC* 2:2; 3:5, 20b; *IWSM: TK* 23:7b-8b contains Wu Wen-yung's memorial (seen February 28, 1841), which reported that Hsu and Liu had heard a rumor from local merchants in Amoy that Imperial Commissioner Ch'i-shan had granted permission in Canton to open trade with Westerners at Amoy. For a description of Chang-chou in October 1843, see W. M. Lowrie, "Narrative of a Recent Visit . . . ," *CR* 12:523-533. Abeel accompanied Lowrie on this visit inland. *SKCC* 2:1b-2.

12. *SKCC* 3:2-4.

13. *CCCY*, pp. 122-123. Yen served as governor general of Min-Che from September 29, 1840 to January 19, 1842. See Yen's memorial (seen June 25, 1841) in *IWSM:TK* 29:18b-20b; *SKCC* 2:1a-b, 2; 3:4b. For a report on Amoy's fall, see *CR* 11:148-157.

14. *SKCC* 1:14b-15. In 1855 Hsu wrote a preface which praised another treatise by this author entitled *Ping-wu wen-chien lu* (A record of things heard and seen [concerning] military [affairs]). Both treatises are found in *Pi Ch'in-hsiang-kung i-shu san-chung ho-k'o* (Three books printed together from the literary collection of Pi-ch'ang; c. 1855).

15. *SKCC* 2:1a-b; 3:4b, 7; Davis, I, 78-80, 157.

16. *SKCC* 3:4b-5. According to H. B. Morse, only ten ships and four steamers were used to attack Amoy on August 26. Hosea Ballou Morse, *The International Relations of the Chinese Empire: The Period of Conflict, 1834-1860* (Shanghai, 1910), I, 291. My translation is abridged.

17. *SKCC* 3:5.

18. *SKCC* 1:7-10. No date is given with this essay, but it was probably written before Hsu arrived in Fukien. Note the use of Hsu's essay on opium suppression in Ch'i Ssu-ho, ed., *Ya-p'ien chan-cheng* (Shanghai, 1954), I, 511-513. For a discussion of the term *Han-chien*, see Frederic Wakeman, Jr., *Strangers at the Gate: Social Disorder in South China, 1839-1861* (Berkeley, 1966), pp. 49-51.

19. *SKCC* 1:7-10.

20. *SKCC* 3:4b. Apparently Mu-chang-a endeared himself even more to the parsimonious Tao-kuang by his part in the confiscation of Ch'i-shan's wealth after the latter's dismissal in February 1841. See Davis, I, 41. After the confiscation of "682 Chinese pounds' weight of gold, 17,940,000 taels in silver, and eleven boxes of jewels . . . , on a second search, by Muhchangah, the prime minister, additional effects were confiscated— 1438 large ingots of Sycee silver, value about 60 dollars each, 46,920 taels in broken silver, 2,561,217 *mows* [*mou*] in land, besides houses, shares in pawn-broking establishments, and transactions in the salt monopoly."

21. Davis, I, 169. Yü-ch'ien's "cry was for [the foreigners'] blood, and he desired 'to flay them alive, and sleep on their skins.'" For an account of the torture of the unfortunate Mr. Stead, see ibid., pp. 169-170.

22. *SKCC* 3:4-7b. This letter was written in early 1842. See I-liang's biography in Hummel, I, 389-390. For some indication of I-liang's tactics to organize Chinese against the British by offering rewards for ships, officers, and men, see *CR* 10:175.

23. Davis, I, 165.

24. Was this concept perhaps derived from contacts with the Chinese trading community?

25. *SKCC* 3:6a-b. This translation is an abridged version.

26. *SKCC* 2:2a-b. Hsieh Pao-chao, p. 301.

III. In Touch with a New World

1. *SKCC* 3:7b; *WTHC* 4:4b; *HPCC* 17:3b.

2. *CSK, lieh-chuan* no. 209, 8b; *HPCC* 17:3b. Brunnert and Hagelstrom, no. 835.

3. *SKCC* 3:7-8; *HPCC* 17:3b.

4. *WTHC* 4:7. See Yang Lien-sheng, "Historical Notes on the Chinese

World Order," in John K. Fairbank, ed., *The Chinese World Order*, pp. 31-33.

5. *SKCC* 3:7.

6. *CCCY*, pp. 123-124. See Hummel, I, 128, 503-505. See various references to Ch'i Kung in Earl Swisher, *China's Management of the American Barbarians: A Study of Sino-American Relations, 1841-1861, with Documents* (New Haven, 1953), p. 44. In an edict dated August 4, 1842 Ch'i Kung and Hsu Chi-yü, among others, are urged to search out talented men who understood barbarian affairs. See *IWSM:TK* 57:16-17. Chang Hsin-pao, p. 58; *CR* 12:333 (1843).

7. Teng Ssu-yü, *Chang Hsi and the Treaty of Nanking, 1842* (Chicago, 1944), p. 170, note 269. Hummel, I, 132.

8. Swisher, pp. 82-88; Fairbank, *Trade*, I, 190-193.

9. *SKCC* 4:24b-25; *CR* 12:328 (1843). The belated notice was based on a report of transfers in the *Peking Gazette*. Ibid., p. 333. His arrival in Canton, noted in the same issue, was given as March 3, 1843. Ibid., p. 328. Although not mentioned in Hsu's work it is likely that John Robert Morrison, son of the first Protestant missionary to China, was one of Hsu's first contacts at this time with the Western community. This was in Canton in late 1842, and possibly early 1843, when Morrison served the British as acting secretary and treasurer under the chief superintendent of trade, Sir Henry Pottinger. See Frederick Wells Williams, *Life and Letters of Samuel Wells Williams* (New York, 1889), pp. 417-418; *CR* 11:114 (1842). The *Chinese Repository* noted with optimism that Hsu "may thus have an opportunity afforded him of removing some imperial misconceptions regarding foreigners." *CR* 12: 333 (1843).

10. Brunnert and Hagelstrom, no. 820A.3, no. 825, no. 826, no. 966, no. 967. Hsieh Pao-chao, pp. 299-300.

11. *CR* 16:488 (1847); 18:446 (1849); Playfair, p. 141.

12. *CR* 15:188 (1846). For a full description of Foochow in 1846 by George Smith, see *CR* 15:185-215 (1846). Also, see *CR* 16:483-500 (1847).

13. Alexander Wylie, *Chinese Researches* (Shanghai, 1897), pp. 68–69, gives an amusing account of William H. Medhurst's visit to this monastery and his effort to convince the monks that their tooth in fact belonged to an elephant.

14. Ho Ping-ti, *Ladder of Success*, p. 247, Table 36.

15. Fairbank, *Trade*, I, 192, 202. *SKCC* 4:25. Ch'i-ying's memorial (seen November 7, 1843) also nominated Huang En-t'ung for Kwangtung, Li T'ing-yü for Chekiang (not accepted), and Hsien-ling for Kiangsu. *IWSM:TK* 69:15–16, 16a-b; 71:6, 22.

16. Davis, I, 155; II, 77; *CR* 15:160 (1846). For details on this early trade, see Hosea Ballou Morse, *The Chronicles of the East India Company Trading to China, 1635-1834* (Oxford University Press, 1926), I, 47-65, 127-134.

17. Westerners in 1846 estimated the population of Amoy between 2 – 300,000. See *CR* 15:160; 363 (1846). But Cressey reported Amoy's population in 1948 as 158,271, so it would seem that even allowing for later emigration, the nineteenth-century figures cited are perhaps somewhat exaggerated. See Cressey, p. 211.

18. *CR* 19:521-522 (1850); *CR* 15:396-398 (1846).

19. *CR* 15:396-398 (1846).

20. *SKCC* 4:25b-26.

21. Fairbank, *Trade*, I, 163-164. Waley, *The Opium War through Chinese Eyes* (London, 1958), p. 91. Abeel (1804-1846), known to the Chinese as *Ya-pei-li*, was born of Dutch-American parentage in New Brunswick, New Jersey. In 1823 he entered the Theological Seminary of the American Dutch Reformed Church at New Brunswick, where he first became interested in missionary work. Despite poor health, Abeel yearned to enter mission work in a foreign land. He was selected as a chaplain to seamen by the American Board of Commissioners for Foreign Missions and the American Seaman's Friend Society in the fall of 1829 to sail with Elijah Bridgman to Canton aboard the merchant vessel *Roman*. He reached the "heathen lands" of China at Canton on February 25, 1830, to begin his work with Western sailors, whom he

found with little desire to "lay up treasures in heaven." Thus he resigned from this work on December 20 of the same year and accepted an appointment with the American Board as missionary to the Chinese. In the following years he traveled widely in Southeast Asia, where he made contacts with Overseas Chinese and learned Fukienese. When Kulangsu fell to the British, Abeel sailed north to survey the site for a mission station which would put him within reach of the nation where "hundreds of millions [were] going mad after their dumb idols." Abeel thanked God for bringing him to this place. "It is the very sphere [for which] I have desired and prayed for many years. This appears more like the beginning of missionary work in China than anything I have yet seen." See G. R. Williamson, *Memoir of the Rev. David Abeel, D. D., Late Missionary to China* (New York, 1849), pp. 40, 69, 217-218.

22.   *CR* 11:505-506 (1842); 12:269 (1843); 13:75 (1844); 15:355 (1846).

23.   *CR* 13:168, 233 (1844); 20:169 (1851). Although Hummel's sketch of Hsu states he met Abeel in 1843, this disagrees with Abeel's own account which puts the meeting in January 1844. The discrepancy probably arises from the overlapping of the solar and lunar calendars, which puts the last 1 1/2 months of the twenty-third year of Tao-kuang into 1844 by Western reckoning. See Hummel, I, 310.

24.   *CR* 13:77 (1844).

25.   *CR* 13:236 (1844).

26.   *CR* 13:236-237 (1844).

27.   ABCFM: Amoy Mission, I (Abeel's Journal), entries of February 29 and March 9, 1844; *CR* 20:170 (1851).

28.   Dorothy Rockwell's account is probably incorrect in assuming that this official was the sub-prefect, Huo Ming-kao. See Rockwell, p. 9. On February 20, 1844 Abeel reported a visit to the sub-prefect. It is unlikely then that a month later Abeel would refer to him as "a young man wearing a white button." Furthermore, it is questionable how "white" the crystal button of the fifth rank would look, while the milk-colored button of the sixth would clearly fit the description. *CR* 13:237-238 (1844). Brunnert and Hagelstrom, no. 966; *CR* 13: 237 (1844).

29. *YHCL* 1: Hsu's preface, 1.

30. *YHCL* 1:4b, 6b; 3:7, 11b (twice); 4:27.

31. *CR* 13:168 (1844); *CR* 20:516 (1851). Also, see Alexander Wylie, *Memorials of Protestant Missionaries to the Chinese* (Shanghai, 1867), p. 129. *YHCL* 5:31b.

32. *CR* 20:516 (1851).

33. Swisher, pp. 145-146; *SKCC* 4:25b.

34. Fairbank, *Trade*, I, 203-204; *IWSM:TK* 72:12; 73:39b. As an example of his comparatively moderate attitude toward China and the Chinese, see George T. Lay, *The Chinese as They Are* (London, 1841).

35. *IWSM:TK* 71:6b. See Jack J. Gerson, *Horatio Nelson Lay and Sino-British Relations, 1854-1864* (Cambridge, Mass., 1972), pp. 5-8; *YHCL* 6:14b, 16b, 26; *CR* 12:135-136 (1843).

36. *IWSM:TK* 73:35-37 (received 12/25/44).

37. Davis, II, 74-75.

38. *CR* 15:190-193 (1846). One is reminded of the same approach in Japan at a later time by the early Meiji authorities.

39. *IWSM:TK* 73:31b.

40. *IWSM:TK* 74:21; *CCCY*, p. 175. Hsu was still acting governor when he signed a memorial received on May 26, 1846; but a memorial received on August 19, 1846 recorded the presence of Cheng Tsu-ch'in. See *IWSM:TK* 75:30b; 76:5. Of the 82 memorials written by Hsu that I have located in the National Palace Museum (most of which date from June 1845 to October 1847), the majority deals with provincial finances. For the history of silver loss, see *TK* 007484; for shipbuilding, 007491, 007944, 008118, 008269, 008413, 008801.

41. *IWSM:TK* 74:21-22.

42. Fairbank, *Trade*, I, 162, 204; *CR* 15:215 (1846).

43. Parliament's increase of the subsidy granted in 1845 to Maynooth College in Ireland was a hot issue with British politicians. The young Gladstone resigned from Peel's ministry over the issue even though he supported the grant. See Llewellyn Woodward, *The Age of Reform, 1815-1870,* 2nd ed. (Oxford, 1962); *CR* 15:216 (1846). Also, see George Smith, *A Narrative of an Exploratory Visit to Each of the Consular Cities of China* (London, 1847), pp. 370-372.

44. *CR* 15:216 (1846).

45. Fairbank, *Trade,* I, 221-222. *IWSM:TK* 75:30b-33b. A rather different version is offered by one of Alcock's biographers; see Alexander Michie, *The Englishman in China during the Victorian Era, As Illustrated in the Career of Sir Rutherford Alcock* (London, 1900), I, 116-119. *IWSM:TK* 76:5-8b.

46. *SKCC* 4:26a-b. This experience noticeably colored Hsu's opinion of most Chinese doctors, supposed practitioners of "benevolent arts." Nearly at the end of his life and unwilling to rely on doctors despite poor health, at 72 *sui* he noted that doctors to be effective in the benevolent arts must first be truly "benevolent"; otherwise, while they are "fooling around with methods to save, what they are really doing is killing—if one does not die of the malady he dies of the medicine." *SKCC* 2:26-27.

47. *SKCC* 4:27a-b.

48. *IWSM:TK* 76:37a-b.

49. For a list of the small number of Westerners who were students of China and the Chinese language in 1842, see *CR* 11:157-161 (1842).

IV. A Victim of Conservatism

1. *CCCY*, p. 176. Hsu received the order on December 24, 1846. See NPM, TK: 009657; 009973.

2. *WTHC* 4:8b; *HPCC* 17:4b; *CCCY*, pp. 176-179.

3. Hsieh Pao-chao, pp. 291, 293. Hummel, I, 388, 583; II, 940. The fate of General Yü Pu-yun, co-defender of Chekiang (beheaded in Peking as

a scapegoat for Chinese defeats at Chinhai and Ningpo), was alone sufficient encouragement for Liu, caught between barbarians and the court, to explore new methods of handling foreigners.

4.   NPM, TK:009973.

5.   NPM, TK:010342; 010506; 010507; 010514; 010596; 101596.

6.   *IWSM:TK* 79:33b-36b (received 2/17/49).

7.   Fairbank, *Trade*, I, 378-379; *IWSM:HF* 1:9b.

8.   *IWSM:HF* 2:10-11.

9.   For more detail, see David T. Roy, "Hsu Chi-yü and the Shen-Kuang Szu Case." Seminar paper, Harvard University, January, 1959. In Professor John K. Fairbank's files.

10. *CSK, lieh-chuan* no. 209, 8b; *HPCC* 17:4.

11. Roy, p. 33; *CR* 19:459-462 (1850); *IWSM:HF* 2:15b-17.

12. *IWSM:HF* 2:17-19b.

13. *IWSM:HF* 2:19b-20, 23.

14. *IWSM:HF* 2:23b-25. *Min Hou hsien-chih* 69:14b. Lin's relationship with Hsu was probably not improved when the emperor called upon Hsu to report whether Lin was truly ill, and whether or not he was able to come to the capital. Hsu had returned to Foochow in early April of 1850, and he visited Lin on or after July 1, 1850. Hsu reported in detail the nature of Lin's alleged affliction, but said he found him much improved. See *SKCC, tsou-su* 1:17b-18b.

15. *IWSM:HF* 2:25b-27b.

16. *IWSM:HF* 2:27b-28b.

17. *IWSM:HF* 3:5b-8.

18. *IWSM:HF* 3:8-11, 15b-16.

19. *IWSM:HF* 3:20-22, 22a-b, 23b-24.

20. Hummel, I, 133; *IWSM:HF* 3:33b-36.

21. *IWSM:HF* 3:38a-b.

22. *IWSM:HF* 3:44-45.

23. *IWSM:HF* 4:1, 6b-7.

24. *IWSM:HF* 4:24b-29b; *CCCY*, p. 179.

25. *CR* 20:433-434 (1851).

26. Mary C. Wright, p. 376 note no. 32.

27. *HPCC* 17:4. Brunnert and Hagelstrom, no. 936B. Hummel's account is mistaken in listing this appointment as subdirector of the Court of Sacrificial Worship. See Hummel, I, 310. Hsu did however receive such an appointment as an expectant subdirector in 1865.

28. See this memorial in *SKCC, tsou-su* 2:19b-25b; *SKCC* 4:25a.

29. *SKCC* 1:12b-14b; 3:22. *CSK, lieh-chuan* no. 209, 10.

V. The Ying-huan chih-lueh

1. For an introduction to some of these materials, see the following: John K. Fairbank and Teng Ssu-yü, "On the Ch'ing Tributary System," in *Ch'ing Administration: Three Studies* (Cambridge, Mass., 1961), pp. 178-191; Alexander Wylie, *Notes on Chinese Literature: With Introductory Remarks on the Progressive Advances of the Art; and a List of Translations from the Chinese into Various European Languages* (Shanghai, 1867). Taipei reprint, 1964, pp. 57-67. Ch'en Kuan-sheng (Kenneth), "The Growth of Geographical Knowledge Concerning the West in China during the Ch'ing Dynasty." Master's thesis, Yenching University, 1934. A copy is held by Harvard-Yenching Library.

2. For a detailed evaluation of the merchant-missionary Society for the Diffusion of Useful Knowledge and its publications on the eve of the

Opium War, see Drake, "Hsu and His *Ying-huan chih-lueh*," pp. 96-113. Tsien Tsuen-hsuin, "Western Impact on China through Translation," *Far Eastern Quarterly* 13:312 (1954) records Gützlaff as the author of *A View of Universal History, History of England,* and *The Introduction to Universal Geography*. This last title appears to have been cited twice in Hsu's *YHCL* as *Wan-kuo ti-li shu*. See *YHCL* 2:31b; 3:55. It also may be the book cited in Fairbank, *Trade*, I, 18-19 as used by Ch'i-ying's assistant in September 1844. It is found in Wang Hsi-ch'i, *Hsiao-fang-hu-chai yü-ti ts'ung-ch'ao tsai-pu-pien, chih* 12:14 (v. 82 of the collection). *Aesop's Fables*, a favorite of translators in East Asia (printed in 1593 as one of Japan's first Western translations and translated by Trigault in 1625 as the first Western literary work into Chinese, for example) was translated for the society by Robert Thom. See Robert Thom, *Esop's Fables in Chinese* (Canton, 1840); *CR* 9:201-210 (1840); 13:98-102 (1844). George B. Sansom, *Japan: A Short Cultural History* (New York, 1962), p. 434. Also, see "List of Books Written and Printed by the Members of the Ultra-Ganges Missions," *CR* 16:371-382 (1847); Wylie, *Memorials*, Index II, pp. 288-306.

3. For a short summary, see Chang Hsi-t'ung, "The Earliest Phase of the Introduction of Western Political Science into China," *The Yenching Journal of Social Studies* 5:1-29 (1950).

4. Liang Ch'i-ch'ao, p. 1.

5. *YHCL* 1: Hsu's preface, 1a-b.

6. *YHCL* 1: *fan-li*, 2b. Matteo Ricci (Li-ma-tou; 1552-1610), Jules Aleni (Ai-ju-lueh; 1582-1649), and Ferdinand Verbiest (Nan-huai-jen; 1623-1688). See Hummel, I, 316, 199, 547. *Ajia rekishi jiten* 9:283a; 1:125a; 8:93a.

7. I have followed Hsu's own account in *YHCL* 1: *fan-li*, 2b. Hsu made exceptions to this rule however. For example, he twice cited a "European" book entitled *Wan-kuo ti-li shu* (Book of geography for all the states of the world; Gützlaff's *Wan-kuo ti-li ch'üan-t'u chi?*). *YHCL* 2: 31b; 3:55. And twice he referred to the work written in 1847 by a Portuguese named Marques. *YHCL* 7:18b, 29b. This work was the *Wai-kuo ti-li pei-k'ao*, cited by Hsu simply as the *Ti-li pei-k'ao*. Hsu even cited Aleni's seventeenth-century work, *Chih-fang wai-chi* (A

record of foreign places from the Chih-fang office). *YHCL* 2:42.
This work was completed in five chüan and published in 1623 to
accompany Ricci's map of the world. See Hummel, I, 453. But while
he generally failed to note his Western sources specifically, he did not
attempt to hide the fact that much of his information came from
Western materials. In reference to friction between Britain and Russia
in the area north of India, he twice mentioned an "English newspaper"
which had been translated at Canton in 1840. *YHCL* 3:17, 3:54. The
latter citation indicates this "newspaper" was a monthly, possibly the
Macao Monthly. See Ch'en Ch'i-t'ien (Gideon Ch'en), *Lin Tse-hsu;
Pioneer Promoter of the Adoption of Western Means of Maritime
Defense in China* (Peking, 1934), p. 10. Also scattered throughout the
book could be found numerous references to "Western" or "European
sources." See, for example, *YHCL* 2:21; 3:30b, 35, 38b, 41, 42b, 44,
56b, 57; 6:11, 12b, 21, 32; 7:13; 8:3b, 5; 10:13, 18b.

8. The Rev. L. B. Peet of Foochow wrote on August 27, 1849 to Rufus
Anderson of the ABCFM that the work was "just published." ABCFM,
Foochow Mission, v. 229, letter no. 334 (8/27/49). According to S.
Wells Williams the book was printed at Hsu's own expense. *CR* 20:170.
This probably meant that Hsu had used the "public" funds available to
his office. The blocks were carved locally by the firm of Sung Chung-
ming at Tung-chieh-k'ou in Foochow. *YHCL* 10:25b. The ten-chüan
work appeared in six ts'e.

The first edition of the book in 1848 included in addition to the
author's, prefaces by P'eng Yun-chang, then commissioner of education
in Fukien; by Lu Tse-ch'ang, a so-called "barbarian expert," and taotai
in Fukien; and a colophon written by Ch'en Ch'ing-hsieh, then financial
commissioner of Fukien and later governor of Shantung from 1849 to
1852. See Hummel, II, 620-621. David Nelson Rowe, ed., *Index to
Ch'ing Tai Ch'ou Pan I Wu Shih Mo* (Hamden, Conn., 1960), pp. 59,
434, 526. *YHCL* 1: Hsu's preface, 1b. Earl Swisher, pp. 103-104, 106.
CCCY, pp. 178-180. Ch'en also appears to have been anathema to the
conservatives under Hsien-feng. The title page informed the reader that
the book had been "inspected," and therefore approved by Liu Yun-k'o,
governor general of Fukien-Chekiang, and Pi-ch'ang, then Tartar General
of Foochow. The table of contents listed Ch'en Ch'ing-hsieh and Lu
Tse-ch'ang as collators; and Huo Ming-kao, a first class sub-prefect, as
"collector [of materials] and translator." *YHCL* 1: Hsu's preface, 1;
mu-lu, 1. Proofreading was done by some of Hsu's relatives, who
apparently were with him in Foochow as personal secretaries. These
were a maternal relative from K'uo-hsien, Shansi, Hsu Hsin-te; Chi-yü's

cousin, Hsu Chi-hsun, from whom he later adopted his son; and a nephew, Po Yü-k'uei, the son of Chi-yü's sister, *YHCL* 1: *mu-lu*, 3.

A second edition appeared in 1850. This edition was printed with the original blocks, but it dropped the author's preface and added one by Liu Yun-k'o (dated the fourth month [April 23-May 21], 1849). Although an 1859 edition has been reported, only the 1861 edition of Hsu's work printed in Japan has been located for this study. See Hummel, I, 310. Harvard holds only the 1861 edition: see Jo Keiyo, *Eikan shiryaku* (1861). This Japanese edition, the *Eikan shiryaku*, was published on the island of Shikoku only seven years after Japan was "opened" by Perry. See title page of *YHCL* (1861 Japanese edition). A "Dutch scholar" wrote in the Dutch equivalents of most of the non-Chinese place names which appear in the work. The two maps of the globe, differing from the Chinese original, appeared in four colors while the remainder were plain. This edition also differed from the earlier Chinese editions held at Harvard and the Library of Congress in that a preface appeared by Liu Hung-ao (dated 1849), governor of Fukien from 1840-1845, and Ch'en Ch'ing-hsieh's colophon was not included.

The book was reprinted in China by the Tsungli Yamen in 1866, with the original blocks, and served as a manual for Restoration leaders. Professor Paul A. Cohen of Wellesley College generously loaned me his personal copy of this edition. It is a duplicate of the 1848 edition except that Liu Yun-k'o's preface appeared as well as a new preface by Tung Hsun. The *WTHC* reported that the original printing blocks had been brought from Foochow to the capital. *WTHC* 4:84. Liu Hung-ao's preface, seen in the Japanese edition, was missing. An additional proofreader was cited in this edition, Chi-yü's cousin, Hsu Chi-ku, who held office in Taiwan during the Hsien-feng reign. *WTHC* 4:34. *YHCL* 1: *mu-lu*, 3.

A final nineteenth-century edition appeared in 1873, the year of the author's death, published in Shanghai for popular consumption, much reduced in size so it could be easily carried. *WTHC* 4:84. Another reprint of the *YHCL* has recently appeared in two small volumes (Taipei, 1968).

9. *CR* 20:171. For Williams's translation of Ch'en Ch'ing-hsieh's colophon, which would seem to disprove his own statement, see *CR* 20:172.

10. *YHCL* 1: Hsu's preface, 1b.

11. *YHCL* 1: *hsu*, 1-2.

12.   *YHCL* 1: *hsu*, 2 (first preface of the 1861 Japanese edition).

13.   *YHCL* 1: *hsu,* 1-2 (second preface of the 1861 Japanese edition).

14.   *YHCL* 1: *pa*, 3; *hsu*, 4-5b.

15.   *YHCL* 1: *hsu*, 9a-b (1866 edition).

16.   *SKCC* 3:20b. This passage is the only reference I have located in Hsu's writings that hints at an imperial request for the compilation. In his book on Tao-kuang, Karl Gützlaff recorded the following: "There have been few emperors who have had a distinct idea of all their vast dominions. Taou-kwang, no doubt, formed an exception; and he even encouraged the publication of geographical works respecting other countries: formerly thought a subject too trivial to be considered worthy of notice. Two foreigners [?] compiled works of this description at the express desire of the Emperor; and some Chinese officers of high rank made similar attempts." Charles Gutzlaff, *The Life of Taou-kwang, Late Emperor of China* (London, 1852), pp. 262-263; *CR* 12:333.

17.   Unfortunately for those like Hsu who wished to import new information, China did not possess a phonetic system which, like the Japanese *katakana* syllabary, could simply reproduce fairly accurate pronunciations of new words without carrying any intrinsic meaning of the characters used to signify the sounds. Since this was not the case in China, Hsu, as did Buddhist missionaries centuries earlier, transliterated polysyllabic foreign names with combinations of monosyllabic characters, most of which in themselves signified a variety of unit-meanings. Like the American expression in Vienna, "donkey field mouse" for "danke viel mals," not only were the original sounds distorted, but the ideographs also conveyed unit-meanings independent of the original. This resulted in written barbarisms that were unpleasant to the Chinese eye.

Nonetheless, one of the truly significant technical achievements of the *Ying-huan chih-lueh* was the selection and standardization of characters which expressed Mandarin pronunciations of foreign proper names. The author, while remaining highly consistent throughout his book in presenting only translations for nouns rather than the inconvenient transliterations given in some of his sources—which had, for example, produced such gobbledygook as *li-po-li-hsien-t'e-ti-fu* in Lin Tse-hsu's book to stand for "representative" in the American congress, was equally faithful in his rule to use only transliterations for names of people and places. See Lin Tse-hsu, *Ssu-chou chih* (1841?), in Wang Hsi-ch'i, *Hsiao-fang-hu-chai, chih* 12:14 (v. 82 of the collection), p. 386. There were exceptions, however, such as Hsu's use of *hsien-shih* for senator. But here the characters themselves had been carefully chosen by the original translator so that their intrinsic meaning conveyed some impression of what at least an ideal senator was: "virtuous scholar." See *YHCL* 9:28b.

Hsu discussed such technical problems in his directions to readers. The following paragraphs partially summarize Hsu's notes. *YHCL* 1: *fan-li*, 3-4. He noted that foreign place names were difficult to distinguish, so that if ten people were to transliterate a name there would be ten characters (*tzu*) for the same sound. Also foreign states had two and three characters which were placed together to make one sound, but China of course did not have this sort of character. Therefore if one used Chinese characters to write foreign words, he would not be able to make the sounds of the characters match the original, and only seven or eight-tenths of the original sound would be retained. Beside this problem, Hsu continued, the Westerners who had studied Chinese to translate materials all had lived in Kwangtung, but Cantonese was not the "true" pronunciation of written Chinese. *Szu, shih*, and *shih* (written with a different character) were used interchangeably. Another *shih* was mixed up with *hsi* and *su*; and so on. Because many characters with different sounds were pronounced alike by Westerners (i.e., because of the dialects they learned), each author differed in his transliterations. Thus confusion and error had been caused to the point that it was almost impossible to distinguish foreign names.

Hsu included an example of the variety of transliterations current in Chinese sources for "Persia," and appeared somewhat perplexed because upon "ordering" a Westerner to pronounce it for him and then to write it down for him to see in Chinese, the sounds still did not tally. Hsu concluded therefore that he would place the various transliterations for names he had encountered in his research after the name of each country. In this way each reader would be able to recognize the place name by the particular transliteration with which he was familiar.

As a further complication, Hsu reported that the languages of the Western states differed from one another. He noted that his book used primarily the transliterations of the English and Portuguese for place names. Those transliterated by the English were done in few characters, but the sound was often incomplete. Those done by the Portuguese, although complete in sound, took eight or nine characters for one place name; this made for harsh sounds which could not be placed together.

Some of these tongue-twisting place names must have seemed almost as difficult to the Chinese as Lake Chargoggaggoggmanchaugagoggchaubunagungamaug in Webster, Massachusetts, appears to Westerners. See *Encyclopedia Britannica* (1959), 23:476.

To further prepare his readers for the complexities of terminology in dealing with the outside world, Hsu reported that each state had a "true name" (i.e., the pronunciation used by the natives of the state). Thus, *Shui-tien* for *Shui-kuo* (Sweden), *Lien-ma* for *Lien-kuo* (Denmark), *I-hsi-pan-ni-ya* for *Hsi-pan-ya* (Spain), and *Po-erh-tu-ko-ya* for *P'u-t'ao-ya* (Portugal). But he concluded that if he were to change all of the names in this manner the reader who was already familiar with some of the standard transliterations would be hard put to recognize the country. Therefore he would keep all of the commonly used names, while at the same time introducing some additional aids for the reader.

18.   For a fascinating treatment of this problem, see Arthur F. Wright, "The Chinese Language and Foreign Ideas," in *Studies in Chinese Thought*, ed. Arthur F. Wright (Chicago, 1953), pp. 286-303.

19.   Tsien Tsuen-hsuin, pp. 320-321.

20.   In the preparation of his book, Hsu's object throughout was clarity. If something could not be readily understood, it was rarely included. If sign posts (such as lines placed alongside the characters to indicate proper names) were necessary to keep readers from becoming confused, they were used in order to render exoteric what had all too long been esoteric, even if this meant sacrificing elegance. Each geographical section was clearly labeled and all of the commonly available transliterations and sometimes even translations, of the place name were included in reduced size immediately following the author's approved form.

VI. Governor Hsu's Image of the World

1.   I have found no evidence or reference in Hsu's materials to the alleged aid "of a Chinese from Hsiangshan [by Macao], who had . . . returned from a four years' sojourn in the United States." See *CR* 20:170. This probably refers to Akin, who had studied at Williams College in 1839. See Rockwell, p. 10.

2.   *YHCL* 1: Hsu's preface, 1; *fan-li*, 1.

3. *YHCL* 1:16. This is Ch'en Lun-ch'iung's *Hai-kuo wen-chien lu*.

4. I have not found any atlas published prior to 1844 which could be identified beyond doubt as Hsu's source. A two-volume set entitled *Maps of the Society for the Diffusion of Useful Knowledge* (London, 1844) may have been used, since many of Hsu's maps reflect idiosyncracies of these maps. However, the date of publication would make it unlikely that these would have appeared in China by the spring of 1844. Another perhaps more likely source was *A General Atlas of the World* (Boston, 1841).

5. *YHCL* 1:4-5b. Throughout I have generally made literal translations of special terms (such as "equator") and names for the oceans only on their first appearance.

6. *YHCL* 1:5b-7b.

7. *CR* 20:179.

8. *YHCL* 1:14a-b.

VII. Danger in China's Maritime Sphere

1. *YHCL* 1:9b-10.

2. "Asia" was apparently derived from "Assiuva," the Hittite name for the northwestern portion of Asia Minor. See M. Cary, ed., *The Oxford Classical Dictionary* (Oxford University Press, 1949).

3. *YHCL* 1:11a-b.

4. Other titles were *Fan-hai hsiao-lu* and *Shih-chou chi* (see Appendix A). *Ajia rekishi jiten* 4:182.

5. *YHCL* 1:20b.

6. *YHCL* 1:16a-b.

7. *YHCL* 1:17.

8. *YHCL* 1:17 ff.

9.   *YHCL* 1:19b-20.

10. *Ajia rekishi jiten* 4:182.

11. See the following articles: Robert K. Sakai, "The Ryukyu (Liu-ch'iu) Islands as a Fief of Satsuma" and Ta-tuan Ch'en, "Investiture of Liu-ch'iu Kings in the Ch'ing Period," in John K. Fairbank, ed., *The Chinese World Order*, pp. 112-134; 135-164.

12. *YHCL* 1:21b.

13. *YHCL* 1:22.

14. *YHCL* 1: *fan-li*, 1b.

15. *YHCL* 1:25 ff.

16. Ch'en Ch'i-t'ien (Gideon Ch'en), *Lin Tse-hsu*, p. 5 (note 7). John Francis Davis cited defense schemes proposed by Chinese after the fall of Amoy which included sending divers to bore holes in the hulls of Western ships. One wonders whether Hsu may have supported such experiments. See Davis, I, 166. Also, note similar efforts elsewhere described, such as in Waley, *Opium War*, p. 115.

17. *YHCL* 1:28b-29.

18. *YHCL* 1:30.

19. *YHCL* 1:31b.

20. By the Treaty of Yandabu (February 24, 1826).

21. *YHCL* 1:32-34.

22. *YHCL* 1:34a-b.

23. *YHCL* 2:19b.

24. *YHCL* 2:3b, 5a-b.

25. *YHCL* 2:4a-b. For a translation from the *Ming History* referring to this Spanish deception, see Matthew Chen, "The Ming Records of

Luzon," in Alfonso Felix, Jr., ed., *The Chinese in the Philippines, 1570-1770* (Manila, 1966), I, 247.

26.   *YHCL* 2:4b.

27.   *YHCL* 2:5 ff. For a discussion of *Fo-lang-hsi*, see Fairbank, *Trade*, I, 10-13.

28.   *YHCL* 2:5b-6. See Rafael Bernal, "The Chinese Colony in Manila, 1570-1770," in Alfonso Felix, Jr., ed., *The Chinese in the Philippines, 1570-1770*, I, 51.

29.   *YHCL* 2:6.

30.   *YHCL* 2:6b.

31.   Note the similar pidgin rendering of "padre" as *pa-te-le*. See William C. Hunter, *The "Fan Kwae" at Canton Before Treaty Days, 1825-1844* (London, 1882), p. 61.

32.   *YHCL* 2:7.

33.   *YHCL* 2:7b-8.

34.   See Fu Lo-shu, *A Documentary Chronicle of Sino-Western Relations, 1644-1820* (Tucson, 1966), I, 31 for the translation of *hua-jen*.

35.   *YHCL* 2:8a-b.

36.   *YHCL* 2:8b-9.

37.   *YHCL* 2:9b-10. The significance of Hsu's use of this ancient term from the *I ching* is discussed in a later chapter. Did Feng Kuei-fen lift this concept from Hsu's book for later popularization?

38.   *YHCL* 2:10b-11b.

39.   *YHCL* 2:14b.

40.   Bantam was captured and annexed by the Dutch only in 1808-1809. Hsu assumed this was much earlier.

41.   *YHCL* 2:16a-b.

42.   *YHCL* 2:15a-b, 19a-b.

43.   *YHCL* 2:17b. This appears to be a quotation taken from *Hai-tao i-chih*.

44.   *YHCL* 2:16b ff., 19b-20.

45.   *YHCL* 2:21a-b.

46.   *YHCL* 2:21b.

47.   *YHCL* 2:22b.

48.   *YHCL* 2:24.

49.   *YHCL* 2:25-26b.

50.   *YHCL* 2:25b.

51.   *YHCL* 2:27-28.

52.   *YHCL* 2:31.

53.   *YHCL* 2:31b-32.

54.   *YHCL* 2:32.

55.   *YHCL* 2:39b, 36b. Hsu had concluded that Ku's *Fo-lang-chi* were the
      French rather than the Portuguese, for he again cited this myth in his
      section for France.

56.   *YHCL* 2:36b.

57.   *YHCL* 2:32b-33.

VIII. Threatened on the Inner Asian Frontier

1.   *YHCL* 1: *fan-li*, 1b.

2.   *YHCL* 1: *fan-li*, 1b; 3:3b-4, 7.

3. *YHCL* 3:5, for example, lists the transliterations which Hsu had found in use at the time of his compilation of the *YHCL*.

4. *YHCL* 3:5b.

5. *YHCL* 3:5b.

6. *YHCL* 3:6a-b.

7. *YHCL* 3:7b.

8. *YHCL* 3:17-18.

9. *YHCL* 3:19.

10. *YHCL* 3:23a-b. This appears to have been taken from the *Hai-lu*.

11. *YHCL* 3:19b-20. This was undoubtedly disturbing news to the Shansi merchants involved in the trade by land with Central Asia.

12. *YHCL* 3:19b.

13. *YHCL* 3:24b-25.

14. *YHCL* 3:18b-19.

15. See *YHCL* 3:30, for example; *YHCL* 3:30b.

16. *YHCL* 3:31.

17. *YHCL* 3:33.

18. *YHCL* 3:33.

19. *YHCL* 3:35-38b.

20. *YHCL* 3:40.

21. *YHCL* 3:45.

22. *YHCL* 3:40b-41.

23. *YHCL* 3:44a-b.

24. *YHCL* 3:49b-50.

25. *YHCL* 3:54.

26. *YHCL* 3:55a-b.

IX. The "Barbarian" Base in Europe

1. *YHCL* 4:3b.

2. *YHCL* 4:3b.

3. *YHCL* 4:3b; 5b-6.

4. *YHCL* 4:6; 8a-b.

5. Note Wang Erh-min's use of this and the following example to stress Hsu's preconceptions of the world. See *Wan-Ch'ing cheng-chih ssu-hsiang shih-lun* (Taipei, 1969), p. 4. See Morohashi Tetsuji, *Dai Kan-Wa jiten* 2:5; 1:465.

6. *YHCL* 4:8b-9.

7. *YHCL* 4:12.

8. *YHCL* 4:12b.

9. *YHCL* 6:5b.

10. *YHCL* 6:10b.

11. *YHCL* 6:9a-b, 10b.

12. *YHCL* 6:13a-b.

13. *YHCL* 6:14-15.

14. *YHCL* 6:16a-b.

15. *YHCL* 6:19.

16. *YHCL* 6:21b-22.

17. *YHCL* 6:22.

18. *YHCL* 6:22b.

19. *YHCL* 6:23.

20. *YHCL* 6:23b. *Wai-i* in China referred to such "outer barbarians" as the Europeans who had not yet admitted Chinese cultural superiority by adopting her calendar, regulations, etc.

21. *YHCL* 6:25a-b.

22. *YHCL* 6:28-29.

23. This undoubtedly refers to the practice in Tibet of selecting a new-born child to replace a lama at his death. *YHCL* 6:29a-b.

24. *YHCL* 6:30.

25. *YHCL* 6:32.

26. *YHCL* 6:34b-36b.

27. *YHCL* 6:36b.

28. *YHCL* 6:37b-38.

29. *YHCL* 6:38b-39.

30. *YHCL* 6:39a-b. Hsu, aware of the secular power and therefore appeal of Western civilization, was arguing here against the simplistic view, still held then by numerous literati, that Christianity constituted the primary threat to China. See Paul A. Cohen, *China and Christianity: The Missionary Movement and the Growth of Chinese Antiforeignism, 1860-1870* (Cambridge, Mass., 1963).

31. *YHCL* 6:40.

32. *YHCL* 7:25b-26.

33. *YHCL* 7:19b; 24b.

34. *YHCL* 6:44b.

35. *YHCL* 6:45.

36. *YHCL* 6:47.

37. *YHCL* 4:17.

38. *YHCL* 4:18.

39. Ibid.

40. *YHCL* 4:23a-b.

41. *YHCL* 4:26a-b.

42. See *YHCL* 4:26b-27, 28-29.

43. *YHCL* 4:27b.

44. *YHCL* 4:27b-28.

45. *YHCL* 7:3-4b.

46. *YHCL* 7:5b.

47. *YHCL* 7:6.

48. *YHCL* 7:6a-b.

49. *YHCL* 7:10b-11.

50. *YHCL* 7:11b-12.

51. See *YHCL* 7:13-14.

52. *YHCL* 7:35-37.

53. *YHCL* 7:37b.

54. *YHCL* 7:39.

55. *YHCL* 7:40.

56. Ibid.

57. *YHCL* 7:43b. This evaluation probably was based on imports to China carried aboard British ships; thus, swallows' nests from Southeast Asia and sand for ballast.

58. *YHCL* 7:44.

59. *YHCL* 7:47-49.

60. *YHCL* 7:48-49.

61. *YHCL* 8:8a-b.

62. *YHCL* 10:7b.

63. *YHCL* 7:49b-50b.

64. *YHCL* 4:31.

65. *YHCL* 4:33b.

66. *YHCL* 5:4b-5.

67. *YHCL* 5:6a-b.

68. *YHCL* 5:11a-b.

69. *YHCL* 5:12.

70. *YHCL* 5:14b.

71. *YHCL* 5:25a-b.

72. *YHCL* 5:31a-b. "Plum Blossom Fountain" refers to the poet T'ao Ch'ien's ideal society. See Ch'en Shou-yi, *Chinese Literature: A Historical Introduction* (New York, 1961), pp. 174-175.

X. Despair in Africa, Hope in America

1. Evariste Regis Huc reported that "it is evident that a European hand has been engaged in [the new Chinese geographies'] composition, and from the flattering strain with which the United States are mentioned in them, it is strongly to be suspected that an American has had something to do with these publications." Evariste Regis Huc, *The Chinese Empire*, 2nd ed. (London, 1855), II, 375. Harvard holds the following three editions of Bridgman's "History of the United States of America":

   a. Kao-li-wen (Cantonese: Kou-lei-men), *Mei-li-ko ho-sheng-kuo chih-lueh* (Singapore, 1838).

   b. *Ya-mo-li-ko ho-sheng-kuo chih-lueh* (Hongkong, 1844).

   c. Pei-chih-wen (Cantonese: P'ei-ch'i-men), *Ta-Mei lien-pang chih-lueh* (Shanghai, 1861). While the transliteration of Bridgman was rendered Pei-chih-wen, Kao-li-wen represented the author's middle name, Coleman, which he commonly used among friends. See Belchertown Historical Association Letters, for example. The letters were for the most part signed "Coleman." For Hsu's use of this work, see my article entitled, "A Nineteenth-Century View of the United States of America from Hsu Chi-yü's *Ying-huan chih-lueh*," *Papers on China* 19:48-49 (1965). East Asian Research Center, Harvard University.

2. *YHCL* 8:3b.

3. *YHCL* 8:4-5.

4. *YHCL* 8:4b.

5. *YHCL* 8:6.

6. *YHCL* 8:11b-12. This ancient slogan was popularized in Meiji Japan as *fukoku kyōhei* ("rich state, strong army").

7. *YHCL* 8:12b.

8. *YHCL* 8:15b.

9. *YHCL* 8:17b; 18b; 21b.

10. *YHCL* 8:19b.

11. *YHCL* 8:20b.

12. *YHCL* 8:25b.

13. Most of the following account of the United States I have taken from my article, "View of the United States." *YHCL* 9:11b, 14b.

14. *YHCL* 9:1.

15. *Wu-kuan*: ears, eyes, nose, mouth, and heart. *YHCL* 9:1a-b, 3.

16. *YHCL* 9:1b, 28, 29b.

17. *YHCL* 9:28b-30.

18. *YHCL* 9:9b-10. The reference is to John Tyler.

19. *YHCL* 9:10b-11.

20. *YHCL* 9:9b-10b.

21. See *Senate Documents*, No. 2, 25th Congress, 3rd session, I, "Report on Finances" (December 3, 1838). "Yuan" appears to be a translation here for American dollar. Although the aggregate revenue is close to the 1838 figure of $39,019,383, expenditures are considerably lower than the official figures, indicating that they may refer to some earlier date. *YHCL* 9:28b-29.

22. *YHCL* 9:29.

23. *YHCL* 9:8, 10.

24. *YHCL* 9:28a-b, 29b.

25. See Michael Gasster, *Chinese Intellectuals and the Revolution of 1911; The Birth of Modern Chinese Radicalism* (Seattle, 1969), pp. 39-40, 104, 196. Four pictures were presented in the first issue of *Min pao* (1905): Ch'in Shih Huang-ti, "the world's first great nationalist;" Rousseau, "the world's first great democrat;" Washington, "the world's first founder of a republic;" and Mo-tzu, "first great advocate of equality and fraternity" (ibid., p. 104).

26. *YHCL* 9:8b-9.

27. *YHCL* 9:9-10.

28. Ch'en Sheng and Wu Kuang: famous rebels, leaders of a peasant revolt,
     against the Ch'in. These figures have naturally taken on new significance
     in China in recent decades. See James P. Harrison, *The Communists and
     Chinese Peasant Rebellions: A Study in the Rewriting of Chinese History*
     (New York, 1969), pp. 145-146 (notes 21, 22), p. 273 (note 18).

29. Ts'ao Ts'ao (155-220 A.D.) and Liu Pei (161-223 A.D.).

30. *Chi-yü t'ien-hsia wei kung.* It should be noted that *"t'ien-hsia wei kung"*
     became a popular slogan of Chinese modernizers, a phrase taken from the
     Li chi (Record of Rituals) which expressed a cosmopolitan ideal in
     Confucianism of a "world . . . shared by all alike." In a modern context
     this suggested a world order predicated on equality and justice. The
     motto was inscribed on Sun Yat-sen's tomb. See William Theodore de
     Bary, comp., *Sources of Chinese Tradition* (New York, Columbia Uni-
     versity Press, 1960), p. 191.

31. *YHCL* 9:10a-b. Late eighteenth and early nineteenth-century Chinese
     export porcelain, produced in Canton, thoroughly exploited Washington's
     popularity. For example, see a porcelain jug with his portrait in Marshall
     B. Davidson, ed., *The American Heritage History of American Antiques
     from the Revolution to the Civil War* (New York, 1968), p. 72; also see
     p. 75 for a Canton painting on glass of the avatar, "Liberty," standing
     on Beacon Hill, with an eagle and the American flag in the background
     (a copy of Edward Savage's "Liberty"); for other examples of United
     States political motifs, quite possibly seen by Hsu due to their popular
     production in Canton, see pp. 133-140. For a remarkable Canton paint-
     ing of Washington's apotheosis—Washington with arms outstretched, a
     Gilbert Stuart face, and lifted upon a sunbeam by two angels while "Lib-
     erty" and an American Indian in the foreground mourn the loss—see
     Ralph K. Andrist, ed., *The American Heritage History of the Making of
     the Nation, 1783-1860* (New York, 1968), p. 66. A fine example of
     Canton painting on glass of Gilbert Stuart's Washington (c. 1800) in
     mirror reverse is found on display in Essex Institute, Salem, Massachusetts.

32. *YHCL* 9:30. Hsu's treatment of Washington in the *YHCL* is found
     inscribed in Chinese inside the Washington Monument in Washington,
     D.C. See below, Chapter XI, note 66. Washington's appeal in China
     appears to have survived from Hsu's time to the present. A recent
     visitor to the People's Republic of China reported that one of the few

items of foreign literature he found in 1972 in the political science reading room of Tsinghua University, along with Edgar Snow's *Red Star
over China*, was a biography of Washington. See Arthur W. Galston,
Daily Life in People's China (New York, 1973), p. 201. This power of
survival is all the more remarkable when one considers the flagrant use
of Washington as a symbol of Western privilege in China, such as the
annual George Washington Ball of treaty port life in Shanghai's Majestic
Hotel, replete with tiny hatchets on the tables in company with red,
white, and blue ice cream. See Enid Saunders Candlin, *The Breach in
the Wall: A Memoir of the Old China* (New York, 1973), p. 121. Sun
Yat-sen nevertheless admitted his admiration for Washington, comparing him to T'ang and Wu of ancient China, founders respectively of the
Shang and Chou dynasties. See Shao Chuan Leng and Norman D. Palmer,
Sun Yat-sen and Communism (New York, 1960), p. 17. In a popular
English-Chinese dictionary of the 1930's, to illustrate the use of the
article "a" is found the following sentence: "We need a Washington.
Wo-men hsu-yao i-ko hsiang Hua-sheng-tun *te jen.*" *A Daily Use English-
Chinese Dictionary* (Shanghai, 1936), p. 1. Theodore H. White's report
of his interview with Mao Tse-tung at Yenan in the 1930's suggests
Washington's appeal, in spite of misinformation, for even a modern
Chinese hero: "Mao said that any wise European who had seen George
Washington's people at Valley Forge would have said that George Wash-
ington was going to lose. It's true, he said, that the Japanese and Chiang
K'ai-shek have electricity, airplanes, tanks and we have nothing, but
then, he said, the British had all those things, and George Washington
didn't have electricity. Yet George Washington won." See Theodore H.
White, *China: The Roots of Madness* (New York, 1968), pp. 84-85.

33.   Waley, *The Analects of Confucius* (New York, 1938), p. 122 (Book VI,
      no. 28).

34.   *YHCL* 10:3b.

35.   *YHCL* 10:4.

36.   *YHCL* 10:7.

XI. Return to China's Heartland

1.   *SKCC* 4:24b-25b.

2.   *SKCC* 4:25.

3. *SKCC* 3:29.

4. *SKCC* 3:17.

5. *SKCC* 3:25b. It was customary for all candidates to "contribute" funds to help cover the expenses of the examiners.

6. *SKCC* 2:27; 3:18b, 25b.

7. *CSK, lieh-chuan* no. 209, 10. Wang was noted for his work in "state-craft," especially for his attention to Ch'ing finances. See Hummel, I, 508; II, 813-814. Hsu apparently first knew Wang in Peking in the 1830's, when their assignments to the Hanlin Academy overlapped. Later they probably met again in Foochow, Wang's home, to which he had returned after his father's death in 1841 to remain till 1846.

8. For Hsu's history of the school, see *SKCC* 4:18b-20.

9. *SKCC* 3:15a-b. For background to the financial basis for local militia, see Philip A. Kuhn, *Rebellion and Its Enemies in Late Imperial China* (Cambridge, Mass., 1970), pp. 87-92.

10. *SKCC* 3:14b-16b.

11. *SKCC* 3:12b, 25. See *Ajia rekishi jiten* 4:405.

12. For example, see Hsu's letter to Wang in *SKCC* 3:8-10b.

13. *SKCC* 3:19.

14. *SKCC* 3:13-14.

15. *SKCC* 3:19, 21, 26b, 29.

16. *SKCC* 3:26b.

17. See the maps of this and the adjacent walled cities of Chieh-hsiu and Fen-yang in *Shan-hsi t'ung-chih* 1:6b-7. Also see "Fen-yang," Map NJ 49-11, Series L500, Army Map Service (Washington, D.C., 1955).

18. *SKCC* 3:25; 4:18b-20.

19.   Chang Hsin-pao, pp. 37-39.

20.   R. W. Swallow, *A Glimpse at Western China; The Province of Shansi* (Manchester, 1906), p. 6.

21.   Ch'en Ch'i-t'ien (Gideon Ch'en), *Shan-hsi p'iao-chuang k'ao-lueh* (Shanghai, 1937), pp. 13-14, 21. See Willard J. Peterson, "The Life of Ku Yen-wu (1613-1682)," (II) in *Harvard Journal of Asiatic Studies*, 29 (1969), pp. 204-205.

22.   Davis, II, 95.

23.   Ch'en Ch'i-t'ien (Gideon Ch'en), *Shan-hsi*, pp. 20-21, 152-154, 158.

24.   *SKCC* 3:10b, 26b-27.

25.   *SKCC* 2:17b-20.

26.   See *SKCC* 4:18b-20.

27.   *SKCC* 4:20.

28.   *SKCC* 3:19; 4:28b-29b.

29.   *SKCC* 3:26a-b.

30.   *SKCC* 3:26b; *SKCC, Liang-Han* . . . , 1a-b.

31.   *SKCC* 3:25b-26.

32.   *SKCC* 4:23a-b.

33.   *SKCC* 1:24b; 3:12b, 16b, 21; 4:30.

34.   *SKCC* 4:14b-16.

35.   *SKCC, Liang-Han* . . . , for example.

36.   Entitled *Wu-t'ai hsin-chih* (New gazetteer of Wu-t'ai). Even in retirement Hsu's dedication to geographic realism could be seen in his strong criticism of gentry who, for the sake of impressing others with their

erudition, used historical geographic names, especially from the Han dynasty, rather than the popular names in current use. See *SKCC* 4:3.

37. *SKCC, Liang-Han* . . . : 1; 2:16-17b.

38. *SKCC* 1:20a-b, 25b; 4:16b-18; *WTHC* 4:7b

39. *SKCC* 1:19b, for example. This preface is dated 1838.

40. *SKCC* 1:24b; 4:14-16.

41. *SKCC* 1:16b-17b, 18b-19, 26; 2:2b; 3:21b-22.

42. *SKCC* 3:10b-12.

43. *SKCC* 3:21b. Whether or not Hsu's influence was felt in Peking on this issue is unclear. Yet in 1860 the Ch'ing government gave some consideration to the use of American merchants to transport rice to the North in steamships. See Stephen C. Lockwood, *Augustine Heard and Company, 1858-1862; American Merchants in China* (Cambridge, Mass., 1971), p. 81.

44. *SKCC* 3:19b-20. It is obvious from the context that Hsu referred here to foreign affairs.

45. *SKCC* 3:19b; Waley, *Analects*, p. 199 (Book XV, 29).

46. *SKCC* 3:19b, 21b, 28a-b; see Waley, *Analects*, p. 187 (Book XIV, 27, 28): "When the Master said, He who holds no rank in a State does not discuss its policies, Master Tseng said, 'A true gentleman, even in his thoughts, never departs from what is suitable to his rank.'"

47. *SKCC* 2:5-6b.

48. *SKCC* 3:25b; 1:16a-b, 18b-19.

49. *SKCC* 3:17a-b.

50. *SKCC* 2:27. A chart of Shansi firms prepared in 1912 lists Tung-yeh-chen as the site of one of the main houses. See Ch'en Ch'i-t'ien (Gideon Ch'en), *Shan-hsi*, p. 196.

51. *SKCC* 3:22b.

52. *SKCC* 2:27; 3:22b. Rowe, p. 537. For a lively discussion of this event, see Wakeman, pp. 11-21.

53. *SKCC* 3:23b.

54. *SKCC* 3:27.

55. *SKCC* 3:27b.

56. *SKCC* 2:4b.

57. *SKCC* 4:30a-b. Tzu-kung and Tzu-lu were disciples of Confucius.

58. *SKCC* 3:22b.

59. *SKCC* 3:3a-b, 22b, 30a-b. *IWSM:TC* 37:16. The importance of this appointment was not missed by contemporary Western observers. See Mary C. Wright, pp. 229-230.

60. *SKCC* 3:30a-b.

61. *SKCC* 3:30b.

62. Ch'ien Shih-fu, *Ch'ing-chi hsin-she chih-kuan nien-piao* (Peking, 1961), p. 3. Brunnert and Hagelstrom, no. 936B. *IWSM:TC* 47:8, 16b. Also, see Knight Biggerstaff, *The Earliest Modern Government Schools in China* (Ithaca, Cornell University Press, 1961), pp. 112-113.

63. *The New York Times*, 17, no. 5151 (March 29, 1868), pp. 4 and 10. The copy was done by a Mr. Pratt of Boston at the request of President Johnson and Secretary of State Seward.

64. Ibid., p. 10. The full text of Burlingame's address is worth noting. "It is now nearly twenty years since you published a geographical history of the countries lying beyond the boundaries of China. You brought to the work great labor, a sound judgment, and the marvelous scholarship of your native land. You passed in review the great men of the countries of which you wrote, and placed Washington before all the rest. You not only did this, but you placed him before the statesmen and

warriors of your own country, and declared that he recalled the three
dynasties whose serene virtues had shed their light along the ages for
4,000 years. Those words have been used and translated by the grateful
countrymen of Washington. To show their appreciation of them, the
President requested the Secretary of State to have made by a distinguished
artist this portrait, and to send it over land and sea to be placed in your
hands. When you look upon its benignant features, do not recall with
sorrow the eighteen [*sic*] years of retirement endured by you on account
of your efforts to make Washington and the countries of the West better
known; but rather, exult with us that an enlightened Government has
for the same reason placed you near the head of the State, to aid in con-
trolling the affairs of 490,000,000 of people; and what is better by a
kind of poetical justice, you have been placed at the head of an institution whose purpose is to advance the views for which you were censured,
and to instruct your people in the language and principles of Washington.
By doing this you will please all the nations, for Washington belonged
not to us alone, but to the world. His life and character were such as to
peculiarly commend him to your countrymen. Like them he honored
agriculture; and like them he was for peace, and only fought in defence
of his country. Like them, he believed that every man is entitled to the
inspiration of fair opportunity, and like them he held to the doctrine of
Confucius, spoken 2,300 years ago, that 'We should not do to others
what we would not that others should do to us.' This great truth came
to Washington, not negatively but positively, from Divinity itself, as a
command unto him, 'Do unto others as you would have others do unto
you.' Why should we not exchange our thoughts? Why should we not
have the moral maxims of Confucius and Mencius, and you the sublime
doctrines of Christianity? Why should we not take your charming manners, your temperance, your habits of scholarship, your improvements
in agriculture, and your high culture . . . , and you our modern sciences,
our railroads and telegraphs, our steamboats? Why should not this great
nation, the mother of inventions, whence comes paper, printing, porcelain, the compass, gunpowder and the great doctrine that 'The people
are the source of power,' follow up their inventions and principles, and
enjoy them in all their development? Why should not the discoverers of
coal have the wealth and strength derived from its use, and those who
made the first water-tight vessels guided by a compass, use the great
steamers whose swiftness makes us your near neighbors, and which
carry a thousand men on their decks? I present this portrait, with all
good will, in the name of the people of the United States, hoping it may
ever recall to you and yours their enduring friendship for your country,
and their love and regard for you, its worthy representative."

65. Ibid., p. 10.

66. Missionaries in China were aware of the monument project at least by 1851. See *CR* 20:189-190 (1851). The stone was presented by "United States citizens" in Foochow probably in 1862. Peter Parker's 1862 translation of the inscription is found in Frederick L. Harvey, *History of the Washington National Monument and Washington National Monument Society* (Washington, 1902), p. 324. Further details on the stone can be found in the National Archives. See Washington National Monument Society, Correspondence of Secretary Whittlesey (Letters Received Regarding Memorial Stones, 1849-1889; box 8; folder entitled: "Stones, 1860-1869"). The inscription is found at approximately the three hundred foot level of the monument.

67. Ch'ien Shih-fu, *Ch'ing-chi hsin-she chih-kuan nien-piao*, p. 4; *WTHC* 4:7b. Brunnert and Hagelstrom, no. 966.

XII. CONCLUSION

1. For information on early Chinese attempts to discover the secrets behind Western ships in the mid-nineteenth century, see Ch'en Ch'i-t'ien (Gideon Ch'en), *Lin Tse-hsu.*

2. See Don C. Price, "The Chinese Intelligentsia's Image of Russia, 1896-1911," Ph. D. dissertation, Harvard University, 1967. Especially see Chapter II, "K'ang Yu-wei, Yen Fu and Peter the Great."

3. See Benjamin Schwartz, *In Search of Wealth and Power: Yen Fu and the West* (Cambridge, Mass., 1964).

4. See Teng Ssu-yü and John K. Fairbank, *China's Response to the West: A Documentary Survey, 1830-1923* (Cambridge, Mass., 1961), p. 50.

5. Ibid., p. 62.

6. *IWSM:HF* 72:6. Hu Sheng, *Imperialism and Chinese Politics, 1840-1925* (Peking, 1955), p. 95.

7. Price, pp. 35, 38. See K'ang Yu-wei, "K'ang Nan-hai tzu-pien nien-p'u" (Chronological autobiography of K'ang Yu-wei) in Chien Po-tsan, ed., *Wu-hsu pien-fa* 4:115 (Shanghai, 1953).

8. Joseph R. Levenson, *Liang Ch'i-ch'ao and the Mind of Modern China* (Cambridge, Mass., 1953), p. 17.

9. Price, p. 19.

10. *SKCC*, preface, p. 1. Mary C. Wright, p. 311, note. Gillin, p. 12.

11. Professor Roy Hofheinz of Harvard University.

BIBLIOGRAPHY

Ajia rekishi jiten アジア歴史事典 (Dictionary of Asian
history). 10 vols. Tokyo, 1959-1962.

American Board of Commissioners for Foreign Missions, Archives.
Cambridge, Mass., Houghton Library, Harvard University.

Andrist, Ralph K., ed., *The American Heritage History of the
Making of the Nation, 1783-1860.* New York, American
Heritage Publishing Co., 1968.

Bernal, Rafael, "The Chinese Colony in Manila, 1570-1770," in
Alfonso Felix, Jr., ed., *The Chinese in the Philippines, 1570-
1770.* Manila, Solidaridad Publishing House, 1966.

Biggerstaff, Knight. *The Earliest Modern Government Schools in
China.* Ithaca, Cornell University Press, 1961.

Boulding, Kenneth E., *The Image.* Ann Arbor, University of
Michigan Press, 1956.

Boxer, Charles R., ed., *South China in the Sixteenth Century.*
London, The Hakluyt Society, 1953.

[Bridgman, Elijah C.] *Ya-mo-li-ko ho-sheng-kuo chih-lueh* 亞
墨理格合省國志略 (A short record of the
United States of America). Hongkong, 1844.

Bridgman Papers, Amherst College Archives.

Brunnert, H. S. and V. V. Hagelstrom. *Present Day Political
Organization of China,* tr. A. Beltchenko and E. E. Moran.
Shanghai, Kelly and Walsh, Ltd., 1912.

Candlin, Enid Saunders, *The Breach in the Wall: A Memoir of the
Old China.* New York, Macmillan Publishing Co., 1973.

Cary, Max, ed. *The Oxford Classical Dictionary.* Oxford, The
Clarendon Press, 1949.

Chan Wing-tsit, tr. *Instructions for Practical Living and Other Neo-Confucian Writings by Wang Yang-ming*. New York, Columbia University Press, 1963.

Chang Ch'i-yun, ed. 張其昀 . *Chung-hua min-kuo ti-t'u chi* 中華民國地圖集 (Atlas of the Republic of China). 5 vols. Taipei, 1960-1963.

Chang Hsi-t'ung. "The Earliest Phase of the Introduction of Western Political Science into China," *The Yenching Journal of Social Studies* 5:1-29 (1950).

Chang Hsin-pao. *Commissioner Lin and the Opium War*. Cambridge, Mass., Harvard University Press, 1964.

Chen, Matthew, "The Ming Records of Luzon," in Alfonzo Felix, Jr., ed., *The Chinese in the Philippines, 1570-1770*. Manila, Solidaridad Publishing House, 1966.

Ch'en Ch'i-t'ien 陳其田 (Gideon Ch'en). *Lin Tse-hsu: Pioneer Promoter of the Adoption of Western Means of Maritime Defense in China*. Peiping, Yenching University, 1934.

――― *Tseng Kuo-fan: Pioneer Promoter of the Steamship in China*. Peiping, Yenching University, 1935.

――― *Shan-hsi p'iao-chuang k'ao-lueh* 山西票莊考畧 (A brief historical study of the Shansi banks). Shanghai, 1937.

――― *Tso Tsung-t'ang: Pioneer Promoter of the Modern Dockyard and the Woolen Mill in China*. Peiping, Yenching University, 1938.

Ch'en Kuan-sheng (Kenneth Ch'en). "The Growth of Geographical Knowledge Concerning the West in China during the Ch'ing Dynasty." Master's thesis, Yenching University, Peiping, 1934.

Ch'en Shou-yi. *Chinese Literature: A Historical Introduction*. New York, The Ronald Press Co., 1961.

Ch'en Ta-tuan. "Investiture of Liu-ch'iu Kings in the Ch'ing Period," in John K. Fairbank, ed., *The Chinese World Order*. Cambridge, Mass., Harvard University Press, 1968.

Ch'i Ssu-ho 齊思和. *Ya-p'ien chan-cheng* 鴉片戰爭 (The Opium War). Shanghai, 1954.

Chien Po-tsan 翦伯贊, ed. *Wu-hsu pien-fa* 戊戌變法 (The reform movement of 1898). Shanghai, 1953.

Ch'ien Shih-fu 錢實甫. *Ch'ing-chi chung-yao chih-kuan nien-piao* 清季重要職官年表 (Chronological tables of important officers in the late Ch'ing). Peking, 1959.

——— *Ch'ing-chi hsin-she chih-kuan nien-piao* 清季新設職官年表 (Chronological tables of officers in newly established posts in the late Ch'ing). Peking, 1961.

Chinese Repository, Elijah C. Bridgman and S. Wells Williams, eds. Macao and Canton, 1832–1851.

Ch'ing-shih kao 清史稿 (Draft history of the Ch'ing dynasty), comp., Chao Erh-hsun 趙爾巽. 536 chüan. 1927.

Ch'ing-tai hsueh-che hsiang chuan 清代學者象傳 (Pictorial biographies of Ch'ing scholars). 1928.

Ch'ou-pan i-wu shih-mo 籌辦夷務始末 (A complete account of our management of barbarian affairs). Peiping, 1930. Tao-kuang period, 80 chüan; Hsien-feng period, 80 chüan; T'ung-chih period, 100 chüan.

Chung-hua chiao-yü chieh 中華教育界 (The world of Chinese education). Shanghai, 1912–?

Cohen, Paul A. *China and Christianity: The Missionary Movement and the Growth of Chinese Antiforeignism, 1860–1870.* Cambridge, Mass., Harvard University Press, 1963.

Conrad, Joseph. *Last Essays.* Garden City, New York, Doubleday, Page and Co., 1926.

Couling, Samuel. *The Encyclopaedia Sinica.* Shanghai, Kelly and Walsh, Ltd., 1917.

Cressey, George B. *Land of the 500 Million.* New York, McGraw-Hill Book Co., 1955.

Daily Use English-Chinese Dictionary, A. Shanghai, The World
 Book Co., Ltd., 1936.

Davidson, Marshall B., ed. *The American Heritage History of
 American Antiques from the Revolution to the Civil War.*
 New York, American Heritage Publishing Co., 1968.

Davis, John Francis. *China During the War and Since the Peace.*
 2 vols. London, 1852.

de Bary, William Theodore, comp. *Sources of Chinese Tradition.*
 New York, Columbia University Press, 1960.

Drake, Fred W. "A Nineteenth-Century View of the United States
 of America from Hsu Chi-yü's *Ying-huan chih-lueh,* " *Papers
 on China* 19:30–54 (1965). Cambridge, Mass., East Asian Research Center, Harvard University.

——— "Hsu Chi-yü and his *Ying-huan chih-lueh* (1848)." Ph.D.
 dissertation, Harvard University, 1970.

——— "A Mid-Nineteenth Century Discovery of the Non-Chinese
 World," *Modern Asian Studies* 6.2:205–224 (April 1972).

Eberhard, Wolfram. *A History of China.* London, Routledge and
 Kegan Paul Ltd., 1950.

——— "Chinese Regional Stereotypes," in *Asian Survey* 5.12: 596–
 608 (1965).

Fairbank, John K. *Trade and Diplomacy on the China Coast: The
 Opening of the Treaty Ports, 1842–1854.* 2 vols. Cambridge,
 Mass., Harvard University Press, 1953.

——— *The Chinese World Order: Traditional China's Foreign Relations.* Cambridge, Mass., Harvard University Press, 1968.

——— and Teng Ssu-yü, "On the Ch'ing Tributary System," in
 Ch'ing Administration: Three Studies. Cambridge, Mass.,
 Harvard University Press, 1961.

Fitzgerald, C. P. *The Horizon History of China.* New York, American Heritage Publishing Co., 1969.

Frodsham, J. D., tr. *The First Chinese Embassy to the West: The Journals of Kuo Sung-t'ao, Liu Hsi-hung, and Chang Te-yi.* Oxford, The Clarendon Press, 1974.

Fu Lo-shu. *A Documentary Chronicle of Sino-Western Relations, 1644-1820.* Tucson, University of Arizona Press, 1966.

Galston, Arthur W. *Daily Life in People's China.* New York, Thomas Y. Crowell Co., 1973.

Gasster, Michael. *Chinese Intellectuals and the Revolution of 1911: The Birth of Modern Radicalism.* Seattle, University of Washington Press, 1969.

General Atlas of the World, A. Boston, 1841.

Gerson, Jack J. *Horatio Nelson Lay and Sino-British Relations, 1854-1864.* Cambridge, Mass., East Asian Research Center, Harvard University, 1972.

Gillin, Donald G. *Warlord: Yen Hsi-shan in Shansi Province, 1911-1949.* Princeton University Press, 1967.

Gutzlaff, Charles. *The Life of Taou-kwang, Late Emperor of China.* London, 1852.

Hardy, E. J. *John Chinaman at Home: Sketches of Men, Manners and Things in China.* New York, T. Fisher Unwin, 1905.

Harrison, James P. *The Communists and Chinese Peasant Rebellions: A Study in the Rewriting of Chinese History.* New York, Atheneum Publishers, 1969.

Harvey, Frederick L. *History of the Washington National Monument and Washington National Monument Society.* Washington, D.C., N. T. Elliott Co., 1902.

Hermann, Albert. *An Historical Atlas of China.* Chicago, Aldine

Publishing Co., 1966. Originally published by Harvard-Yenching Institute, 1935.

Ho Ping-ti. *Studies on the Population of China, 1368-1953.* Cambridge, Mass., Harvard University Press, 1959.

——— *The Ladder of Success in Imperial China.* New York, Columbia University Press, 1962.

Hsieh Pao-chao. *The Government of China, 1644-1911.* Baltimore, Johns Hopkins University Press, 1925.

Hsu Chi-yü 徐繼畬. *Ying-huan chih-lueh* 瀛環志畧 (A short account of the maritime circuit). 10 chüan. Foochow, author's preface, 1848.

——— *Ch'ou yun Hsi-mi ts'e-lueh* (To devise a policy of importing Western rice). 1858.

——— *T'ui-mi-chai i-chi* (Remaining writings from the T'ui-mi study). See *Sung-k'an hsien-sheng ch'üan-chi.*

———, ed. *Wu-t'ai hsin-chih* (New gazetteer of Wu-t'ai [Shansi]), 4 chüan. Wu-tai, Shansi, 1884.

Hsu, Immanuel C.Y. *The Rise of Modern China.* New York, Oxford University Press, 1970.

Hsu Jun-ti 徐閏第. *Tun-ken-chai i-shu* 敦艮齋遺書 (Remaining writings from the Tun-ken Study). 17 chüan. c. 1831.

Hu Sheng. *Imperialism and Chinese Politics, 1840-1925.* Peking, Foreign Languages Press, 1955.

Huc, Evariste Regis. *The Chinese Empire.* 2 vols. 2nd ed., London, 1855.

Hummel, Arthur W., ed. *Eminent Chinese of the Ch'ing Period, 1644-1912.* 2 vols. Washington, D.C., U.S. Government Printing Office, 1944.

Hunter, William C. *The "Fan Kwae" at Canton Before Treaty Days, 1825-1844.* London, 1882.

Jo Keiyo 徐繼畬. *Eikan shiryaku* 瀛環志畧 (A short account of the maritime circuit). 1861. The Japanese version of the *Ying-huan chih-lueh.*

K'ang Yu-wei 康有為. "K'ang Nan-hai tzu-pien nien-p'u" 康南海自編年譜 (Chronological autobiography of K'ang Yu-wei) in vol. 4 of Chien Po-tsan, ed., *Wu-hsu pien-fa.*

Kao-li-wen 高理文 (E. C. Bridgman). *Mei-li-ko ho-sheng-kuo chih-lueh* 美利哥合省國志畧 (A brief record of the United States of America). Singapore, 1838.

Kuhn, Philip A. *Rebellion and Its Enemies in Late Imperial China.* Cambridge, Mass., Harvard University Press, 1970.

Latourette, Kenneth Scott. "Voyages of American Ships to China, 1784–1844," *Transactions of the Connecticut Academy of Arts and Sciences* 28:237–271 (1927).

Lay, George T. *The Chinese as They Are.* London, 1841.

Leng Shao-chuan and Norman D. Palmer. *Sun Yat-sen and Communism.* New York, F. A. Praeger, 1960.

Leonard, Jane Kate. "Wei Yuan and the *Hai-kuo t'u-chih:* A Geopolitical Analysis of Western Expansion in Maritime Asia." Ph.D. dissertation, Cornell University, 1971.

Levenson, Joseph R. *Liang Ch'i-ch'ao and the Mind of Modern China.* Cambridge, Mass., Harvard University Press, 1953.

Liang Ch'i-ch'ao. *Intellectual Trends in the Ch'ing Period,* tr. Immanuel C. Y. Hsu. Cambridge, Mass., Harvard University Press, 1959.

Lin Tse-hsu 林則徐. *Ssu-chou chih* 四洲志 (Record of the four continents, 1841?) in Wang Hsi-ch'i, ed., *Hsiao-fang-hu-chai yü-ti ts'ung-ch'ao tsai-pu-pien. Chih* 12:14 (vol. 82).

Liu Kwang-ching. "Nineteenth-Century China: The Disintegration of the Old Order and the Impact of the West," in Ho Ping-ti and Tang Tsou, eds., *China's Heritage and the Communist Political System,* vol. 1, bk. 1. The University of Chicago Press, 1968.

Lockwood, Stephen C. *Augustine Heard and Company, 1858–1862: American Merchants in China.* Cambridge, Mass., East Asian Research Center, Harvard University, 1971.

Lu Hsun. "The True Story of Ah Q," in *Selected Works of Lu Hsun,* vol. 1. Peking, Foreign Languages Press, 1956.

Maps of the Society for the Diffusion of Useful Knowledge. 2 vols. London, 1844.

Mayers, William F. *The Chinese Government: A Manual of Chinese Titles, Categorically Arranged and Explained with an Appendix.* Shanghai, 1897.

Michie, Alexander. *The Englishman in China during the Victorian Era, As Illustrated in the Career of Sir Rutherford Alcock.* 2 vols. London, W. Blackwood & Sons, 1900.

Min Hou hsien-chih 閩侯縣志 (Gazetteer of Foochow). 1933.

Mitchell, Peter MacVicar. "Wei Yuan (1794–1857) and the Early Modernization Movement in China and Japan." Ph.D. dissertation, Indiana University, 1970.

Morohashi Tetsuji 諸橋轍次. *Dai Kan-Wa jiten* 大漢和辭典 (Great Chinese-Japanese dictionary). 13 vols. Tokyo, 1943–1960.

Morse, Hosea Ballou. *The International Relations of the Chinese Empire: The Period of Conflict, 1834–1860.* London, Longmans, Green and Co., 1910–1918.

——— *The Chronicles of the East India Company Trading to China, 1635–1834.* 5 vols. Oxford, The Clarendon Press, 1926–1929.

Nivison, David S. "The Problem of 'Knowledge' and 'Action' in Chinese Thought since Wang Yang-ming," in Arthur F. Wright, ed., *Studies in Chinese Thought*. The University of Chicago Press, 1953.

——— "Aspects of Traditional Chinese Biography," *The Journal of Asian Studies* 21:457–463 (1962).

Pei-chih-wen 裨治文 (E. C. Bridgman). *Ta-Mei lien-pang chih-lueh* 大美聯邦志略 (A short record of the United States of America). Shanghai, 1861.

Pei-chuan chi, hsu-chi 碑傳集續集 (A supplementary collection of epitaphs), ed., Miao Ch'üan-sun 繆荃孫 Soochow, 1910.

Peterson, Willard J. "The Life of Ku Yen-wu (1613–1682)," (II), *Harvard Journal of Asiatic Studies* 29:201–247 (1969).

Pi-ch'ang 壁昌 . *Shou-pien chi-yao* 守邊輯要 (A summary of items to protect the border), in *Pi Ch'in-hsiang-kung i-shu san-chung ho-k'o* 壁勤襄公遺書三種合刻 (Three books printed together from the literary collection of Pi-ch'ang). c. 1855.

——— *Ping-wu wen-chien lu* 兵武聞見錄 (A record of things heard and seen concerning military [affairs]), in *Pi Ch'in-hsiang-kung i-shu san-chung ho-k'o*. c. 1855.

Playfair, G. M. H. *The Cities and Towns of China*. Shanghai, Kelly and Walsh, 1910.

Price, Don C. "The Chinese Intelligentsia's Image of Russia, 1896–1911." Ph.D. dissertation, Harvard University, 1967.

Rockwell, Dorothy Ann. "The Compilation of Governor Hsu's *Ying-huan chih-lueh*," *Papers on China* 11:1–28 (1957). East Asian Research Center, Harvard University.

Rowe, David Nelson, ed. *Index to Ch'ing-tai ch'ou-pan i-wu shih-mo.* Hamden, Conn., The Shoe String Press, 1960.

Roy, David T. "Hsu Chi-yü and the Shen-Kuang Szu Case at Foochow in 1850." Seminar paper, Harvard University, January 1959. In Professor John K. Fairbank's files.

Sakai, Robert K. "The Ryukyu (Liu-ch'iu) Islands as a Fief of Satsuma," in John K. Fairbank, ed., *The Chinese World Order.* Cambridge, Mass., Harvard University Press, 1968.

Sansom, George B. *Japan: A Short Cultural History.* New York, Appleton-Century-Crofts, 1962.

Schwartz, Benjamin. *In Search of Wealth and Power: Yen Fu and the West.* Cambridge, Mass., Harvard University Press, 1964.

Shan-hsi t'ung-chih 山西通志 (Gazetteer of Shansi [province]), comp. Ch'u Ta-wen 儲大文 . Shansi, 1734.

Smith, George. *A Narrative of an Exploratory Visit to Each of the Consular Cities of China.* London, 1847.

Snow, Edgar. *Red China Today.* New York, Random House, 1970.

Sung-k'an hsien-sheng ch'üan-chi 松龕先生全集 (The collected works of Hsu Chi-yü), comp. Yen Hsi-shan 閻錫山 . 9 chüan. Wu-t'ai, Shansi, 1915.

Swallow, Robert William. *A Glimpse at Western China: The Province of Shansi.* Manchester, Sherratt and Hughes, 1906.

Swisher, Earl. *China's Management of the American Barbarians: A Study of Sino-American Relations, 1841-1861, with Documents.* New Haven, Yale University Press, 1953.

Teng Ssu-yü. *Chang Hsi and the Treaty of Nanking, 1842.* University of Chicago Press, 1944.

——— and John K. Fairbank. *China's Response to the West: A Documentary Survey, 1839-1923.* Cambridge, Mass., Harvard University Press, 1961.

Teng T'ing-chen 鄧廷楨. "Teng T'ing-chen kuan-yü Ya-p'ien chan-cheng te shu-hsin" 鄧廷楨關於鴉片戰爭的書信 (Letters of Teng T'ing-chen concerning the Opium War), in Ch'i Ssu-ho, ed., *Ya-p'ien chan-cheng*.

Thom, Robert. *Esop's Fables in Chinese*. Canton, 1840.

Tsien Tsuen-hsuin. "Western Impact on China through Translation," *Far Eastern Quarterly* 13:305–327 (1954).

Twitchett, Denis. "Problems of Chinese Biography," in Arthur F. Wright and Denis Twitchett, eds., *Confucian Personalities*. Stanford University Press, 1962.

Wakeman, Frederick, Jr. *Strangers at the Gate: Social Disorder in South China, 1839–1861*. Berkeley, University of California Press, 1966.

Waley, Arthur. *The Opium War through Chinese Eyes*. London, George Allen and Unwin, Ltd., 1958.

——— tr. *The Analects of Confucius*. New York, George Allen and Unwin, Ltd., 1938.

Wang Erh-min 王爾敏. *Wang-Ch'ing cheng-chih szu-hsiang shih-lun* 晚清政治思想史論 (A history of political thought in the late Ch'ing [dynasty]). Taipei, 1969.

Wang Hsi-ch'i 王錫祺. *Hsiao-fang-hu-chai yü-ti ts'ung-ch'ao tsai-pu-pien* 小方壺齋輿地叢鈔再補編 (Supplement to collected texts on geography from the Hsiao-fang-hu Study). Shanghai, 1897.

Wei Yuan 魏源. *Hai-kuo t'u-chih* 海國圖志 (An illustrated gazetteer of the countries overseas). 1844.

White, Theodore H. *China: The Roots of Madness*. New York: W. W. Norton & Co., Inc., 1968.

Williams, Frederick Wells. *Life and Letters of Samuel Wells Williams*. New York, 1889.

Williams, Samuel Wells. *The Middle Kingdom*. 2 vols. New York, 1883.

Williamson, G. R. *Memoir of the Rev. David Abeel, D.D., Late Missionary to China.* New York, 1849.

Woodward, Ernest Llewellyn. *The Age of Reform, 1815-1870.* 2nd ed. Oxford, The Clarendon Press, 1962.

Wright, Arthur F. "The Chinese Language and Foreign Ideas," in Arthur F. Wright, ed., *Studies in Chinese Thought.* The University of Chicago Press, 1953.

Wright, Mary C. *The Last Stand of Chinese Conservatism: The T'ung-chih Restoration, 1862-1874.* Stanford University Press, 1957.

Wylie, Alexander. *Memorials of Protestant Missionaries to the Chinese.* Shanghai, 1867.

——— *Notes on Chinese Literature: With Introductory Remarks on the Progressive Advancement of the Art; and a List of Translations from the Chinese into Various European Languages.* Shanghai, 1867. Taipei reprint, 1964.

——— *Chinese Researches.* Shanghai, 1897.

Yang Lien-sheng. "Historical Notes on the Chinese World Order," in John K. Fairbank, ed., *The Chinese World Order.* Cambridge, Mass., Harvard University Press, 1968.

GLOSSARY

Ai-ti
哀帝

chan-kuo 戰國

Chang Ch'ien 張騫

Chang-chou 漳州

Ch'ang-ch'i 長崎

Chao Ssu-wei 趙思位

Ch'ao-chou 潮州

Ch'ao-shan shu-yuan
超山書院

Ch'en Ch'ing-hsieh 陳慶偕

Ch'en Lun-ch'iung 陳倫烱

Ch'en Sheng 陳勝

Cheng Chao 鄭昭

Cheng Tsu-ch'in 鄭祖琛

cheng-t'ung-ling 正統頒

Chi I-chai 冀一齋

Chi-li-szu-te-na
基利斯的那

chi-mi 羈縻

Chi-ts'ui szu 積翠寺

Chi-tzu 箕子

chi-yü t'ien-hsia wei kung
幾於天下為公

Ch'i-hsien

Ch'i Kung 祈墳

Ch'i-shan 琦善

Ch'i-ying 耆英

chia-pan-ch'uan 夾板船

chia-pi-tan 甲必丹

Chia-ying 嘉應

Chieh-hsiu 介休

Chin-chiang 晉江

chin-shih 進士

Chin-t'ien-ts'un 金田村

Chin-yang 晉陽

Chin-yang shu-yuan
晉陽書院

Ch'in-chou 欽州

ching-shih 經史

ch'iu 酋

ch'iu-chang 酋長

Chou Chih-kuei 周攡圭

Chou i 周易

ch'ou-pan 籌辦

chu 誅

ch'uang-yeh chih tsu
創業之祖

chueh-shen 爵紳

chung 家

Chung-shan 中山

chü-jen 舉人

Ch'üan-chou 泉州

ch'ün
群

fan 番

fan-pu 番部

fan-seng 番僧

257

fan-t'an 番攤
Fang Pao 方苞
Fang Tung-shu 方東樹
fen 分
Fen Shui 汾水
Fo-lang-chi 佛郎機
Fo-lang-hsi 佛郎西
fu-ch'iang 富強
fukoku kyōhei
富國強兵
Ha Fen 哈芬
Hai-ch'eng 海澄
Han-chien 漢奸
Han Yü 韓愈
hao 號
hei-i 黑夷
Heng-ch'un 恆春
Heng Fu 恒福
Ho-chung-kuo 合衆國
Ho Kuan-ying 何冠英
Hou-kuan 候官
Hsi-jen 西人
Hsi-nai Shan 西奈山
Hsia 夏
Hsiang-p'ing 襄平
hsiang-shen 鄉紳
Hsien-feng 咸豐
Hsien-li 顯理
hsien-shih 賢士
Hsin-chou 忻州
hsing 星
Hsing-Ch'üan-Yung 興泉永

hsing t'ui-che 行推擇
Hsu Chi-hsun 徐繼壎
Hsu Chi-ku 徐繼穀
Hsu Chi-wan 徐繼畹
Hsu Chi-wu 徐吉午
Hsu Chi-yü 徐繼畬
Hsu Chien-nan 徐健男
Hsu Ching-ju 徐敬儒
Hsu Hsin-te 續新德
Hsu Jun-ti 徐潤第
Hsu K'o-chia 續克家
Hsu Kuang-chin 徐廣縉
Hsu Shu 徐樹
Hsu Sung-k'an 徐松龕
Hsu Sung-ya 徐松芽
hsuan 選
Hsueh Huan 薛煥
Hsun Chiang 潯江
Hsun-chou 潯州
Hu-t'o Ho 濾沱河
Hua-ch'i-kuo 花旗國
huai-jou 懷柔
Huang En-t'ung 黃恩彤
Hung-mao 紅毛
Hung-mao-ch'ien 紅毛淺
Huo Ming-kao 霍明高
huo-shen 火神

i 役
I ching 易經
I-hsin 奕訢
i-k'ou 夷寇

i-kuo 夷國
I-li-pu 伊里布
I-liang 怡良
I-na-ku 義納孤
i-shih-t'ing
議事廳
ju-shih
儒士
K'ai-hua szu 開化寺
Kan-ming 甘明
k'ao-cheng-hsueh 考證學
K'o-lun 可崙
Ku-lang-hsu (Kulangsu)
鼓浪嶼
Ku Shan 鼓山
Ku Yen-wu 顧炎武
Kuang-hsuan hsien-sheng
廣軒先生
Kuei-p'ing 桂平
k'un 鯤
kung-hui 公會
kung-lun 公論
kuo 國
kuo-chia 國家
kuo-chu 國主
kuo-fu, ping-ch'iang
國富兵強
Kuo Meng-ling 郭夢齡
kuo-t'i 國體
kuo-tu 國都
kuo-wang 國王
K'uo-hsien 崞縣

li 里 (1/3 mile)
li 理 (principle)
li-min 黎民
li-po-li-hsien-t'e-ti-fu
里勃里先特底甫
Liang T'ing-nan 梁廷枏
Liang Wen-ch'ing 梁問青
Liang Yung-chou 梁蓉洲
Lin Tse-hsu 林則徐
Lin Yang-tsu 林楊祖
Liu Hung-ao 劉鴻鷔
Liu Pei 劉備
Liu-shih 呹氏
Liu Yao-ch'un 劉耀椿
Liu Yun-k'o 劉韻珂
Lo-i 雒邑
Lu Hsiang-shan 陸象山
Lu-i 路易
Lu Tse-ch'ang 鹿澤長
Lung-ch'i
龍溪
Ma 馬
Ma Chih-chai 馬祉齋
Ma-erh-ko An-to-ni-yueh
馬爾各安多尼約
Ma-li-ya 馬利亞
Mi-li-chien 米利堅
mi-sa 彌卅
Mi-yeh (?)-ku 彌耶穀
Min 閩
min 民
Mo-ha-mai 摩哈麥

Mo-hsi 摩西
mou 畝
Mu-chang-a 穆彰阿
nan-huang 南荒
ni-i p'o-ts'e 逆夷叵測
nü-chu 女主
pa-ku-wen 八股文
pa-kua 八卦
pa-li 巴禮
pai-hsing 百姓
pao-chia 保甲
pao-kuo 報國
P'eng Yun-chang 彭蘊章
Pi-ch'ang 璧昌
P'ing-yang 平陽
P'ing-yao 平遙
pu 部
pu-lo 部落
Sa-szu-ma 薩岷馬
san-tai 三代
Shai-ko-lo 灑哥落
Shan-nan 山南
Shan-pei 山北
Shang-tang 上黨
shen 神
shen-ch'i 紳耆
Shen-kuang szu 神光寺
shen-shih 紳士
shen-t'ien 神天

Shen-tu 身毒
shih-ta-fu 士大夫
shih-tan 史丹
Shih-wan-shan 十萬山
shu-kuo 屬國
shu-min 庶民
shu-yuan 書院
Ssu-ma Hsiang-ju 司馬相如
sui 歲
Sun Ming-en 孫銘恩
Sung Chung-ming 宋鐘鳴
Sung-k'an 松龕
Ta-Ch'in 大秦
ta-ch'iu 大酋
Ta-erh-chi-szu-tan 達爾給斯丹
Ta-Hsi-yang 大西洋
Ta-ta-li 韃韃里
t'ai-chi-ch'üan 太極拳
T'ai-ku 太谷
T'ai-yuan 太原
Tao-kuang 道光
Tao-shan kuan 道山觀
Te-hsiu 德修
Teng T'ing-chen 鄧廷禎
T'ien 天
T'ien-chu 天竺
t'ien-chu 天主
T'ien-chu-chiao 天主教
T'ien Feng-lu 田逢露

t'ien-hsia 天下
t'ien-hsia shih 天下事
t'ien-kuo 天國
t'ien-shen 天神
Ting-hsiang 定襄
T'ing-Chang-Lung 汀漳龍
Ts'ao Ts'ao 曹操
Tse-chou 澤州
tsung-t'ung-ling 總統領
tu 度
T'u-erh-ch'i mai-no
土耳具買諾
t'u-man 土蠻
Tui-ma-tao 對馬島
t'ui-che 推擇
t'ui-chü 推舉
t'ui-hsuan 推選
t'ui-li 推立
T'ui-mi-chai 退窣齋
Tung-chieh-k'ou 東街口
Tung Hsun 董恂
Tung-yeh-chen 東冶鎮
T'ung-an 同安
T'ung-ch'eng 桐城
T'ung-ho 通和
tzu 字
tzu-ch'iang 自强
tzu-li 自立
tzu li wei kuo 自立為國
Tz'u-an (Hsiao-chen)
慈安 (孝貞)
Tz'u-hsi (Hsiao-ch'in)
慈禧 (孝欽)

wai-i 外夷
wang 王
Wang Ch'ing-yun 王慶雲
Wang Ch'iu-pao 王秋寶
Wang Ch'un-yeh 王春埜
Wang-kuang 王光
Wang Yang-ming 王陽明
Wang Yueh-t'an 王月潭
Wei-to-li-ya 維多里亞
Wei Yuan 魏源
Wen-hsiang 文祥
Wo-nu 倭奴
wu-kuan 五官
Wu Kuang 吳廣
Wu Lai-yü 武來雨
Wu-szu 烏斯
Wu-t'ai Shan 五臺山
Wu Wen-yung
吳文鎔
Ya-pei-li 雅裨理
Ya-po-la-han 亞伯拉罕
Yang-ch'eng 陽城
yeh-i 野夷
Yeh-su 耶蘇
Yeh-su-chiao 耶蘇教
Yen-Chien-Shao 延建邵
Yen-p'ing 延平
Yen-P'ing-Ta-So-Ning-Hsin
   Tai-Pao
雁平大朔寧忻代保
Yen Po-t'ao 顏伯燾
yin-cheng 印證

Yin-tu 印度
Ying-chi-li 嘆咭唎
Ying Kuei 英桂
Ying-lun 英倫
yuan 圓
Yuan-ch'ü 垣曲

Yueh-se-fu 約色弗
Yü-ch'ien 裕謙
Yü Pu-yun 余步雲
Yü-t'ai 裕泰
Yü-tz'u 榆次

INDEX

Abeel, David: 34–37, 43, 60, 65, 99, 125; interpreter for Gribble and Hsu Chi-yü, 34–35; gives maps and books to Hsu, 34–37; opinion of Hsu, 35

Abraham, 119

Aden, 107, 141

Administrative reforms: recommended by Hsu, 15

Afghan War, First (1839–1842), 109

Afghanistan, 104

Africa: general description of, 64, 150–151; European encroachment in, 150–151; slave trade in, 150; characterization of, 154

Africa, Central, 152

Africa, East, 152–153

Africa, North: states of, 151

Albuquerque, Afonso d', 99

Alcock, Rutherford: 40–41, 43, 50; wife's globe to Hsu, 41; on Hsu, 40–41; on Hsu's dismissal, 50

Aleni, Jules, 54

Alexander the Great, 105, 122, 194

Alexandria, Virginia, 160

Alfred, 135

Algeria, 152

Alligator, H.M.S., 21

America: general description of, 64–65, 155; balance to European power, 150; Spanish occupation of, 155–156

American Indians, 155

American Presbyterian Board, 37

American Revolution, 154, 163–164

Amoy, 1–2, 19–23, 25–26, 32–37, 39

Amoy Bay, 32

Analects, 165

An-nan chi-ch'eng, 55, 79

Anglo-French War with China, 182–185

Antarctica: exploration of, 65

Anti-Manchu sentiment, 20, 31

Antony, Mark, 124

"Appeasement" party, 21, 29

Arabia, 106–107

Asia: general, 63–64, 69–72; European invasion of, 24

Assam: tea cultivation in, 101

Australia, 65

Austria, 143–144

Babylon, 105, 118

Badakshan, 104, 108

Balboa, 189

Bali, 93

Baluchistan, 104

Bangka, 96

Bantam: Dutch at, 91

"Barbarian" experts, 29

Batavia, 20

Bengal, 100–101

Bering, 130, 189

Berlin, 145

Bhutan: buffer state between China and India, 101

Biblical history: Hsu's use of, 119, 151

Black Rock Hill, Foochow, 39, 43, 46–47

Board of Civil Appointments, 50

Board of Revenue, 182
Bohea tea district, 18
Bolor, 108
Bombay, 101–102
Boone, William J., 34
Borneo, 20, 90
Bremer, 184
Bridgman, Elijah Coleman, 2, 53, 150; Lin Tse-hsu warned by, 2
British, 24
Buddhism, 9, 31, 107, 179
Bukhara, 108, 109
Burlingame, Anson, 187
Burma, 64, 80–82
Burut, 63
Byzantium, 124

Caesar, Julius, 124, 135, 194
Calcutta, 101–102
Canaan, 119
Cannon: Chinese invention taken to Europe, 113
Canton, 2, 28, 29; ransom of, 24
Cantonese linguists, 41
Cape of Good Hope, 62
Cape Horn, 62
Carthage, 151–152, 194
Cartography, Western, 60–61
Catherine the Great, 129, 194
Catholicism, 116–117, 121–122, 136, 179
Celebes, 88–89
Celts, 135
Chang Ch'ien, 189
Chang-chou, 19, 21, 23
Chang Ping-lin, 162
Ch'ang-an, 12
Ch'ang-ch'i (Nagasaki), 73
Chao Ssu-wei, 178
Ch'ao-shan Shu-yuan, 173, 175–176
Charlemagne, 131

Ch'en Ching-hsieh, 55–56
Ch'en, helmsman in Fukien, 96
Ch'en Lun-ch'iung, 72
Ch'en Sheng, 164
Cheng Ch'eng-kung (Koxinga), 31, 127
Cheng Ho, 83, 104
Cheng Tsu-ch'in, 44
Chi I-chai, 175
Chi-mi, 28, 45
Chi-ts'ui Temple, 43, 46
Chi-tzu, 68
Ch'i (state of), 197
Ch'i Ch'un-yuan, 104
Ch'i-hsien, 9
Ch'i Kung, 29
Ch'i-shan, 21, 24, 29
Ch'i-ying, 29, 32, 44, 46, 49
Chia-pi-tan: in Java, 91–92
Chieh-hsiu, 10–11, 175, 185
Chin (state of), 197
Chin-t'ien-tsun, 17
Chin-yang, 10
Chin-yang Shu-yuan, 173
Ch'in (state of), 197
Ch'in dynasty, 148, 192
Ch'in Shih Huang-ti, 151
China, 66, 68; exports and imports of, 8; military weakness of, 25–27; Hsu's description of, 63–64
Chinese Repository: editors' view of Hsu's dismissal, 49–50
Chinese "traitors", 24, 26, 45, 75, 91, 96
Ching-shih School, 3, 5, 190
Ch'ing empire, 63–64, 68
Ch'ing tributary system, 19, 63–64, 68, 192
Ch'ing-hai, 68
Chinkiang, 2
Chou Chih-kuei, 12
Chou Hai-shan, 76

Chou i, 10, 196
Chou Kung, 107
Ch'ou yun Hsi-mi ts'e-lueh, 181
Christianity, 106–107, 118, 124–125
Christina, 143
Chu Hsi, 179
Ch'u (state of), 197
Ch'üan-chou, 19, 26, 72
Chuang people, 17
Chuang-tzu, 66
Chuenpi Convention, 24
Chung-shan chih, 76
Church Missionary Society, 40
Cochin China, 63, 79
Colombia, 158
Columbia, District of, 159–161
Columbus, 126, 158, 165, 189
Conciliation policy, 28, 46
Confucian Classics, 11, 178
Confucian education, 12–14, 176–178
Confucian literati: parochialism of, 1, 52–53; bewildered by Westerners, 1; view of "barbarians", 1, 38, 52–53, 191; realism of some, 2, 55–57, 98, 190
Confucian world view, 1, 4
Confucius, 107, 182
Constantinople, 118
Cook, James, 189
Cornwallis, H.M.S., 28
Cortez, 158, 165
Court of the Imperial Stud, 50, 169, 187
Court of Sacrificial Worship, 186
Cumming, William Henry, 34, 37, 147
Cushing, Caleb, 37

Daniel, 118–119

Darfur, 152
Darius, 105
David, 119
Davis, John Francis, 23, 26, 39
Denmark, 142–143
Dominicans, 19
Draco: legalism of, 122

Egypt, 119, 150–151
Eight Trigrams theories, 115, 147, 154
Eleuths, 108
Elizabeth I, 136
Elliot, George, 21
Erh ya, 178
Europe: general description of, 64, 115–116; location and history of, 112–113; trade with China, 113–115; products and commerce of, 116; languages of, 117; religious wars in, 120

Fan-hai hsiao-lu, 76
Fan-t'an, 31
Fang Pao, 11
Fang Tung-shu, 11
Fen River, 8
Fen Valley, 7, 173
Feng-en, 34
Feng Kuei-fen, 195–196
Ferdinand and Isabella, 126
"Five Indias", 100
Flores, 93
Fo-lang-hsi, 85, 135
Foochow, 19–20, 29–32, 38–49
Foreign countries, Chinese literature on, 52, 55–56
Foreign trade: China's need to participate in, 97–98
France, 131–135
Franciscans, 19
Frederick William III, 146

Fu-ch'iang, 24, 121
Fuju (Foochow), 30
Fukien, 18–23, 30–32, 40, 44, 52, 190
Fukuzawa Yukichi, 181

Galileo, 191
Gama, Vasco da, 99
Geographical misconceptions, of Hsu, 66
Georgetown, 160
Grand Secretariat, 186
Great Britain: miliary power of, 23; Hsu's early characterization of, 24–26, 48; dependent on trade, 26; a source of wealth and power in India, 103; history of, 135–137; description of, 138; products of, 138–139; industry and trade of, 139; government of, 139–140; military of, 140–141; customs and people of, 142
Greece, 120–122, 151–152, 193
Gribble, Henry, 34–35
Grand Council, 47
Guatemala, 166
Guinea, 153
Gunpowder: from China to Europe, 113
Gurkha: a buffer zone between India and China, 101
Gützlaff, Karl Friedrich August, 53, 96, 146

Ha-fen, 171
Hai-ch'eng, 22–23
Hai-kuo t'u-chih, 3, 56
Hai-kuo wen-chien lu, 55, 72, 78, 80, 83, 84, 85, 87, 90, 96
Hai-lu, 83, 90, 96
Hai-tao i-chih, 83, 90, 92
Hakka people, 17

Hakluyt, Richard, 189
Han Learning, 11
Han shu, 12, 173, 177
Han Yü, 50, 179
Hangchow, 31
Hanlin Academy, 7, 12, 14, 15, 30, 181
Heilungkiang, 68
Heng-ch'un, 171, 172
Heng Fu, 181
Henry the Navigator, 99
Henrys, of England, 136
Hepburn, James C., 37
Himalayas, 68
Ho Kuan-ying, 48
Holland, 126–128
Hong Kong, 28, 196
Hottentots, 151
Hou Han shu, 73, 76
Hou-kuan (district), 31
Hsi-yü wen-chien lu, 104–105
Hsiang-p'ing, 68
Hsieh Ch'ing-kao, 83
Hsien-feng Emperor, 46–50
Hsin-chou, 177, 184–185
Hsing-Ch'üan-Yung Circuit, 21
Hsiung-nu, 108
Hsu, rise of family in Shansi, 9–10
Hsu Chi-hsun, 176
Hsu Chi-wan, 11
Hsu Chi-wu, 177
Hsu Ching-ju, 10
Hsu Jun-ti, 10–11
Hsu K'o-chia, 11–12
Hsu Kuang-chin, 46, 49
Hsu pei-chuan chi, 11
Hsu Shu, 176
Hsu Sung-ya, 177–178
Hsuan-tsang, 189
Hsueh Huan, 186
Hsun-chou, 16–17
Hsun River (West River), 17

Hu-t'o River, 9
Huai-ch'eng (Tsinyang), 171
Huang En-t'ung, 29
Huang I-hsien, 86
Hung Hsiu-ch'üan, 18
Huo Ming-kao, 36–37, 60

I-hsin (Prince Kung), 186–187
I-li-pu, 24
I-liang, 25
India, 99–103, 109, 195
Ireland: characterization of the
    people of, 138
Islam, 106, 151–153, 179
Italy, 122–124
Ivan, 128

Jackson, Robert B., 43
Jacob, 119
Japan, 64, 72–76; pirates from, 53,
    73, 75
Java, 20, 90–93
Jesuits, 1, 53
Jesus, 119; teachings and disciples
    of, 124–125
Jews, 107, 119; characterization of,
    120
Joan of Arc, 131
Joseph (father of Jesus), 119, 124
Joshua, 119
Judaism, 106; base of Western reli-
    gion, 119
Judas, 124
Justinian, 124

K'ai-hua Temple, 42
K'ang-hsi Emperor, 9
K'ang Yu-wei, 5, 196
K'ao-cheng hsueh, 13, 53, 56, 190
Karnovoy, 8
Kashmir, 101
Kazakhs, 108

Keelung, 47
Khiva, 109
Kirghiz, 63
Kokand, 108
Kokonor, 63
Kordofan, 152
Korea, 63, 68
Koxinga, see Cheng Ch'eng-kung
Ku-shan, 31
Ku-Yen-wu, 13, 53, 55, 72, 96,
    135; in Shansi, 174, 179
Kuang-hsu Emperor, 196
Kuei-p'ing, 17
Kulangsu, 23, 25, 35, 37; English
    graves on, 32; Western occupa-
    tion of, 34
Kuo Meng-ling, 171–172
Kuo Sung-tao, 5
K'uo-hsien, 10
Kwangsi, 17, 44
Kwangtung, 28–29, 52, 190

Lamaism, 179
Land routes, Europe to China, 108
Laos, 64
Latin America, 165; economic po-
    tential of, 166
Lay, George Tradescant, 38–40, 43,
    46, 120
Legalism, 6, 148, 197
Lesser Khingan Mountains, 68
Liang Ch'i-ch'ao, 5–6, 196
Liang T'ing-nan, 29
Liang Wen-ch'ing, 14–15, 182–183
Liang Yung-chou, 178
Liao-chou, 172
Liao-yang, 68
Liberia, 153
Lin Tse-hsu, 2–3, 21, 25–26, 47,
    56, 190
Lin Yang-tsu, 47
Liu-ch'iu, 19, 49, 63, 69, 76–77;

marooned fishermen from, 40; Chinese tributary, 76–77; Japanese influence in, 76–77
Liu Hung-ao, 28, 40, 56
Liu Pei, 164
Liu Yao-ch'un, 21–22, 26–27, 184
Liu Yun-k'o, 38–41, 43, 45–49, 56
London, 138
Lu-an, 172
Lu Hsiang-shan, 179
Lu Tse-ch'ang, 48, 55–56
Lu-Wang School, 13
Lü-sung chi-lueh, 55, 86–87
Luichow Peninsula, 17
Lung River, 23
Luther, Martin, 116, 123, 125
Luzon, 84–88
"Luzon dollars", 126

Ma Chih-chai, 21–22
Macao, 19, 114, 153
Macassar natives: respected by Dutch, 88–89
Madras, 101
Magellan, 126
Maine, 154–155
Malacca, 20; Western rivalry in, 95
Malacca Strait, 95
Malaya, 20
Manchu invasion, 10, 53
Manchuria, 63
Manila, 87
Mao Tse-tung, 5
Maps, Western-style, 53, 60, 104; Hsu's use of, 60–63, 189
Martin, W. A. P., 187
Mary (mother of Jesus), 124
Maryland, 159
Masloff, 8
Maynooth grant, 41
McKay, Donald, 30
Medhurst, Walter H., 53

Mencius, 194
Mexico, 158, 165–166
Mezeritsky, 8
Mi-sa ("mass"), 87
Military power, Chinese inferiority, 25, 27, 89
Milne, William, 53
Min (district), 31
Min dialect, 20
Min pao, 162
Min River, 18, 30–31, 44
Ming court, 31
Ming-shih (History of the Ming dynasty), 84
Mithraism, 106
Miyako, 73
Mo-tzu, 10, 13
Mohammed, 106
Molucca Islands, 20, 93
Mongolia, 63, 68, 179
Mongols, 8; Hsu critical of, 75–76, 189
Morrison, M. C., 43
Morrison, Robert, 53
Morocco, 152
Moscow, 8
Moses, 106–107; ten precepts of, 119
Moslem tribes, 64
Mozambique, 153
Mu-chang-a, 15, 21, 44, 46, 49
Muscat: commercial treaty with Britain and the United States, 106–107

Nanchang, 28
Nanking, 196
Nantai Island, 30, 41, 49; Western missionaries on, 49
Napoleon, 92, 132, 151, 194
National Institute of Compilation and Translation, 58

Naval power: important in ancient West, 152
Negroes, 151
Nelson, Mary, 38
Neo-Confucianism, 11, 13, 53, 98
New Guinea (Papua), 93
New Hampshire, 155
Nien Rebellion, 172, 184-185
Ningpo, 2; fall of, 24
Noah, 118; and sons, 151
Norway, 142-143

Opium, 24, 102, 117, 174, 178
Opium War, 1, 3, 20-27, 31, 190
Overseas Chinese, 195; from Fukien, 20; in Vietnam, 79; in Siam, 80; in Southeast Asia, 83, 96-97; in Luzon, 85, 87; in Borneo, 90; in Penang, 95

Pa-ku-wen (eight-legged essay), 177, 181
Pa-li, 86
Pagoda Anchorage, 30
Pao-chia, 18
Palmerston, Lord, Foreign Secretary, 46
Panama: canal possible at, 142, 166
Paris, 133
Parkes, Harry, 41
Parsees, 102
Patani, 80
Peking, 10, 182-183, 185-186, 190, 197
Peking Gazette, 182
Penang, 95
P'eng-hu, 19
P'eng Yun-chang, 56
Persia, 104-105, 151; ancient history of, 105; characterization of the people of, 105
Peter the Great, 5, 128-129, 194, 196

Philippines, 20, 84-88
Phoenicia, 151-152
Pi-ch'ang, 22
Pilate, 124
P'ing-yang, 12
P'ing-yao, 9, 173-174, 178-181, 183-185
Po-hai fan-yü lu, 85, 90, 96
Poetry: written by Hsu in retirement, 180
Polo, Marco, 30, 52, 189
Pondicherry, 101
Portugal: same as Ta-Hsi-yang, 114; navigational techniques of, 125; ships sent to China, 126
Portuguese, 125-126; located at Macao, 126
Pottinger, Sir Henry, 38
Proserpine, H.M.S., 39
Protestantism, 116-117, 123, 145-146, 179
Protestant missionaries, 53-55
Protestant publications, 54
Prussia, 144-147
P'u-t'o-shan, 73
Punic Wars, 123-124

Quemoy Island, 32

Rattlesnake, H.M.S., 21
Religion: a tool for control, 179
Remus, 123
Ricci, Matteo, 54
Rome, 122, 123, 151-152, 194
Roman Empire (Ta Ch'in), 107-108, 112, 192
Romulus, 123
Russia, 8, 128-131

Sa-szu-ma (Satsuma), 73
Sahara Desert, 151
Samuel, 119

San-yuan-li, 184
Saul, 119
Scotland: characterization of the people, 138
Sea routes: Europe to China, 107
"Self-strengthening", 195–196; in Southeast Asia, 98
Senegambia, 153
Shansi, 7–9, 169–176, 180–185
Shang-tang, 172, 176
Shao Hsing-yen, 85
Shen-kuang Temple, 46–49
Shen-tu, 100
Shenyang, 68
Shih chi, 12, 177
Shih-chou chih, 76
Shih-tan, in Java, 92
Ship construction, 40
Shou-pien chi-yao, 22
Siam, 20, 64, 80, 93–94
Siberia, 129, 130
Silk Route, 8
Singapore: strategic position of, 94
Sinkiang, 63, 68
Slave trade, 150, 153
Smith, George, 40
Society for the Diffusion of Useful Knowledge in China, 96
Solomon, 119
Solon: reforms of, 122
Soochow, 31
Southeast Asia, 24, 77–78, 81–83, 96–98
Spain, 126
Ssu-ma Hsiang-ju, 50
Stuart, Gilbert, 187
Sudan, 152
Suez, Isthmus of, 107, 141, 142, 166
Sulu, 19, 89–90, 196
Sun Ming-en, 47
Sun-tzu, 1

Sunda Strait, 90–91
Sumatra, 95
Sumba, 93
Sumbawa, 93
Sungora, 80
Sweden, 142–143
Switzerland, 147, 194
Szechwan, 50, 170

Tai, 9
T'ai-chi-ch'üan, 173
T'ai-chou, 73
T'ai-ku, 9, 171–172, 185
T'ai-yuan, 7, 10, 171, 173
Taiping Rebellion, 4, 17–18, 44, 107, 125, 171–172, 175, 183
Taiwan, 19–20, 47
Tamerlane, 100
Tao-kuang Emperor, 14–15, 16, 21, 29, 44–46, 182, 190
Tao-shan Temple, 48–49
Taoism, 179–180
Tartary, 108
Tashkent, 108
Tasman, 189
Teng T'ing-chen, 18, 21
Theseus, King, 121
Tibet, 63, 68, 179; British threat to, 101
T'ien-chu, 100
T'ien Feng-lu, 180
T'ien-hsia, 191
T'ien-hsia chün-kuo li-ping shu, 55, 72, 74, 75, 78, 80, 81, 83, 92, 95, 96, 135
Tienshan Mountains, 68
Timor, 93
Ting-hsiang, 178
T'ing-Chang-Lung Circuit, 19, 28, 169
Tinghai, 2, 21, 25
Transportation, revolution in, 141

Treaty of Nanking, 28–29
Trengganu, 80
Triad Society, 20, 31
Tripoli, 151
Ts'ai T'ing-lan, 79
Ts'ao Ts'ao, 164
Tse-chou, 171–172
Tseng Kuo-fan, 167, 196
Tso chuan, 177
Tsou Jung, 162
Tsungli Yamen, 186–187, 196
Tui-ma-tao (Tsushima), 73
T'ui-mi-chai, 170
Tun-ken-chai i-shu, 11
Tung Hsun, 56–57, 134, 186, 196
Tung-yeh-chen, 171, 183, 185
T'ung-ch'eng School, 11, 13
T'ung-chih Emperor, 186
T'ung-chih Restoration, 5, 185–
    186, 196
T'ung-ho kiln, 183
T'ung-meng-hui, 162
T'ung-wen kuan, 5, 187
Tunisia, 151
Turfan, 68
Turkestan, 63, 68, 108
Turkey, 151
"Turkey Minor", 69
Turkish Empire: cradle of Western
    civilization, 117 ff.
Tzu-kung, 165, 185
Tzu-lu, 185
Tz'u-an, 185
Tz'u-hsi, 185, 197

United States: 154–165, 194, 196;
    Hsu's fascination with, 150;
    general description of, 154–155,
    160; use of Chinese analogues,
    155; history of, 155, 162; cli-
    mate of, 158; products of, 158;
    British colonization of, 158;
    government of, 158–160; elec-
    tions, 159–160, 164; population
    of, 161; revenues of, 161; mili-
    tary power of, 161; flag of, 161–
    162; transportation in, 162;
    scholars in, 161–162; religion of,
    162; appeal of federalism to
    Chinese, 167

Verbiest, Ferdinand, 54, 119, 151
Victoria, Queen, 138
Vienna, Congress of, 122, 143
Vietnam: 78–79; Chinese tributary,
    78; Chinese influence in, 78; suc-
    cess in fighting Western ships,
    78–79; West's fear of, 78
Virginia, 159

Wan-kuo ti-li shu, 96, 109
Wang Ch'ing-yun, 171–172
Wang Ch'iu-pao, 12
Wang Ch'un-yeh, 184
Wang Ta-hai, 83
Wang Yang-ming, 3, 14, 179; influ-
    ence on Hsu, 13, 190
Wang Yueh-t'an, 12
War junks, construction of, 40
Warring States period, 4, 131, 148,
    192, 197
Washington, George: 5, 131, 137,
    154, 159, 161–163, 187–188,
    194; compared to Chinese
    heroes, 164; imitated by Latin
    American leaders, 165
Washington National Monument,
    188
Waterloo, Battle of, 138
Wei Yuan, 3, 56
Wen-chou, 73
Wen-hsiang, 186
Western calendar, 117
Western civilization: superior

technology of, 112, 193; accomplishments of, 148–149; evolution of, 192, 195; threat to China, 192–193; penetration of the world, 193; political forms of, 193–194; military power of, 194–195

Western information: Hsu's use of, 54–58, 61

"Western Region": 63, 68; buffer zone between Russia and China, 108; Anglo-Russian rivalry in, 108–109; Russian position in, 109

Western ships, 141

Williams, S. Wells, 55, 68, 187

Wo-nu, 73

World: Hsu's general description of, 61–67; oceans of, 61–66; climate of, 61–62; continents of, 62–66

World geography: effect of its introduction to China, 3, 58–59, 67–68

Wu Kuang, 164

Wu Lai-yü, 172, 184

Wu-szu, 68

Wu-t'ai (city), 9–10, 177, 183

Wu-t'ai (district), 9, 11, 34, 50,

171, 180, 197

Wu-t'ai hsin-chih (New gazetteer of Wu-t'ai), 44

Wu-t'ai Mountains: Buddhist monasteries in, 9

Wu Wen-yung, 18–19, 21, 28, 57

Yang-ch'eng, 171

Yellow River, 8, 171–172

Yen (state), 197

Yen-Chien-Shao Circuit, 18, 169

Yen Fu, 195–196

Yen Hsi-shan, 6, 197

Yen-P'ing-Ta-So-Ning-Hsin-Tai-Pao Circuit, 9

Yen Po-t'ao, 22–23, 28

Yenp'ing, 44

Yin-tu, 100

Ying-chi-li, 48

Ying-i, 46

Ying Kuei, 184, 186

Yü-ch'ien, 24

Yü-t'ai, 49

Yü-tz'u, 185

Yuan-ch'ü, 171

Yuan Shih-tsu (Khubilai Khan), 75

Zayton, 19

HARVARD EAST ASIAN MONOGRAPHS

1. Liang Fang-chung, *The Single-Whip Method of Taxation in China*. 1956. 79 pp.

2. Harold C. Hinton, *The Grain Tribute System of China, 1845-1911*. 1956. 171 pp.

3. Ellsworth C. Carlson, *The Kaiping Mines, 1877-1912*. 1971. 235 pp.

4. Chao Kuo-chün, *Agrarian Policies of Mainland China: A Documentary Study, 1949-1956*. 1957. 290 pp.

5. Edgar Snow, *Random Notes on Red China, 1936-1945*. 1957. 164 pp.

6. Edwin George Beal, Jr., *The Origin of Likin, 1835-1864*. 1958. 204 pp.

7. Chao Kuo-chün, *Economic Planning and Organization in Mainland China: A Documentary Study, 1949-1957*. Vol. I: 275 pp. 1959. Vol. II: 280 pp. 1960.

8. John K. Fairbank, *Ch'ing Documents: An Introductory Syllabus*. Vol. I: 141 pp. Vol. II: 41 pp. 1965.

9. Helen Yin and Yi-chang Yin, *Economic Statistics of Mainland China, 1949-1957*. 1960. 110 pp.

10. Wolfgang Franke, *The Reform and Abolition of the Traditional Chinese Examination System*. 1960. 110 pp.

11. Albert Feuerwerker and S. Cheng, *Chinese Communist Studies of Modern Chinese History*. 1961. 313 pp.

12. C. John Stanley, *Late Ch'ing Finance: Hu Kuang-yung as an Innovator*. 1961. 313 pp.

13. S. M. Meng, *The Tsungli Yamen: Its Organization and Functions*. 1962. 152 pp.

14. Ssu-yü Teng, *Historiography of the Taiping Rebellion*. 1962. 188 pp.

15. Chun-Jo Liu, *Controversies in Modern Chinese Intellectual History: An Analytic Bibliography of Periodical Articles,*

Mainly of the May Fourth and Post-May Fourth Era.
1964. 215 pp.

16. Edward J. M. Rhoads, *The Chinese Red Army, 1927-1963:
An Annotated Bibliography.* 1964. 202 pp.

17. Andrew J. Nathan, *A History of the China International
Famine Relief Commission.* 1965. 114 pp.

18. Frank H. H. King (ed.) and Prescott Clarke, *A Research
Guide to China-Coast Newspapers, 1822-1911.* 1965.
245 pp.

19. Ellis Joffe, *Party and Army: Professionalism and Political
Control in the Chinese Officer Corps, 1949-1964.* 1965.
210 pp.

20. Toshio G. Tsukahira, *Feudal Control in Tokugawa Japan:
The Sankin Kōtai System.* 1966. 240 pp.

21. Kwang-Ching Liu, ed., *American Missionaries in China:
Papers from Harvard Seminars.* 1966. 316 pp.

22. George Moseley, *A Sino-Soviet Cultural Frontier: The Ili
Kazakh Autonomous Chou.* 1966. 171 pp.

23. Carl F. Nathan, *Plague Prevention and Politics in Manchuria,
1910-1931.* 1967. 112 pp.

24. Adrian Arthur Bennett, *John Fryer: The Introduction of
Western Science and Technology into Nineteenth-Century
China.* 1967. 169 pp.

25. Donald J. Friedman, *The Road from Isolation: The Campaign of the American Committee for Non-Participation
in Japanese Aggression, 1938-1941.* 1968. 132 pp.

26. Edward Le Fevour, *Western Enterprise in Late Ch'ing
China: A Selective Survey of Jardine, Matheson and
Company's Operations, 1842-1895.* 1968. 223 pp.

27. Charles Neuhauser, *Third World Politics: China and the
Afro-Asian People's Solidarity Organization, 1957-1967.*
1968. 107 pp.

28. Kungtu C. Sun, assisted by Ralph W. Huenemann, *The
Economic Development of Manchuria in the First Half
of the Twentieth Century.* 1969. 134 pp.

29. Shahid Javed Burki, *A Study of Chinese Communes, 1965.* 1969. 117 pp.

30. John Carter Vincent, *The Extraterritorial System in China: Final Phase.* 1970. 134 pp.

31. Madeleine Chi, *China Diplomacy, 1914-1918.* 1970. 213 pp.

32. Clifton Jackson Phillips, *Protestant America and the Pagan World: The First Half Century of the American Board of Commissioners for Foreign Missions, 1810-1860.* 1969. 380 pp.

33. James Pusey, *Wu Han: Attacking the Present through the Past.* 1970. 94 pp.

34. Ying-wan Cheng, *Postal Communication in China and Its Modernization, 1860-1896.* 1970. 150 pp.

35. Tuvia Blumenthal, *Saving in Postwar Japan.* 1970. 120 pp.

36. Peter Frost, *The Bakumatsu Currency Crisis.* 1970. 87 pp.

37. Stephen C. Lockwood, *Augustine Heard and Company, 1858-1862: American Merchants in China.* 1970. 125 pp.

38. Robert R. Campbell, *James Duncan Campbell: A Memoir by His Son.* 1970. 145 pp.

39. Jerome Alan Cohen, ed., *The Dynamics of China's Foreign Relations.* 1970. 139 pp.

40. V. V. Vishnyakova-Akimova, *Two Years in Revolutionary China, 1925-1927,* tr. Steven I. Levine. 1971. 345 pp.

41. Meron Medzini, *French Policy in Japan during the Closing Years of the Tokugawa Regime.* 1971. 267 pp.

42. *The Cultural Revolution in the Provinces.* 1971. 267 pp.

43. Sidney A. Forsythe, *An American Missionary Community in China, 1895-1905.* 1971. 152 pp.

44. Benjamin I. Schwartz, ed., *Reflections on the May Fourth Movement: A Symposium.* 1972. 140 pp.

45. Ching Young Choe, *The Rule of the Taewŏn'gun, 1865-1873: Restoration in Yi Korea.* 1972. 287 pp.

46. W. P. J. Hall, *A Bibliographical Guide to Japanese Research on the Chinese Economy, 1958-1970.* 1972. 113 pp.

47. Jack J. Gerson, *Horatio Nelson Lay and Sino-British Relations, 1854-1864.* 1972. 350 pp.

48. Paul Richard Bohr, *Famine and the Missionary: Timothy Richard as Relief Administrator and Advocate of National Reform.* 1972. 301 pp.

49. Endymion Wilkinson, *The History of Imperial China: A Research Guide.* 1973. 234 pp.

50. Britten Dean, *China and Great Britain: The Diplomacy of Commercial Relations, 1860-1864.* 1974. 223 pp.

51. Ellsworth C. Carlson, *The Foochow Missionaries, 1847-1880.* 1974. 259 pp.

52. Yeh-chien Wang, *An Estimate of the Land-Tax Collection in China, 1753 and 1908.* 1973. 192 pp.

53. Richard M. Pfeffer, *Understanding Business Contracts in China, 1949-1963.* 1973. 147 pp.

54. Han-sheng Chuan and Richard Kraus, *Mid-Ch'ing Rice Markets and Trade, An Essay in Price History.* 1975. 238 pp.

55. Ranbir Vohra, *Lao She and the Chinese Revolution.* 1974. 199 pp.

56. Liang-lin Hsiao, *China's Foreign Trade Statistics, 1864-1949.* 1974. 297 pp.

57. Lee-hsia Hsu Ting, *Government Control of the Press in Modern China, 1900-1949.* 1974. 318 pp.

58. Edward W. Wagner, *The Literati Purges: Political Conflict in Early Yi Korea.* 1974. 238 pp.

59. Joungwon A. Kim, *Divided Korea: The Politics of Development, 1945-1972.* 1975. 445 pp.

60. Noriko Kamachi, John K. Fairbank, and Chuzo Ichiko, *Japanese Studies of Modern China Since 1953: A Bibliographical Guide to Historical and Social-Science Research on the Nineteenth and Twentieth Centuries, Supplementary Volume for 1953-1969.* 1975. 610 pp.

61. Donald A. Gibbs and Yun-chen Li, *A Bibliography of Studies and Translations of Modern Chinese Literature, 1918-1942.* 1975. 239 pp.

62. Robert H. Silin, *Leadership and Values: A Cultural Theory of Organization in Taiwanese Enterprises.* 1975.

63. David Pong, *A Critical Guide to the Kwangtung Provincial Archives Deposited at the Public Record Office of London.* 1975.

64. Fred W. Drake, *China Charts the World: Hsu Chi-yü and His Geography of 1848.* 1975.

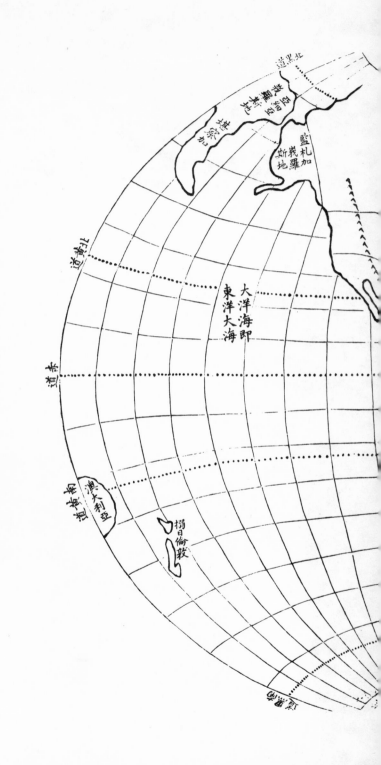